Politics by Other Means

Politics by Other Means

Politicians, Prosecutors, and the Press from Watergate to Whitewater

THIRD EDITION

Benjamin Ginsberg

Martin Shefter

W. W. Norton & Company
New York · London

The text of this book is composed in Garamond 3
with the display set in Garamond 3 Italic
Composition by Gina Webster

Library of Congress Cataloging-in-Publication Data

Ginsberg, Benjamin.
Politics by other means : politicians, prosecutors, and the press in the post-electoral era /
Benjamin Ginsberg, Martin Shefter.—3rd ed.
p. cm.
Includes bibliographical references and index.
ISBN 0-393-97763-3 (pbk.)
1. Political participation—United States. 2. Political parties—United States. 3. Elections—
United States. 4. Governmental investigations—United States. 5. Mass media—Political
aspects—United States. 6. United States—Politics and government—1945–1989. 7.
United States—Politics and governement—1989– I. Shefter, Martin, 1943– II. Title.

JK1764.G56 2002
320.973—dc21   2001055767

W. W. Norton & Company, Inc., 500 Fifth Avenue, New York, N.Y. 10110
http://www.wwnorton.com

W. W. Norton & Company Ltd., Castle House, 75/76 Wells Street, London W1T 3QT

    3 4 5 6 7 8 9 0

For our families

Contents

Preface to the Third Edition   9

1   Electoral Decay and Institutional Conflict   13

2   Electoral Deadlock   46

3   The Democrats and the Domestic State   81

4   The Republican Offensive   102

5   Institutional Combat   132

6   Bush v. Gore: The Fracas Over Florida   170

7   Electoral Mobilization, Institutional
Combat, and Governmental Power   212

Notes   233

Index   249

Preface to the
Third Edition

Since the initial publication of *Politics by Other Means* eleven years ago, the patterns of nonelectoral politics we described have become even more prominent features of American political life. The first edition discussed Watergate and the Iran-contra affair. The second edition revised and extended the discussion to include the political struggles of the Clinton era. During the past ten years, competing forces have continued to perfect nonelectoral weapons of political combat even as they have continued to fail to mobilize voters to participate in democratic electoral politics. We concluded the first edition by remarking that America seemed to be on the verge of entering a postelectoral political era in which elections might be eclipsed in importance by "other means" of political conflict. We began the revised edition by observing that such an era had arrived. The third edition extends our account with a discussion of the dramatic struggle in Florida and before the U.S. Supreme Court that decided the 2000 presidential election. Over the past several decades contending political forces have learned how to circumvent electoral outcomes. In 2000 they took this knowledge a step further and employed nonelectoral institutions to decide the election.

When George W. Bush took office in 2001, Republicans initially held both houses of Congress. This, of course, offered the new president some protection from attack. Sen. James Jeffords's (I-V.) defection from the GOP camp, however, gave the Democrats control of the Senate and increased the potential for institutional conflict. Of course,in the wake of the September 11 terrorist attacks in 2001, domestic political struggle was somewhat muted. Indeed, for a number of weeks the Senate was barely able to conduct business because Senate offices had been contaminated by anthrax spores. But, as fear of terrorism subsided, opposing forces returned to politics as usual and searched for ways to use matters such as the Enron scandal against one another.

The readers and reviewers of the first edition offered many helpful comments, for which we are grateful. We want to thank our editor at W. W. Norton, Steve Dunn, for encouraging us to undertake a new edition of *Politics by Other Means.* It is always a pleasure to work with Steve on a book project. Our thanks to Todd Rankin, our copy editor, and Lory Frenkel, our project editor, who saved us from many errors. We also wish to fondly remember the late Martin Kessler, who in his capacity as publisher and president of Basic Books edited and published the first edition.

Politics by Other Means

1

Electoral Decay and Institutional Conflict

BILL CLINTON WAS ELECTED to the presidency in 1992 and re-elected by a comfortable margin in 1996. During much of his tenure in office, Clinton was besieged by media revelations, congressional hearings into his conduct in office, and a multiyear independent counsel probe that examined his financial dealings, official conduct, and personal morality. Clinton's administration may come to be remembered as much for his innovative defenses against investigations as for his policy innovations. To thwart the independent counsel Kenneth Starr, Clinton and his aides made use of a special damage control office in the Democratic National Committee and joint legal defense agreements with staffers whose testimony might otherwise prove embarrassing. The president also sought to turn the tables on the independent counsel by launching an investigation of Starr's staff.

Clinton of course has not been the only prominent elected official to become the subject of investigations and prosecutions in recent years. Ronald Reagan's second term was marred by the Iran-contra probe. Richard Nixon was forced to resign from office as a result of the Watergate investigations. In addition, several congressional leaders, including former House Speaker Newt Gingrich, have come under serious attack for their conduct in office. Taken together, all these cases reflect a major change in the conduct of American politics. In particular, the pattern of investigations and prosecutions directed against Clinton, Reagan, Nixon, Gingrich, and many others reflects the declining place of democratic elections and the growing importance of "politics by other means" in the United States. The declining place of electoral politics in the United States was brought into even sharper focus by the 2000 presidential election, a struggle decided by institutional combat rather than popular mobilization. In 2000 voter turnout was low, the popular vote winner lost the race, and the president of the United States was, in effect, chosen by the courts. The postelectoral era had arrived.

FOR MUCH OF AMERICA'S HISTORY, elections have been central arenas of popular choice and political combat. In recent years, however, elections have become less decisive as mechanisms for resolving conflicts and constituting governments in the United States. As a result of the development of new weapons of political warfare, political struggles have come more frequently to be waged elsewhere and crucial choices more often made outside the electoral realm. Rather than engage in an all-out competition for votes, contending political forces have come to rely upon such weapons of institutional combat as congressional investigations, media revelations, and judicial proceedings to defeat their foes. In contemporary America, electoral success often fails to confer the capacity to govern, and political forces have been able to exercise considerable power even if they lose at the polls or, indeed, do not compete in the electoral arena.

The use of institutional weapons of political combat is not without precedent in American history. Even during the heyday of classic American party politics, political elites sought to gain influence over public policy by techniques other than (or in addition to) competitive electoral mobilization. The fine art of political compromise was one such technique. The celebrated compromises of the antebellum era saw political leaders (from different sections of the nation and different parties) colluding with one another, rather than engaging in all-out political warfare. The most significant of these accords concerned the extension of slavery, the subject of a series of compromises extending from the Missouri Compromise of 1820 through the Compromise of 1850 and the Kansas-Nebraska Act.

This series of sectional compromises was interrupted by the Civil War. Southern Democrats reacted to the election of Abraham Lincoln not by seeking to strike deals with the leader of the newly organized Republican party but rather by seceding from the Union. Failing to prevail over their opponents by mobilizing a larger number of voters in electoral campaigns, the leaders of the pro- and antislavery forces undertook to defeat each other by mobilizing soldiers in military campaigns. And the era of Reconstruction following the war was brought to an end by the Compromise of 1876 between northern and southern political elites, not by a realignment of voters.

The Progressives also undertook to enact "reforms" without mobilizing voters, and they sought to institutionalize their victories outside the party system. The Progressives sponsored political reforms that were among the most important in American history, but these major changes in the political order were achieved without securing a realignment of the electorate. Rather than line up the unwashed, the Progressives demobilized much of the electorate, weakened political parties, and ultimately made it more difficult to achieve political change through voting.

As these examples suggest, during the course of American political history, contending elites have not always employed electoral mobilization as the chief means to achieve their goals. Indeed, the significance of elections in American politics should be viewed as a variable, rather than assumed to be a constant. During a number of eras in American history contending forces have fought key battles outside the electoral arena, through such institutions as the judiciary, executive agencies, and the news media. Over the past three decades, however, politics outside the electoral arena has become the norm, rather than an episodic deviation from the routine pattern of American politics. During this time the importance of these institutional weapons has increased while the significance and decisiveness of elections have diminished. This development has profound consequences for the nation's domestic affairs and international standing. Because contemporary elections fail to establish conclusively who will— or will not—exercise power, conflict over this question continues to rage throughout the political system. This exacerbates the historic fragmentation of government in the United States, further weakening the American state and making it difficult to achieve collective national purposes. Contending political groups are increasingly able to seize portions of the state apparatus and pursue divergent and often contradictory goals even in the face of serious domestic problems and international challenges. In short, contemporary political patterns often produce a government that cannot govern.

FROM ELECTORAL TO INSTITUTIONAL COMBAT

During the nineteenth and early twentieth centuries, political conflicts in the United States were mainly fought in the electoral arena.

Full white manhood suffrage was achieved in the United States in the Jacksonian era, and the American electorate was highly mobilized. By the end of the nineteenth century, electoral turnout exceeded 80 percent of eligible voters in presidential elections and approached 70 percent in midterm congressional races. Outside the South, presidential election turnout stood at nearly 90 percent.[1]

These high levels of voting participation were achieved because contending political forces waged their struggles largely through competitive popular mobilization. Debates about policies and battles for power among rival elites were not confined to the conference rooms and corridors of the Capitol. Instead, political struggles typically extended into the electoral arena. In a pattern that E. E. Schattschneider characterized as "expanding the scope of conflict," opposing parties mobilized their supporters throughout the country, "lining up the unwashed," as V. O. Key put it, in an effort to defeat their political opponents by outvoting them.[2]

The resulting style of nineteenth-century political campaigns has been characterized as "militarist."[3] Contending political forces were organized and active in every constituency. Voters in each precinct were "drilled" by party "captains," who in turn were provided with help and intelligence by a well-staffed and well-financed organization. Party propaganda was disseminated by a rabidly partisan press. Throughout the country hundreds of thousands of party workers marched from house to house on election day, handing out leaflets, helping voters to the polls, and, on occasion, offering voters financial inducements to support the candidate of *their* choice.

When the stakes were high, as during the critical election of 1896, party machines were capable of extraordinary feats of popular mobilization. During William McKinley's "front porch" campaign of 1896, 750,000 persons—about 13 percent of GOP voters that year—were brought from all over the United States to the candidate's Ohio home by Republican party workers. Workers for the two parties led nearly 90 percent of all eligible voters outside the South to the polls on election day. This prodigious feat, in a semiagrarian nation in which the horse and buggy were still a major mode of transportation, illustrates the close relationship between elite struggle and electoral mobilization in nineteenth-century America. Each side devoted its energies to mobilizing the maximum number of votes. To be sure, political contention during the late nineteenth century was not solely a matter of electoral mobilization.[4] And fraudulent voting was commonplace in elections.[5] But the attempt to mobilize maximum support in elections was a central strategy for anyone seeking to control the government and to influence public policy.

The nineteenth-century pattern of active public involvement is a far cry from how politics is conducted in present-day America. Recent voter turnout has been extremely low. In the lowest electoral turnout since 1924, fewer than 49 percent of those eligible to vote actually voted in the 1996 presidential election. In midterm congressional elections, barely one-third of eligible voters go to the polls. Interestingly, however, these low levels of voter turnout are not associated with a decline in political conflict. For example, conflict within Congress, as measured by the closeness of roll call votes, has *increased* significantly in recent years.[6]

It is indicative of the intensity of conflict in contemporary American politics that many political forces castigated President Clinton for his willingness to compromise with their opponents. For example, two assistant secretaries of health and human services, Mary Jo Bane and Peter Edelman, resigned to protest Clinton's signing welfare reform legislation that had been introduced by conservative Republicans. Similarly, the top leaders of the congressional Democratic party initially denounced the budget compromise hammered out by Clinton and the Republican leadership as an unacceptable "deal."

During the 1950s and 1960s most observers of American politics considered the tendency of American politicians to compromise with their opponents a virtue, reflecting the "genius of American politics."[7] Nowadays, by contrast, a number of political commentators have asserted that President Clinton's compromises are a sign of his complete lack of moral convictions.[8]

Also indicative of the intensity of conflict among elites in contemporary American politics is the number of Clinton's legislative proposals that were filibustered by Republicans in the Senate.

Moreover, many bills embodying the administration's program encountered unanimous opposition among both Republicans in the Senate and the House. For his part, President George W. Bush was unable to persuade the Democrat-controlled Senate to act on key administration nominees and resorted to a large number of recess appointments to circumvent the Senate. However, it is noteworthy that such struggles among contending political forces no longer lead to major efforts to mobilize voters in elections.

In view of the intensity of contemporary political struggles concerning such questions as how to cope with international crises and whether abortions should be publicly financed or totally outlawed, the limited involvement of the mass electorate in recent years is striking. During the nineteenth century, voter mobilization (as manifested in electoral turnout) and elite conflict (as manifested in close congressional roll calls) were directly associated. In recent years, however, the relationship between levels of conflict at the elite and mass levels has collapsed.[9] In sharp contrast with the militarist elections of the nineteenth century, contemporary political forces no longer seem willing to engage in all-out struggles in the electoral arena.

Competing political forces in America today, to be sure, do seek to appeal to voters. Indeed, politicians are currently spending enormous sums on election campaigns. Campaign spending during the 2000 national election may have reached an unprecedented three billion dollars when national, state, and local spending totals are taken together. Much of this money, however, was spent on television advertising during the last month of the campaign. This advertising is aimed primarily at middle-class Americans who are already registered and likely to vote. In contrast with the nineteenth-century pattern of reaching out to the "unwashed," neither party has made much of an effort to defeat its opponents by attempting to mobilize the tens of millions of generally poorer and less educated Americans who are not currently part of the electorate.[10]

This failure to mobilize new voters actively is especially striking given the fact that since the late 1960s neither major party has been able to win a decisive edge in the electoral arena. Though the two parties have spent huge sums campaigning for the support of existing voters, the results have been inconclusive and control of the government has been divided during most of the past thirty years. Why, then, has neither party seen fit to engage in nineteenth-century–style all-out voter mobilization in an attempt to overwhelm its opponent at the polls? One reason is that both political parties are afraid of the implications of a strategy of mobilization. For the Republicans, expansion of the electorate could threaten an influx of poor voters who wouldn't seem likely to be supporters of the GOP. As for the Democrats, whatever the potential benefits to the party as a whole, an influx of millions of new voters would represent a "leap into the dark" for current of-ficeholders at the local, state, and congressional levels. Moreover, various interests allied with the Democrats—notably upper-middle-class environmentalists, public interest lawyers, antinu-clear activists, and the like—could not be confident of retaining their influence in a more fully mobilized electoral environment. Finally, though it is seldom openly admitted, the truth is that many members of both the liberal and the conservative camps are wary of fuller popular participation in American politics. Conser-vatives fear blacks, and liberals often have disdain for working- and lower-middle-class whites.

American politicians purport to deplore the nation's low levels of voter turnout. It is interesting to note, however, that even modest ef-forts to boost voter turnout inspire only lukewarm support in Wash-ington. For example, the so-called Motor Voter Act, signed into law by President Clinton in 1993, was bitterly opposed by most Re-publicans.[11] For their part, congressional Democrats were willing to delete those portions of the bill that were most likely to maximize registration among the poor, such as providing automatic voter reg-istration to all clients at welfare offices. Indeed, many Democrats had been happy to see the bill vetoed by President Bush in 1992, even though Motor Voter was expected to have only a modest effect on the size and composition of the electorate. Thus far, at least, few of the individuals registered under the act have actually gone to the polls to cast their ballots. In 1996 the percentage of newly registered voters who appeared at the polls actually dropped.[12] Mobilization requires more than the distribution of forms. In 2000, both parties claimed to be undertaking major voter mobilization efforts. In reality, with the partial exception of Democratic efforts to register new black voters in Florida and new blue-collar voters in Michigan and Pennsylvania, both the Democrats and Republicans focused mainly on turning out their established supporters. Overall, voter turnout in 2000 remained at roughly the 50-percent level that has been the norm in recent decades.

INSTITUTIONAL COMBAT

Rather than mobilize voters to attempt to overpower their foes in the electoral arena, over the past thirty years politicians have perfected alternative weapons of political combat. These weapons, deployed outside the electoral arena, have allowed opposing forces to compete for power without exposing them to the uncertainties of full-scale voter mobilization.

President and Congress

To begin with, both parties have sought to make maximum political use of the elective institutions they controlled to undermine and disrupt institutions controlled by their rivals. In the 1970s and 1980s Republicans responded to their inability to win control of Congress by seeking to enhance the powers of the White House relative to the legislative branch. Thus, President Nixon impounded billions of dollars appropriated by Congress and sought, through various reorganization schemes, to bring executive agencies under closer White House control while severing their ties to the House and Senate. Presidents Reagan and Bush tolerated budget deficits of unprecedented magnitude in part because these precluded new congressional spending; they also sought to increase presidential authority over executive agencies and diminish the authority of Congress by centralizing control over administrative rule making in the Office of Management and Budget (OMB). In addition, Reagan undertook to circumvent the legislative restrictions on presidential conduct embodied in the War Powers Act. Finally, Reagan and his successor, George Bush, also sought to secure a line-item veto power to strengthen the president's hand in the legislative process. Ironically, by the time this power was secured the presidency was in Democratic hands and Democrat Bill Clinton became the first U.S. president with the power to excise portions of spending bills. Subsequently, the Supreme Court in a 1998 decision declared the line-item veto unconstitutional. President George W. Bush has made expansive claims of executive privilege and used executive orders and recess appointments to circumvent his foes in Congress.

During the same period the Democrats responded to the Republican presidential advantage by seeking to strengthen the Congress while reducing the powers and prerogatives of the presidency, a sharp contrast with Democratic behavior from the 1930s to the 1960s, when that party enjoyed an advantage in presidential elections. In the 1970s Congress greatly expanded the size of its committee and subcommittee staffs, thus enabling the House and Senate to monitor and supervise closely the activities of executive agencies. Through the 1974 Budget and Impoundment Act, Congress sought to increase its control over fiscal policy. Congress also enacted a number of statutory restrictions on presidential authority in the realm of foreign policy, including the Foreign Commitments Resolution and the Arms Export Control Act.

Finally, of course, when they controlled the Congress, Democrats launched a number of major legislative investigations aimed at embarrassing or discrediting Republican presidents and other officials of the executive branch. The Watergate and Iran-contra investigations discussed below were of course the most important. After the GOP won control of Congress in 1994, the investigative tables were turned. Republicans used their control over congressional investigative committees to launch inquiries into allegations that the Clinton administration had sought to use confidential FBI files for political purposes. Following the 1996 national elections, Congress launched a major probe of the Clinton campaign's fund-raising practices in an effort to demonstrate that Clinton and Vice President Al Gore had committed numerous violations of campaign finance laws, including accepting money from foreign business interests and possibly money that originated with Chinese government intelligence agencies. Republicans promised to use their investigative powers to harass Clinton for the remainder of his presidency. "Clinton will be debilitated," predicted one Republican official.[13] At first, Republicans had little or no interest in actually impeaching Clinton. Instead, Republicans saw the never-ending investigative process as a means of harassing Clinton and preventing him from pursuing any serious legislative agenda. Later of course, the GOP decided to actually impeach the president, leading to an enormous partisan struggle in Congress.

Institutional struggle of the sort that has characterized American politics in recent years is most likely to occur when the major branches of government are controlled by hostile political forces. This condition is neither exclusively nor necessarily associated with divided partisan control of Congress and the presidency.[15] On the one hand, during periods of unified partisan control, institutional combat can occur when hostile factions of the same party are entrenched in different branches of government. For example, right-wing Republicans led by Joseph McCarthy in the early 1950s and antiwar Democrats led by J. William Fulbright in the mid-1960s used legislative investigations to attack presidents belonging to their own parties. On the other hand, divided control is not likely to result in intense institutional struggles in the absence of deep cleavages between the two parties. For instance, in the mid- and late 1950s, when moderates and internationalists controlled both the Democratic and Republican parties, relations between the Eisenhower White House and the Rayburn-Johnson Congress were reasonably amicable. However, when divided partisan control of government does coincide with sharp cleavages between the two parties, the importance of institutional conflict relative to electoral competition is likely to increase. This state of affairs has characterized American politics since the Vietnam and Watergate eras.

The Courts and the Media as Political Weapons

Contending political forces have sought to use not only Congress and the presidency but also the federal judiciary and the mass media as instruments of political combat. These institutions in turn have been able to ally with such forces and to bolster their own autonomy and power. Through this process, institutions that are not directly subject to the control of the electorate have become increasingly significant players in contemporary American politics.

The Judiciary. One important substitute for electoral mobilization in contemporary politics is the growing political use of a powerful nonelectoral weapon—the criminal justice system. Between the early 1970s and 2000 there was more than a tenfold increase in the number of indictments brought by federal prosecutors against national, state, and local officials not including those political figures (such as Ronald Reagan's attorney general Edwin Meese and former Democratic House Speaker Jim Wright) who were targets of investigations that did not result in indictments.

Many of the individuals indicted have been lower-level civil servants, but large numbers have been prominent political figures— among them more than a dozen members of Congress, several federal judges, and numerous state and local officials. Some of these indictments were initiated by Republican administrations, and their targets were primarily Democrats. At the same time, a substantial number of high-ranking Republicans in the executive branch—including former Defense Secretary Caspar Weinberger, former Assistant Secretary of State Elliott Abrams, presidential aides Michael Deaver and Lyn Nofziger, and, of course, national security official Oliver North—were the targets of criminal prosecutions stemming from allegations or investigations initiated by

Democrats. Weinberger and Abrams, along with several other figures in the Iran-contra case, were pardoned by President George
Bush in December 1992, just before he left office. In justifying the
pardons, Bush charged that Democrats were attempting to crimi-
nalize policy differences.

During the first two years of the Clinton administration, the
powerful chair of the House Ways and Means Committee, Dan
Rostenkowski (D-Ill.), was forced to give up his post after being indicted on corruption charges. In 1994 and 1995 charges of improper conduct were leveled at Agriculture Secretary Mike Espy,
Transportation Secretary Henry Cisneros, and Commerce Secretary
Ron Brown, among others. Espy and Cisneros were forced to resign
and were ultimately indicted on fraud and corruption charges.
Brown died tragically in an airplane crash before the investigation
into his conduct was completed. During the same period President
Clinton himself became the target of an intensive probe that led to
the jailing of several of his closest associates on charges including
fraud and conspiracy. This investigation is discussed in more detail
below. While this investigation continued, in February 1998 Attorney General Janet Reno requested the appointment of still another independent counsel to look into charges that Interior
Secretary Bruce Babbitt had lied to Congress about his decision to
award an Indian gambling casino license to a group that had made
major contributions to the 1996 Democratic campaign.

On Capitol Hill, House Speaker Newt Gingrich was subjected
to an ethics investigation prompted by Democratic complaints
about his fund-raising tactics. Acting on a formal complaint from
Democratic House members, the House Ethics Committee began
in 1994 to investigate whether a college course organized by Gingrich with tax-deductible contributions was actually a partisan political endeavor. This would violate federal laws prohibiting
tax-exempt charities from engaging in partisan efforts. In 1996
the committee and its counsel, James M. Cole, broadened the scope
of their investigation to examine the relationship between the
course and GOPAC, a political action committee once headed by

Gingrich. GOPAC raised an enormous amount of money for Republican congressional candidates. The House Ethics Committee
is also looking at the Progress and Freedom Foundation, a conservative think tank associated with Gingrich. At issue are whether
the tax-exempt foundation was actually a shelter for partisan efforts
and whether Gingrich's college courses were actually tied to
GOPAC.[16] Gingrich was eventually forced to pay a fine of several
hundred thousand dollars. More important, the investigation undermined Gingrich's leadership of the House and helped derail the
GOP's legislative agenda.

There is no particular reason to believe that the level of political
corruption or abuse of power in America actually increased tenfold
over the past two decades, as the figure above would seem to indicate. It could be argued, however, that this sharp rise reflects a
heightened level of public concern about governmental misconduct.
However, as we shall see, both the issue of government ethics and the
growing use of criminal sanctions against public officials have been
closely linked to struggles for political power in the United States.
In the aftermath of Watergate, institutions such as the Office of the
Independent Counsel were established and processes to investigate
allegations of unethical conduct on the part of public figures were
created. Since then political forces have increasingly sought to make
use of these mechanisms to discredit their opponents. When scores
of investigators, accountants, and lawyers are deployed to scrutinize
the conduct of a Bill Clinton or a Newt Gingrich, it is all but certain that something questionable will be found. The creation of these
investigative processes, more than changes in the public's tolerance
for government misconduct, explains why public officials are increasingly being charged with ethical and criminal violations.

The growing use of criminal indictments as a partisan weapon
has helped enhance the political importance of the judiciary. The
prominence of the courts has been heightened by the sharp increase in the number of major policy issues that have been fought
and decided in the judicial realm rather than in the arena of electoral politics.[17] The federal judiciary has become the main insti-

tution for resolving struggles over such issues as race relations and abortion, and it has also come to play a more significant role in deciding questions of social welfare and economic policy.[18] The number of suits brought by civil rights, environmental, feminist, and other liberal groups seeking to advance their policy goals increased dramatically during the 1970s and 1980s, reflecting the willingness and ability of these groups to fight their battles in the judicial arena. For example, the number of civil rights cases brought in federal courts doubled during this period. After the emergence of a conservative majority on the Supreme Court in 1989, forces from the political right began to use litigation to implement their own policy agenda. In recent years a number of conservative legal foundations have pursued aggressive strategies of litigation against their opponents on the left. For example, the Paula Jones suit against Bill Clinton was partly financed by the Rutherford Institute, a foundation that champions conservative causes through the courts. The growing importance of the federal judiciary explains why judicial confirmation battles have sometimes been so bitterly fought in recent years. The growing importance of the judiciary also set the stage for the court battles that decided the outcome of the 2000 presidential election. Both sides presumed that the courts could and should settle the issue. Of course, the Bush and Gore campaigns differed over the question of which courts should settle the matter.

The Independent Counsel. The political importance of the federal judiciary was further enhanced by the 1978 Ethics in Government Act, which created the Office of the Special Prosecutor. This official, unlike the attorney general or other prosecutors, is independent of the executive branch and, though in principle subject to presidential removal, could only be fired at enormous political cost to the president. The idea of the independent counsel was Congress's response to Richard Nixon's dismissal of the Watergate counsel Archibald Cox in the infamous Saturday Night Massacre. Under the terms of the independent counsel provision, which was subject to renewal every five years (it was most recently renewed in 1994 but allowed to lapse in 1999), Congress could initiate a request for the appointment of a special counsel if its own investigations gave it reason to believe that the president or some other high-ranking executive branch official might have committed some illegal act. The independent counsel provision did not apply to Congress itself. Congress created the independent counsel to undertake investigations of the executive branch; it had no interest in subjecting itself to similar investigations by government prosecutors. The independent counsel provision of the Ethics in Government Act expired not long after the Clinton impeachment imbroglio. However, independent counsels can and will still be appointed on an ad hoc basis when Congress and the attorney general deem them to be useful.

Under the special counsel law, Congress or another interested party asked the attorney general to go before a statutory three-judge panel to request the appointment of a special counsel to ascertain whether or not a crime had indeed been committed by an executive official. The attorney general had some discretion and could assert that there was insufficient evidence of criminal action to warrant going further. For example, in 1997 and 1998 Attorney General Janet Reno refused to request the appointment of an independent counsel to look into allegations that the 1996 Clinton-Gore campaign violated federal election finance laws. Usually, however, the attorney general had no desire to become the target of the firestorm of criticism from Congress and the media likely to ensue if he or she failed to accede to Congress's wishes. As a result, Congress was generally able to have its way when it requested the appointment of an independent counsel.

Once appointed, an independent counsel can be a powerful figure, exercising far more prosecutorial discretion than other federal or state prosecutors. First, the independent counsel is not appointed to investigate a specific crime that has already taken place. Instead he or she is assigned to determine if a crime has been committed. This vague mandate allows the independent counsel to look into a variety of events that seem suspicious without having to worry much about their relationship to the matters that triggered congressional concern in the first place.

Second, the independent counsel is often far more generously funded than other prosecutors. Unlike routine inquiries, the independent counsel's investigation is funded directly by Congress. Since, almost by definition, special counsels are conducting investigations that Congress eagerly sought, the legislative branch has every reason to provide them with ample resources. For example, Congress gave Whitewater independent counsels Robert Fiske and Kenneth Starr nearly forty million dollars over a four-year period to seek evidence of wrongdoing on the part of President Clinton and his associates. Such generous levels of funding give special counsels the ability to follow even the most unlikely leads, interview numerous witnesses, collect huge quantities of evidence, and prosecute several cases simultaneously. The independent counsel's resources are likely to overwhelm those of all but the most powerful defendant.

Finally, the independent counsel has extremely broad leeway to expand the scope of his or her investigation from its initial focus to seemingly unrelated matters. Ordinary federal prosecutors, by contrast, normally must confine themselves to the initial subject matter of an investigation. They are not free to pursue leads into unrelated areas.

In 1994 a special counsel was appointed by the Justice Department to investigate charges that President Clinton and his wife had engaged in illegal activities growing out of their partnership in the Whitewater Development Corporation while Clinton was governor of Arkansas. The same special counsel, Robert Fiske, also investigated the activities of a number of Clinton aides accused of making illegal contacts with the Treasury Department on behalf of the White House. In August 1994 Fiske was replaced by former federal prosecutor Kenneth Starr. Fiske had been appointed by Attorney General Janet Reno before Congress had restored the lapsed independent counsel provision of the Ethics in Government Act.

Once this portion of the act was restored by Congress, a three-judge federal panel ruled that because Fiske had been appointed to investigate Clinton by a member of Clinton's own cabinet, there was a potential for conflict of interest.

Starr, a Republican who often had been critical of the Clinton administration, expanded his jurisdiction several times and was, by 1998, investigating charges that Clinton had had an affair with a White House intern, Monica Lewinsky, in 1996 and had subsequently pressed Lewinsky to perjure herself. An ordinary federal prosecutor would probably have been laughed out of court if he or she sought to convince a judge that an alleged Washington affair in 1996 had any relevance to real estate dealings in Arkansas in the 1980s. Starr, however, had no difficulty persuading the attorney general and the three-judge panel supervising his investigation to allow him to expand the scope of his probe. Reno was not willing to endure another storm of protest on the heels of congressional outrage at her refusal to appoint an independent counsel to investigate Clinton's fund-raising activities. For its part, the three-judge panel was simply following precedent. The leading precedent in this matter is the 1996 case of *United States v. Tucker,* in which the Eighth Circuit Court of Appeals held that independent counsels should be given broad latitude to expand the scope of an ongoing investigation.[19] The Supreme Court declined to review this decision.

Taken together, its broad mandate, generous funding, and easily expanded investigative purview make the independent counsel a powerful instrument. In effect, when the independent counsel launches an investigation of a president or other high government official, his or her office has the resources and latitude to investigate almost any aspect of that individual's life and career. Unlike most judicial inquiries, which are aimed at specific acts, the independent counsel's mission is to identify and prosecute evidence of *any* wrongdoing on the part of the individual under investigation. In the case of executive branch officials other than the president, the special counsel may secure a grand jury criminal indictment if he or she believes that the facts warrant such action. In the case of presidential misconduct, the special counsel is limited to providing Congress with information for a possible impeachment proceeding.

When the office was initially established in 1978, congressional Democrats viewed what was then called the special prosecutor as an important weapon in their struggle with the executive branch. Until 1994 Democratic members of Congress were the office's chief defenders, while Republicans typically railed against it. In 1994, of course, the GOP won control of both houses of Congress, and the two parties changed their respective tunes. Now Democrats called for reining in Starr and the other independent counsels. Republicans, on the other hand, defended Starr and the other independent counsels probing former Clinton administration officials Henry Cisneros and Mike Espy. So long as they control the Congress, Republicans had little interest in attacking an office that the former Reagan administration official Terry Eastland once called "a loaded gun pointed at the executive branch."[20]

The Media. Another institution whose power has risen dramatically over the past three decades is the news media. The political power of the media has increased through the growing prominence of "adversarial journalism," a form of journalism in which the media adopt a hostile posture toward the government and public officials.

During the nineteenth century American newspapers were completely subordinate to the political parties. Newspapers depended upon official patronage—legal notices and party subsidies—for their financial survival and were controlled by party leaders. (A vestige of that era survived into the twentieth century in such newspaper names as the *Springfield Republican* and the *St. Louis Globe-Democrat*.) At the turn of the century, with the development of commercial advertising, newspapers became financially independent. This made possible the emergence of a formally nonpartisan press.

Presidents were the first national officials to see the opportunities in this development. By communicating directly to the electorate through newspapers and magazines, Theodore Roosevelt and Woodrow Wilson established political constituencies for themselves independent of party organizations and strengthened their own power relative to Congress. President Franklin D. Roosevelt used the radio, notably in his famous fireside chats, to reach out to voters throughout the nation and to make himself the center of American politics. FDR was also adept at developing close personal relationships with reporters that enabled him to obtain favorable news coverage despite the fact that in his day a majority of newspaper owners and publishers were staunch conservatives. Following Roosevelt's example, all subsequent presidents have sought to use the media to enhance their popularity and power. For example, through televised news conferences, President John F. Kennedy mobilized public support for his domestic and foreign policy initiatives.

In the 1950s and early 1960s a few members of Congress also made successful use of the media—especially television—to mobilize national support for their causes. Senator Estes Kefauver of Tennessee became a major contender for the presidency and won a place on the 1956 Democratic national ticket as a result of his dramatic televised hearings on organized crime. Senator Joseph McCarthy of Wisconsin made himself a powerful national figure through his well-publicized investigations of alleged Communist infiltration of key American institutions. These senators, however, were more exceptional than typical. Through the mid-1960s the executive branch continued to generate the bulk of news coverage, and the media served as a cornerstone of presidential power.

The Vietnam War shattered this relationship between the press and the presidency. During the early stages of U.S. involvement, American officials in Vietnam who disapproved of the way the war was being conducted leaked information critical of administrative policy to reporters. Publication of this material infuriated the White House, which pressed publishers to block its release; on one occasion, President Kennedy went so far as to ask the *New York Times* to reassign its Saigon correspondent. The national print and broadcast media—the network news divisions, the national news weeklies, the *Washington Post,* and the *New York Times*—discovered, however, that there was an audience for critical coverage among segments of the public skeptical of administration policy. As the Vietnam conflict dragged on, critical media coverage fanned antiwar sentiment. Moreover, growing opposition to the war among liberals encouraged some members of Congress, notably Senator J. William Fulbright, chair of the Senate Foreign Relations Committee, to break with the president. In turn these shifts in popular and congressional sentiment emboldened journalists and publishers to continue to present critical news reports. Through this process, journalists developed a commitment to adversarial journalism, while a constituency emerged that would rally to the defense of the media when they came under White House attack.

This pattern, established during the Vietnam War, endured through the 1970s and into the 1990s. Political forces opposed to presidential policies, many members of Congress, and the national news media began to find that their interests often overlapped. Liberal opponents of the Nixon, Carter, Reagan, and Bush administrations welcomed news accounts critical of the conduct of executive agencies and officials in foreign affairs and in such domestic areas as race relations, the environment, and regulatory policy. In addition, many senators and representatives found it politically advantageous to champion causes favored by the antiwar, consumer, and environmental movements because by conducting televised hearings on such issues, they were able to mobilize national constituencies, to become national figures, and in a number of instances to become serious contenders for their party's presidential nomination.

For their part, aggressive use of the techniques of investigation, publicity, and exposure allowed the national media to enhance their autonomy and carve out a prominent place for themselves in American government and politics. In essence, the media came to have a stake in finding and revealing damaging information about prominent politicians. Increasingly, media coverage has come to influence politicians' careers, the mobilization of political constituencies, and the fate of issues and causes. Inasmuch as liberal political forces in the 1970s and 1980s benefited from the growing influence of the press, they were prepared to rush to its defense when it came under attack. For example, this constituency could be counted upon to denounce any move by the White House or its supporters to curb media influence as an illegitimate effort to manage the news, chill free speech, and undermine the First Amendment. It was the emergence of these overlapping interests, more than an ideological bias, that often led to a de facto alliance between liberal political forces and the national news media.

This confluence of interests was in evidence during the 1996 presidential campaign. Most journalists endeavored to be evenhanded in their coverage of the candidates. The media subjected all the major campaigns to regular scrutiny and criticism. However, as several studies have since indicated, during the course of the campaign the media tended to be more critical of Dole and more supportive of Clinton. Republican economic proposals were generally dismissed by the media as gimmickry. Republican efforts to question President Clinton's ethics—a topic the media had enjoyed probing during the previous years—were rejected as inappropriate for a serious national campaign. Even the Republican National Convention was dismissed, not without cause, as a staged event not worthy of much news coverage. A major network news program, *Nightline,* showed its disdain for the GOP's convention by leaving before it ended, host Ted Koppel proclaiming, "Nothing surprising has happened."[21] One British observer wrote in reaction to these events, "Dole got his most sympathetic and in-depth coverage when he fell off the stage in Chico, California."[22] This was an almost inevitable outgrowth of the de facto alliance that developed over a number of years between the media and liberal forces. Like any long-standing relationship, this one tends to shape the attitudes and perceptions of the participants. Without any need for overt bias or sinister conspiracy, journalists tend naturally to provide more favorable coverage to liberal politicians and causes.

The linkage between substantial segments of the media and liberal interest groups is by no means absolute. Indeed, over the past several years a conservative media complex has emerged in opposition to the liberal media. This complex includes two major newspapers, the *Wall Street Journal* and the *Washington Times,* several magazines such as the *American Spectator,* and a host of conservative radio and television talk programs. These radio programs, in particular, helped Republicans win the 1994 congressional elections. Conservative religious leaders like the Reverends Jerry Falwell and Pat Robertson, leader of the Christian Coalition, have used their television shows to attack the president's programs and to mount biting personal attacks on both Clinton and his wife. For example, a videotape promoted by Falwell accuses Clinton of arranging for the murder of an Arkansas investigator who allegedly had evidence of the president's sexual misconduct. Other conservative groups not associated with the religious right have also launched sharp assaults against the president. Nationally syndicated talk show host Rush Limbaugh is a constant critic of the administration. Floyd Brown, leader of Citizens United, a group with forty employees and a three-million-dollar annual budget, attacks Clinton on a daily radio show and faxes anti-Clinton news bulletins to more than twelve hundred journalists and talk show hosts.

The emergence of this conservative media complex has meant that liberal policies and politicians are virtually certain to come under attack even when the "liberal" media are sympathetic to them. For example, charges that President Clinton and his wife were involved in financial improprieties as partners in the Whitewater Development Corporation, as well as allegations that while governor, Clinton had sexually harassed an Arkansas state employee, Paula Jones, were first publicized by the conservative press. Only after these stories had received a good deal of coverage in the *Washington Times* and the *American Spectator* did the mainstream "liberal" media begin to highlight them. Of course, once the stories

broke, the *Washington Post,* the *New York Times,* and the major television networks devoted substantial investigative resources and
time to them. In due course the "liberal" media probably gave the
Whitewater and Jones charges just as much play as the "conservative" media, often with just as little regard for hard evidence.[23]
Later Clinton's opponents were able to gather evidence suggesting
that the president had an affair with White House intern Monica
Lewinsky. Once again, the "liberal" media gave the story enormous play. Interestingly, however, liberal news organizations made
certain to point out that the story originated with Clinton's right-
wing foes. For example, in its front-page coverage on January 24,
1998, the *Washington Post* revealed that the initial effort to gather
evidence against Clinton had been the brainchild of a conservative
activist and ardent Clinton foe.[24] In this way the *Post* appeared to
be deflecting attention from the allegations against Clinton to the
tactics of his enemies.

Providing the media with information is an enormous set of
ancillary institutions, including conservative and liberal "think
tanks," various consulting firms specializing in developing damaging information on their clients' enemies (a tactic known as opposition research), and public relations firms. These enterprises,
located mainly in Washington and New York, serve up an endless
supply of press releases. Conservative institutions provide damaging information about liberal politicians, while liberal entities provide damaging information about conservative politicians. The
press hardly needs to engage in any investigative work of its own.
It can choose the most tempting tidbits from the torrent of rumors,
innuendos, accusations, and occasional facts conveniently delivered to newsrooms via fax on a daily basis.[25]

Revelation, Investigation, Prosecution

Taken together, the expanded political roles of the national news
media and the federal judiciary have given rise to a major new
weapon of political combat: revelation, investigation, and prosecution. The acronym for this, RIP, forms a fitting political epitaph

for the public officials who have become its targets. The RIP weaponry was initially forged by opponents of the Nixon administration in their struggles with the White House, and through the Reagan years it was used primarily by congressional Democrats to attack their foes in the executive branch. Beginning in the 1980s, however, Republicans began to wield the RIP weapon against Democrats.

In 1972, after his reelection, President Nixon undertook to expand executive power at the expense of Congress by impounding funds appropriated for domestic programs and reorganizing executive agencies without legislative authorization. In addition, the White House established the so-called plumbers squad of former intelligence agents and mercenaries to plug leaks of information to Congress and the press, and (its opponents claimed) it sought to undermine the legitimacy of the federal judiciary by appointing unqualified justices to the Supreme Court. The administration's adversaries also charged that it tried to limit Congress's influence over foreign policy by keeping vital information from it, notably the "secret bombing" of Cambodia from 1969 to 1973.

At the same time Nixon sought to curtail the influence of the national news media. His administration brought suit against the *New York Times* in an effort to block publication of the *Pentagon Papers* and threatened, using the pretext of promoting ideological diversity, to compel the national television networks to sell the local stations they owned. The president's opponents denounced the administration's actions as abuses of power—which they surely were—and launched a full-scale assault upon Richard Nixon in the Watergate controversy.

The Watergate attack began with a series of revelations in the *Washington Post* linking the White House to a break-in at the Watergate Hotel headquarters of the Democratic National Committee. The *Post*'s reporters were quickly joined by scores of investigative journalists from the *New York Times, Newsweek, Time,* and the television networks.

As revelations of misdeeds by the Nixon White House proliferated,

the administration's opponents in Congress demanded a full legislative investigation. In response, the Senate created a special committee, chaired by Sam Ervin, to investigate White House
misconduct in the 1972 presidential election. Investigators for the
Ervin committee uncovered numerous questionable activities on
the part of Nixon's aides, and these were revealed to the public during a series of dramatic, nationally televised hearings.

Evidence of criminal activity unearthed by the Ervin committee led to congressional pressure for the appointment of a special
prosecutor. Ultimately a large number of high-ranking administration officials were indicted, convicted, and imprisoned. Impeachment proceedings were initiated against President Nixon,
and when evidence linking him directly to the cover-up of the Watergate burglary was found, he was forced to resign from office.
Thus, with the help of the RIP weaponry the Nixon administration's antagonists achieved a total victory in their conflict with the
president. Although no subsequent president has been driven from
office, opponents of presidential administrations have since used
the RIP process to attack and weaken their foes in the executive
branch.

The RIP process became institutionalized when Congress
adopted the 1978 Ethics in Government Act, which established
procedures for the appointment of independent counsels (initially
called special prosecutors) to investigate allegations of wrongdoing
in the executive branch. The act also defined as criminal several
forms of influence peddling in which executive officials had traditionally engaged, such as lobbying former associates after leaving
office. (Such activities are also traditional on Capitol Hill, but Congress chose not to impose the restrictions embodied in the act upon
its own members and staff.) Basically Congress created new crimes
that executive branch officials could be charged with. The independent counsel provision of the act lapsed during the Bush administration but was restored by Congress in 1994.

The extent to which the RIP process had come to be a routine
feature of American politics became evident during the Iran-contra

conflict, when Democrats charged that the Reagan administration had covertly sold arms to Iran and used the proceeds to provide illegal funding for Nicaraguan contra forces, in violation of the Boland amendments, which prohibit such help. After the diversion of funds to the contras was revealed, it was universally assumed that Congress should conduct televised hearings and the judiciary should appoint an independent counsel to investigate the officials involved in the episode. Yet this procedure is really quite remarkable. Officials who in other democracies would merely be compelled to resign from office are now threatened with criminal prosecution in the United States.

The institutionalization of the RIP process became even more clear during the Clinton administration. RIP began with the Whitewater probe, in which the president's critics charged that he and his wife had been guilty of a variety of conflicts of interest and financial improprieties while involved in a partnership with a shady Arkansas banker and real estate developer. An independent counsel was appointed to look into the charges, and Republicans demanded that congressional hearings on the issue be scheduled. Democrats opposed hearings, arguing that the Republicans merely sought to embarrass the administration prior to major congressional votes and the 1994 congressional elections. Finally, hearings were scheduled, but under very limited conditions that Democrats hoped would protect the president from potentially embarrassing disclosures.

The president's critics also questioned the circumstances under which Hillary Clinton had been able to earn a profit of more than a hundred thousand dollars in a short time, through a series of highly risky and speculative commodities trades. Critics noted that the First Lady, who had no experience in the commodities market, had been guided by an attorney for Tyson Foods, Inc., a huge Arkansas-based poultry producer that stood to gain from the friendship of then Governor Clinton. Although the White House denied any wrongdoing on her part, the charges produced at least the appearance of impropriety.

After the GOP took control of both houses of Congress in 1994, new investigations were launched by the House and Senate banking committees and the House Oversight Committee. In 1995, as he investigated the Clintons' involvement in the Whitewater matter, special counsel Kenneth Starr indicted Arkansas Governor Jim Guy Tucker and former Clinton Whitewater partners James and Susan McDougal for bank fraud and conspiracy. All three were convicted, but Starr was not immediately able to wrest incriminating testimony about the president from them. Another Clinton associate had already been sent to prison as a result of evidence turned up during the various investigations of the Clintons' business dealings in Arkansas. Former Hillary Clinton law partner and Associate U.S. Attorney General Webster Hubbell began serving a prison term in 1994 for scheming to defraud his Rose law firm partners of $482,000.

In March 1996 the scope of Starr's investigation was broadened to include the so-called Travelgate affair, in which the administration is alleged to have sought to cover up the details surrounding the firing of members of the White House travel office. In June 1996 the scope of Starr's investigation was expanded again to include Filegate, allegations that the White House had improperly obtained FBI files on some nine hundred individuals.

As noted above, in 1998 Starr once again expanded the scope of his investigation to probe charges that Clinton had been sexually intimate with a young White House intern, Monica Lewinsky, and then sought to induce Lewinsky to perjure herself by denying the story in a deposition. Lewinsky had been deposed by attorneys for Paula Jones, who was bringing an ultimately unsuccessful civil suit against Clinton for an alleged act of sexual harassment when he was governor of Arkansas and she was a state employee. Jones's attorneys were seeking to show that Clinton made a practice of seeking sexual favors from employees. They had learned about Lewinsky from a former White House employee, Linda Tripp, who brought Lewinsky's name to the attention of both Jones's lawyers and Starr's office. Starr offered to grant Lewinsky limited immunity from prosecution in exchange for her testimony against the president and his close friend and adviser Vernon Jordan. Starr believed that Clinton and Jordan had sought to persuade Lewinsky to perjure herself in the Jones civil suit and that Jordan offered to find her a job as a form of "hush money." Jordan admitted to helping Lewinsky find a position in New York but said he acted simply to be helpful to the young intern. Clinton vehemently denied all the allegations and launched a vigorous campaign to discredit Starr's investigation as nothing more than a right-wing smear campaign.

In August 1998, Clinton was forced to appear before Starr's grand jury and acknowledge the affair with Lewinsky. The president claimed that technically he had not perjured himself when denying sexual contact with Lewinsky in his deposition in the Jones case, but admitted engaging in improper behavior. Clinton delivered an extraordinary televised address to the nation, acknowledging the relationship with Lewinsky, but also attacking Starr and his other political opponents. In the ensuing weeks, Clinton was compelled to travel the country repeating humiliating apologies and requests for forgiveness. In September, the House Judiciary Committee began an impeachment inquiry to ascertain whether Clinton's offenses constituted "high crimes and misdemeanors" stipulated by the Constitution as grounds for removing a president from office. To further humiliate Clinton, the committee released a complete tape of his testimony before the Starr grand jury. The entire four-hour tape was aired on national television and viewed by millions of Americans.

In the wake of Clinton's humiliation, congressional Republicans eagerly looked forward to the 1998 elections. They assumed that voter disgust with Clinton's actions would give Republican candidates an edge in elections for House and Senate seats. Republican predictions were proven wrong, however. Most voters did not see Clinton's character as the central issue of the campaign. Moreover, as the GOP focused on Clinton's misdeeds, the party's leadership appeared to ignore other national issues. This provided Democratic candidates an opportunity emphasize issues that voters cared about, such as education and Social Security. The results of the 1998 elections were a rebuke to the Republicans. In most midterm elections, the president's party loses seats in Congress; in 1998, however, the Democrats more than held their ground. In the House, Democrats posted a net gain of five seats, leaving the Republicans with a razor-thin 223-to-211 majority. In the Senate, the party balance remained unchanged at 55 to 45.

Initially, the 1998 results seemed to discourage the GOP from pursuing its effort to impeach Bill Clinton. The electorate was clearly weary of the relentless attack on the president, and many Republicans hoped that some compromise coud be reached between Clinton and his opponents. Within a few days, however, the House GOP leadership resolved to resume the offensive against the president, and in December 1998, Clinton was impeached by the House of Representatives on an almost straight party-line vote. Two months later, after a relatively brief trial, Clinton was acquitted in the Senate.

The 1998 election also brought an end to the career of House Speaker Newt Gingrich. Many Republicans blamed Gingrich for the party's poor showing in the elections and demanded that he step down. Two days after the election, Gingrich became convinced that he could not be reelected to the Speakership and announced that he would resign his House seat. Though Gingrich was the individual most responsible for leading the GOP to victory in 1994, many Republicans were now convinced that he had run out of ideas and lacked the skills needed for day-to-day management of the government. Gingrich's star had been fading since the politically disastrous 1995–1996 government shutdown. The 1998 election sealed his fate.

Gingrich was initially replaced by Bob Livingston (R-La.), chairman of the House Appropriations Committee. In a surprising turn of events, however, Livingston resigned from Congress after it was revealed that he had engaged in a number of extramarital affairs. Livingston urged President Clinton to follow his course. The president declined. The information about Livingston's transgressions had been released by Larry Flynt, publisher of *Hustler* magazine, who had made it his business to defend President Clinton by offering cash rewards to individuals who could prove that prominent Republicans were guilty of misdeeds similar to the president's. Such is the character of politics in America today that pornographers have been transformed into king makers. Livingston was replaced by Dennis Hastert of Illinois, an individual little-known outside the House who was, at least, able to assure his colleagues of his moral probity.

RIP FOR DEMOCRATIC POLITICS

During the political struggles of the past decades, politicians sought to undermine the institution associated with their foes, disgrace one another on national television, force their competitors to resign from office, and, in a number of cases, send their opponents to prison. Remarkably, one tactic that has not been so widely used is the mobilization of the electorate. Of course Democrats and Republicans have contested each other and continue to contest each other in national elections. Voter turnout even inched up in 1992, before dropping again in 1996. However, neither side has made much effort to mobilize *new* voters, to create strong local party organizations, or in general to make full use of the electoral arena to defeat its enemies.

It is certainly not true that politicians don't know how to mobilize new voters and expand electoral competition. Voter mobilization is hardly a mysterious process. It entails an investment of funds and organizational effort to register voters actively and bring them to the polls on election day. Occasionally politicians demonstrate that they *do* know how to mobilize voters if they have a strong enough incentive. For example, a massive get-out-the-vote effort by Democrats to defeat neo-Nazi David Duke in the 1991 Louisiana gubernatorial election led to a voter turnout of over 80 percent of those eligible—twice the normal turnout level for a Louisiana election. In the 1990s it was the GOP, through its alliance with conservative religious leaders, that made the more concerted effort to bring new voters into the electorate. This effort was limited in scope, but it played an important part in the Republican party's capture of both houses of Congress in 1994. The GOP's gains from this limited strategy of mobilization demonstrate what could be achieved from a fuller mobilization of the national electorate.

How extraordinary, then, that politicians stop short of attempting to expand the electorate to overwhelm their foes in competitive elections. Why is this? To expand upon a point made earlier, a large part of the answer to this question is that the decline of political party organizations over the past several decades strengthened politicians in both camps who were linked with and supported by the middle and upper middle classes. Party organization is an especially important instrument for enhancing the political influence of groups at the bottom of the social hierarchy—groups whose major political resource is numbers. Parties allowed politicians to organize the energies of large numbers of individuals from the lower classes to counter the superior financial and institutional resources available to those from the middle and upper classes.

The decline of party organization that resulted in large measure from the efforts of upper- and middle-class "reformers" over the years has undermined such politicians as union officials and Democratic and Republican "machine" leaders who had a stake in popular mobilization, while it has strengthened politicians with an upper-middle- or upper-class base. As a result of these reforms, today's Democratic and Republican parties are dominated by different segments of the American upper middle class. For the most part, contemporary Republicans speak for business and professionals from the private sector, while Democratic politicians and political activists are drawn from and speak for upper-middle-class professionals in the public and not-for-profit sectors.

Both sides give lip service to the idea of fuller popular participation in political life. Politicians and their upper-middle-class constituents in both camps, however, have access to a variety of different political resources—the news media, the courts, universities, and interest groups—to say nothing of substantial financial resources. As a result, neither side has much need for or interest in political tactics that might, in effect, stir up trouble from below. Both sides prefer to compete for power without engaging in full-scale popular mobilization. Without mobilization drives that might encourage low-income citizens or minorities to register and actually to vote, the population that does vote tends to be wealthier, whiter, and better educated than the population as a whole. There are marked differences in voter turnout linked to ethnic group, education level, and employment status. This trend has created a political process whose class bias is so obvious and egregious that if it continues, it may force Americans to begin adding a qualifier when they describe their politics as democratic. Perhaps the terms "semidemocratic," "quasi-democratic," and "neodemocratic" are in order to describe a political process in which ordinary voters have as little influence as they do in contemporary America. As we shall see, the consequences of these undemocratic political patterns reverberate throughout the American political system.

2

Electoral Deadlock

ONE OF THE REASONS that the importance of elections has declined in relation to that of other weapons of political combat in recent decades is that elections in the United States have been marked by a pattern of divided and inconclusive results. From the 1960s through the 1980s Republicans controlled the White House while Democrats controlled Congress. In the 1990s this pattern appeared to have reversed itself with Democrats controlling the White House and Republicans entrenched in Congress. In 2000, of course, Republicans took control of the executive branch after an extraordinary postelection struggle in Florida. During the same year, Democrats seemed to lose both the House and Senate but regained control of the upper chamber after Senator James Jeffords of Vermont switched his affiliation from Republican to independent. Thus, control of two of the nation's most important elective institutions was decided in postelectoral processes which further encouraged both sides to rely more heavily on nonelectoral means of defeating their opponents and securing power. In this chapter we shall examine the pattern of partisan competition from the 1960s through the Clinton era. The peculiar conduct of the 2000 national election will be examined in Chapter 6.

NATIONAL PARTY POLITICS, 1968–1998

From the 1930s through the mid-1960s the Democratic party was the nation's dominant political force, led by a coalition of southern white politicians and northern urban machine bosses and labor leaders. The party drew its votes primarily from large cities, from the South, and from minorities, unionized workers, Jews, and Catholics.

Though occasionally winning presidential elections and, less often, control of Congress, the Republicans had been the nation's minority party since Franklin Roosevelt's presidential victory and the beginnings of the New Deal in 1933. The Republicans were led by northeastern and midwestern Protestants with deep roots in the business community. They drew their support primarily from middle- and upper-middle-class suburban voters from the Northeast, from rural areas, and from the small towns and cities of the Midwest.

In the 1960s two powerful tidal waves brought about the reconstruction of both national party coalitions: the anti–Vietnam War movement and the civil rights movement. The anti–Vietnam War movement galvanized liberal activists in the Democratic party. These activists attacked and, during the late 1960s, destroyed much of the power of the machine bosses and labor leaders who had been so prominent in Democratic party affairs. Liberal activists organized a number of public interest groups to fight on behalf of such liberal goals as consumer and environmental regulation; an end to the arms race; expanded rights and opportunities for women, gays and lesbians, and the physically disabled; and gun control. These groups supported the election of liberal congressional and presidential candidates, as well as legislation designed to achieve their aims. Their efforts were effective; during the 1970s liberal forces in Congress were successful in enacting significant pieces of legislation in many of these areas.

For its part, the civil rights movement attacked and sharply curtailed the power of the southern white politicians who had been the third leg of the Democratic party's leadership troika. In addition, the civil rights movement enfranchised millions of African American voters in the South, nearly all of whom could be counted upon to support the Democrats. These developments dramatically changed the character of the Democratic party.

First, the new prominence and energy of liberal activists in the Democratic party after the late 1960s greatly increased the Democratic advantage in local and congressional elections. Democrats had usually controlled Congress and a majority of state and local offices since the New Deal and therefore already possessed an edge in elections because of the benefits of incumbency. Because incumbents have many electoral advantages, more often than not they are able to secure reelection. Particularly advantageous of course is the ability of incumbents to bring home pork in the form of federal projects and spending in their districts. In general, the more senior the incumbent, the more pork he or she can provide for constituents. Thus, incumbency perpetuated Democratic power by giving voters a reason to cast their ballots for the Democratic candidate regardless of issues and ideology.

The advantage of incumbency was enhanced in the 1960s and 1970s, when Congress enacted a large number of new programs for local economic development, housing, hospital construction, water and air pollution control, education, and social services. These programs made available tens of billions of dollars each year that members of Congress could channel into their constituencies. By using their influence over the allocation of these funds, incumbent representatives and senators could build political support for themselves at home. In this way, incumbents greatly enhanced their prospects for reelection. Since the Democrats held a solid majority in Congress when this process began, it helped perpetuate their control for several decades.

Incumbency effects, however, were not the only key to Democratic success in local and congressional races. At least until recent years these races tended to be fought on the basis of local concerns rather than the national issues that dominated presidential contests. Moreover, while presidential elections were usually fought through the national media, especially television, victory in congressional and local races has depended upon the capacity of candidates to recruit volunteers to hand out leaflets, call voters, post handbills, and engage in the day-to-day efforts needed to organize constituency support. Liberal activists, along with organized labor, gave Democratic candidates a ready-made cadre of supporters willing to engage in these forms of political work. Prior to the 1990s, at least, Republicans did not appeal to any comparable group. Liberal activists, generally drawn from the not-for-profit and public sectors, had a strong stake in working for the election of Democrats, who generally supported the high levels of federal domestic expenditures upon which the public and not-for-profit sectors depended. Their liberal activist and trade union cadres gave the Democrats a reach, depth, and institutional base throughout the nation that were unmatched by the Republicans and allowed the Democrats to dominate the congressional arena until the mid-1990s despite frequent GOP success in presidential elections.

The same liberal activism, however, that helped propel the Democrats to victory in congressional elections often became a hindrance in the presidential electoral arena. Particularly after the 1968 Democratic National Convention and the party's adoption of new nominating rules, liberal activists came to play a decisive role in the selection of Democratic presidential candidates. Although liberal Democrats were not always able to nominate the candidates of their choice, they were in a position to block the nomination of candidates they opposed.

The result was that the Democratic nominating process often produced candidates who were considered too liberal by much of the general electorate. This perception contributed to defeat after defeat for Democratic presidential candidates. In 1972, for example, Democratic candidate George McGovern suffered an electoral drubbing at the hands of Republican Richard Nixon after proposing to decrease the tax burden of lower-income voters at the expense of middle- and upper-income voters. Similarly, in 1984 Walter Mondale was routed by Ronald Reagan after pledging to increase taxes and social spending if elected.

The Democratic party's difficulties in presidential elections were compounded by the aftermath of the civil rights movement. The national Democratic party had helped bring about the enfranchisement of millions of black voters in the South. To secure the loyalty of these voters, as well as to cement the loyalty of black voters in the North, the national Democratic leadership supported a variety of civil rights and social programs designed to serve the needs of African Americans.

Unfortunately, however, the association of the national Democratic party with civil rights and the aspirations of blacks alienated millions of white Democrats, including southerners and blue-collar northerners, who believed that black gains came at their expense. White voters defected en masse to support George Wallace's third-party presidential candidacy in 1968. Subsequently many began voting for Republican presidential candidates.

Efforts by Democratic presidential candidates to rebuild their party's support among southern whites and blue-collar northerners were hampered by the harsh racial arithmetic of American politics. In the wake of the Voting Rights Act, the Democratic party depended upon African Americans for more than 20 percent of its votes in national presidential elections. Yet at the same time, and for a more or less equal percentage of votes, the Democrats relied upon whites who, for one or another reason, were unfriendly to blacks. Efforts by Democratic candidates to bolster their support among blacks by focusing on civil rights and social programs wound up losing them as much support among whites as they gained among blacks. Conversely, those Democratic candidates who avoided overtly courting black support in order to maintain white backing were hurt by declines in black voter turnout. For example, in 1984 Walter Mondale assiduously courted black support and was abandoned by southern white Democrats. In 1988 Michael Dukakis carefully avoided too close an association with blacks and was punished by a steep decline in black voter turnout.

Thus, liberal activism and civil rights combined to weaken the Democratic party in national presidential elections. From 1968 on, the Republicans moved swiftly to take advantage of this weakness. Their presidential candidates developed a number of issues and symbols designed to show that the Democrats were too liberal and too eager to appease blacks at the expense of whites. For instance, beginning in 1968, Republicans emphasized a "southern strategy," consisting of opposition to school busing to achieve racial integration and resistance to affirmative action programs.

At the same time Republicans took on a number of issues and positions designed to distinguish their own candidates from what they declared to be the excessive liberalism of the Democrats. Republican platforms included support for school prayer and opposition to abortion, advocacy of sharp cuts in taxes on corporations and on middle- and upper-income voters, a watering down of consumer and environmental federal regulatory programs, efforts to reduce crime and increase public safety, and increased spending on national defense. Accordingly, during the Reagan and Bush presidencies, taxes were cut, defense spending was increased, regulatory efforts were reduced, support for civil rights programs was curtailed, and at least token efforts were made to restrict abortion and reintroduce prayer in the public schools.

These Republican appeals and programs proved successful in presidential elections. Southern and some northern blue-collar voters were drawn to the Republicans' positions on issues of race. Socially conservative and religious voters were energized and mobilized in large numbers by the Republicans' strong opposition to abortion and support for school prayer. Large numbers of middle- and upper-middle-class voters were drawn to Republicanism by tax cuts. The business community responded positively to Republican efforts to reduce the government's regulatory efforts and to the prospect of continuing high levels of defense spending. These issues and programs carried the Republicans to triumph in five of six presidential contests between 1968 and 1992. The South and West, in particular, became Republican strongholds in presidential elections and led some analysts to assert that the Republicans had a virtual lock on the electoral college.

Nevertheless, the issues that allowed the Republicans to achieve such an impressive record of success at the presidential level during this period still did not translate into GOP victories in the congressional, state, or local races. Presidential races are mainly media campaigns in which opposing forces compete for the attention and favor of the electorate through television spot ads, media events, and favorable press coverage. This form of politics emphasizes the use of issues and symbols. Congressional and local races, by contrast, were typically fought "on the ground" by armies of volunteers. The national media could devote little attention to any individual local race, while local media tended to focus on local issues and personalities. As a result, national issues, for the most part, had little effect upon the outcomes of local races.

Frequently, Democratic members of Congress, making vigorous use of the federal pork barrel, won handily in the same districts that were carried by the Republican presidential candidate. Presidential and congressional elections seemed to exist in different political universes. Voters who supported a Richard Nixon or a Ronald Reagan at the presidential level seemed still to love their Democratic congressional representatives.

Senatorial elections have some of the characteristics of national races and some of the characteristics of local races. Both media and activists can be important. Therefore, though Republicans had greater success in capturing the White House than the Senate, they had a better record in Senate races than in contests for the House.

Thus, for thirty years the pattern of American politics was Republican control of the White House and Democratic control of Congress, especially of the House of Representatives. Indeed, this pattern seemed to have become such a permanent feature of the

American political landscape that each party began to try both to fortify its own institutional stronghold and to undermine its opponent's. Democrats sought to strengthen Congress while weakening the presidency. Republicans tried to expand presidential powers while limiting those of Congress.

For this reason, Democratic Congresses enacted such legislation as the War Powers Act, the Budget and Impoundment Control Act, and the Arms Export Control Act, all of which sought to place limits upon the use of presidential power at home and abroad. In a similar vein, the Ethics in Government Act gave Democratic Congresses a mechanism for initiating formal investigations and even the prosecution of executive branch officials—usually Republican appointees. The Iran-contra investigations, for example, led to indictments of a number of high-ranking Republicans.

For their part, Republicans sought to weaken Congress with sharp cuts in the domestic spending programs upon which congressional Democrats rely to build constituency support. Republicans also built a record of successful presidential faits accomplis in foreign affairs, such as the Reagan administration's invasion of Grenada and bombing of Libya. The favorable popular reaction to these presidential initiatives undermined the War Powers Act and untied the hands of the White House in foreign and military affairs.

Although engaged in these sorts of institutional struggles, each party also sought to devise strategies to capture its opponent's political base. Moderate and conservative Democrats argued that the party could win presidential elections if it nominated an ideologically centrist candidate who ran on issues that would appeal to the middle-class voters who had rejected more liberal Democratic nominees. Moderate Democrats organized the Democratic Leadership Council (DLC), which sought to develop new issues and advance the political fortunes of moderate candidates. Many Democrats also advocated a version of the GOP's southern strategy, arguing that a moderate southerner would be the party's ideal presidential candidate. Such an individual not only might attract middle-class voters in the North but also might lead southern whites, who had defected to the Republicans in presidential elections, to return to their Democratic roots.

While Democrats pondered ways in which they might capture the presidency, some Republicans considered strategies that might allow them to storm the seemingly impregnable Democratic fortress on Capital Hill. In the 1970s and 1980s the Republican National Committee (RNC) embarked upon an effort to recruit politically attractive candidates for congressional and local races. It also sought to create a national fund-raising apparatus to replace, or at least augment, the historically decentralized fund-raising that characterized both American political parties. The RNC was able to create a nationwide direct-mail fund-raising machine that allowed it to raise millions of dollars through small contributions. These funds could then be allocated to those local races where they might do the most good.

At the same time Republicans began to reach out to antiabortion forces and religious conservatives. These groups represented important voting blocs. Even more important, however, was the possibility that the religious fervor of these groups could be converted into political activism. If so, these forces could become a source of Republican volunteers and activists in the same way that the fervent anti-Vietnam forces fueled Democratic activism for years. In other words, religious conservatives could give the Republicans the infantry needed to compete effectively in local and congressional races.

Finally, Republican strategists looked for ways to "nationalize" congressional and local races. For thirty years, such issues as taxes, defense, and abortion had brought the GOP victory in presidential contests. Yet these issues did not appear to have much impact at the subpresidential level. Indeed, local Democratic candidates usually tried to avoid identification with national issues and ideologies, calculating that they could only be hurt by them. The question for Republicans, then, was how to tie popular local Democrats to the national party's often unpopular issues and ideological stances.

The Democratic southern and moderate strategy produced two presidential victories: the election of Jimmy Carter in 1976 and the election of Bill Clinton in 1992. Carter seemed to be the ideal Democratic candidate. He was a white southerner with a good civil rights record. His political views seemed to be centrist. Carter's victory over incumbent Republican Gerald Ford led some Democrats to hope that their party's presidential problems were over.

Unfortunately, the moderate bent that allowed Carter to win the presidential election proved a handicap in office. Carter's middle-of-the-road programs and policies alienated liberal Democrats in Congress, who quickly attacked his presidency. Liberals were so offended by what they saw as Carter's conservative leanings that they supported a fierce challenge to his renomination in 1980 and gave him only lukewarm support against Reagan in the general election. Liberal Democrats, it would seem, supported the idea of a centrist campaign but did not go so far as to support a centrist administration. The party's liberal wing had what appeared to be incompatible goals: It wanted a centrist campaign that would win the election, followed by a liberal administration to govern the nation. In 1992 a solution to this dilemma seemed to be at hand.

THE 1992 ELECTION

First, however, the Democrats had to put their own party's house in order. Since the early 1970s Democratic candidates had been handicapped by problems of a liberal ideology and racial issues. During this period moderate Democrats had argued that the party needed to present a more centrist image if it hoped to be competitive in national elections. The major organizational vehicle for the centrists was the Democratic Leadership Council (DLC), an organization based in Washington and funded by business firms with ties to the Democratic party. Throughout the Reagan and Bush years the DLC organized networks of state and local party officials and sought to develop political themes that could both bring about a measure of party unity and appeal to the national electorate.[1]

In 1992 the DLC and its moderate allies were able to dominate the Democratic party's presidential nominating processes as well as its national convention. The party chose as its presidential and vice presidential candidates Governor Bill Clinton and Senator Al Gore, both founding members of the DLC. The platform adopted at the party's national convention was widely perceived to be the most conservative in decades, stressing individual responsibility and private enterprise while implicitly criticizing welfare recipients. Though the platform mentioned the importance of protecting the rights of women, gays, and minorities, gone were the calls for expanded rights for criminals and welfare recipients that had provided Republicans with such convenient political targets in previous years.

Democrats sought to deal with their party's racial divisions by keeping black politicians and racial issues at arm's length and relying upon economic appeals to woo both working-class white and black voters. Democratic strategists calculated that black voters and politicians would have no choice but to support the Democratic ticket. Given the nation's economic woes, which afflicted blacks even more than whites, Democratic leaders reasoned that they did not need to appeal explicitly for black support. This freed the party to seek the votes of conservative whites. One step in this direction was of course the creation of a ticket headed by two southerners. Democrats hoped that the Clinton-Gore ticket would appeal directly to the southern white voters who once had been Democratic stalwarts but had made the Deep South a Republican bastion during the Reagan years.

Clinton went out of his way to assure conservative whites in both the North and South that unlike previous Democratic candidates, he would not cater to blacks. He thus became the first Democratic presidential candidate in two decades who was neither burdened by an excessively liberal image nor plagued by the party's racial division. With Democratic strategists believing they had stabilized the party's traditional southern, African American, and blue-collar base, Clinton and his allies moved to expand the Democratic coalition into Republican electoral territory: business and the middle class. For this purpose, the Democrats fashioned an economic message designed to appeal to business and the middle class without alienating the party's working-class constituency.

Against the backdrop of continuing economic recession and Republican disarray, the Democrats' economic program and new posture of moderation on racial issues and ideology helped the Clinton-Gore ticket take a commanding lead in the polls in August 1992, after the Democratic National Convention. The Republican ticket's difficulties became fully evident during the nationally televised presidential and vice presidential debates in October. While the Democratic candidates focused on the nation's economic distress, constantly reminding voters of the need for programs and policies designed to improve the nation's economy, Bush and Quayle, for their part, had considerable difficulty articulating an affirmative message and were left to talk about character. Not surprisingly, the debates attracted few new voters to the Republican camp. The Clinton-Gore ticket achieved a comfortable victory, winning 43 percent of the popular vote and 370 electoral votes. Bush and Quayle received 38 percent of the popular vote and only 168 electoral votes. Economic recession, the end of the Cold War, and the Democrats' newfound moderation on matters of race and ideology combined to oust the Republicans from the White House for the first time in twelve years.

According to national exit poll results reported by the *Washington Post* immediately after the election, the single issue with the largest impact upon the election's outcome was the economy.[2] Nearly half the voters surveyed cited jobs and the economy as their central concerns, and these voters supported the Democrats by a two to one margin. Among voters who believed that their own economic prospects were worsening, Clinton won by a five to one margin. "Family values," a major Republican campaign theme, was of concern to only one voter in seven. Similarly, only one voter in twelve cited foreign policy as a major worry. The once-powerful Republican tax issue had completely lost its potency in the face of

Bush's failure to adhere to his own pledge never to raise taxes. Only one voter in seven cited taxes as an important issue. Twenty percent of those surveyed said that Bush's failure to keep his promise on taxes was "very important."

At the same time the Democrats' racial strategy was successful. Democratic strategists had opted to ignore blacks and to court conservative whites, calculating that the economic hard times left blacks no choice but to support the Clinton ticket. This calculation proved to be correct. Conservative white voters in the North and South responded positively to Clinton's well-publicized conflicts with Jesse Jackson and other Clinton gestures designed to distance himself from blacks. For their part, African American voters supported the Democratic ticket in overwhelming numbers, helping Clinton carry a number of southern states.

1994: A Democratic Debacle

Despite their decades of success in local and congressional elections, the Democrats suffered a stunning defeat in the November 1994 elections. For the first time since 1946 Republicans won simultaneous control of both houses of Congress and were now in a position to block President Clinton's legislative efforts and to promote their own policy agenda.

In Senate races the Republicans gained 8 seats to achieve a 52 to 48 majority. Immediately after the election Senator Richard Shelby of Alabama, a conservative Democrat who frequently voted with the Republicans, announced that he was formally joining the GOP. In March 1995 another Democrat, Senator Ben Nighthorse Campbell of Colorado, changed his affiliation to the Republican party. These moves gave the Republicans a 54 to 46 advantage in the upper chamber. In House races the Republicans gained an astonishing 52 seats to win a 230 to 204 majority (1 House seat is held by an independent). Gaining control of the House was a significant achievement for the Republicans, for although they had controlled the Senate as recently as 1986, the

House of Representatives had been a Democratic bastion since 1954.

Republicans also posted a net gain of 11 governorships and won control of 15 additional chambers in state legislatures. A number of the Democratic party's leading figures were defeated, including Governor Mario Cuomo of New York, former House Ways and Means Committee Chair Dan Rostenkowski of Illinois, House Judiciary Committee Chair Jack Brooks of Texas, three-term Senator Jim Sasser of Tennessee, and, most shocking of all, the Speaker of the House, Thomas Foley of Washington. Foley became the first sitting Speaker to be defeated for reelection to his own congressional seat since 1860. All told, 34 incumbent Democratic representatives, 3 incumbent Democratic senators, and 4 incumbent Democratic governors went down to defeat. On the Republican side, in contrast, not one of the 10 incumbent senators, 15 incumbent governors, or 155 incumbent House members seeking reelection was defeated. The South, which had voted Republican in presidential elections for twenty years, now seemed to have turned to the Republicans at the congressional level as well. Republicans posted gains among nearly all groups in the populace, with white male voters in particular switching to the GOP in large numbers. The nation's electoral map had been substantially altered overnight. Interest in the hard-fought race had even produced a slight increase in voter turnout, albeit to a still-abysmal 39 percent.

Two important factors help explain the 1994 Democratic defeat and Republican victory. The first is the electorate's reaction to President Clinton's first two years in office. The second is the strategy developed by the GOP since Ronald Reagan's election in 1980.

Clinton: Running "Right" and Governing "Left"

Clinton's centrist strategy had helped bring about a Democratic electoral victory in 1992. Once in office, however, Clinton shifted to a more liberal stance. As many commentators observed, Clinton "ran right but governed left." Some critics, like Representative Newt Gingrich, charged that Clinton was only showing his true "Great Society, counterculture, McGovernik" colors.

Clinton's shift, however, can be understood better as a matter of political calculus than as one of personal predilection. Personally Clinton seemed willing to do whatever worked. The reality of his position was that he could not govern effectively without the support of the powerful liberal wing of the Democratic party in Congress.

To be sure, the extent of Clinton's shift to the left should not be overstated. A number of the new president's policies were decidedly centrist and even won the support of the business community and broad segments of the Republican party. In the realm of economic policy, for example, the president allied himself with congressional Republicans to secure the passage of the North American Free Trade Agreement (NAFTA), which promised to create new opportunities for American firms in the world economy. At the same time the president's 1992 and 1993 budgets aimed to bring about some reduction in the nation's huge budget deficit. This limited the opportunity for new social programs. In 1994 barriers to interstate banking were relaxed with the expectation that this would encourage competition in the banking and financial services industries. With the president's backing, Congress also approved a new loan program for college students, an initiative popular with middle-class voters. Clinton also worked to "reinvent" government by cutting the size of the government's work force. This too was a measure designed to appeal to middle-class taxpayers.

Despite these ideologically middle-of-the-road programs, a number of Clinton's other initiatives seemed calculated to please liberals. Soon after his election Clinton postponed calls for a middle-class tax cut and instead called for tax increases on more affluent Americans. Clinton enraged social conservatives and the religious right by supporting efforts to end discrimination against homosexuals in the military.

The president also became embroiled in an ideologically charged area when he supported gun control efforts. Clinton tried to expand federal social spending under the rubric of "social investment." When this effort was defeated, the president added social programs to his omnibus crime control bill under the title of "crime prevention." He also made race and gender diversity a major criterion for federal appointments.

Most important, the White House crafted a health care reform proposal, under the direction of First Lady Hillary Rodham Clinton, that at least appeared to set the stage for the creation of vast new bureaucracies and a federal takeover of the nation's health care system. Liberal Democrats, who generally favored a Canadian-style system totally operated by the government, thought the president's proposal did not go far enough in the direction of government management of health care. Conservatives and even moderates, however, came to fear that Clinton's initiative would increase the cost and reduce the quality and availability of health care services to middle- and upper-middle-class Americans.[3]

THE REPUBLICAN STRATEGY

The Republican effort to win control of Congress actually began during the late 1980s, with an attempt to discredit the Democratic party's congressional leadership. In 1989 Newt Gingrich initiated charges of financial impropriety that led to the resignations of the Democratic House Speaker, Jim Wright, and the House Democratic whip, Tony Coelho. Then, in 1991, Gingrich and his allies launched attacks upon the operations of the House bank and post office, attacks that undermined public confidence in Congress and its Democratic leadership. These attacks culminated in the resignation and criminal indictment of one of the most powerful Democratic committee chairmen, Representative Dan Rostenkowski of Illinois. The Rostenkowski indictment depicted the Democratic leaders of Congress as displaying a greater interest in venality and corruption than in the concerns of ordinary voters.

The second element in the Republican effort to win control of Congress was the full-scale mobilization of the religious and social conservatives, small-business owners, gun enthusiasts, and other conservatives who had been building grassroots organizations over the previous years. This mobilization was extremely important. While presidential elections are largely fought and won through media campaigns, congressional races still require armies of volunteer workers to canvass every community in a legislative district, distribute literature, remind voters to go to the polls—that is, congressional elections reward campaign workers, who engage in all the traditional and mundane tasks of electioneering in a democracy. During the years 1968–1992 a major reason that the Democrats consistently controlled Congress, even though the GOP dominated presidential elections, was that liberal public interest groups provided the Democrats with an infantry force of activists prepared to engage in this type of political work in virtually every congressional district in the nation. Republicans could win elections for the presidency with the personalities, issues, and themes that GOP candidates presented on television, but these were not sufficient to prevail in congressional elections.

By 1994, however, the GOP was able to deploy massive political infantry forces, while the Democrats found their ranks somewhat depleted. One consequence of the shift by the Democrats to a strategy of litigation in the late 1980s was that many liberal public interest groups had been transformed from membership associations to staff organizations. Litigation required a professional staff, legal talent, and financing, not battalions of grassroots volunteers. As a result, by 1994 most liberal public interest groups neither had active local chapters nor asked their nominal members to participate in any activity beyond writing checks in response to direct-mail or phone solicitations.[4]

The Republicans, by contrast, were able to call upon activists mobilized by a host of grassroots conservative groups. Christian Coalition members, for example, played a role in many congressional races, including a number in which Republican candidates were not especially identified with the religious right. One postelection survey suggested that more than 60 percent of the more than six hundred GOP candidates supported by Christian Coalition activists were successful in state, local and congressional races in 1994.[5] The National Rifle Association (NRA) and the National Federation of Independent Business (NFIB) also mobilized thousands of volunteers to work in congressional and local elections. The effort of Republican activists to bring voters to the polls is one major reason that in 1994 turnout among Republicans exceeded Democratic turnout in a midterm election for the first time since 1970. Turnout increases were especially large in the South, where the Christian Coalition was most active.

The third key to the GOP's successful assault on Congress was conservative talk radio. Talk radio served to nationalize congressional elections. For thirty years Democratic congressional and local candidates had been able to insulate themselves from the Republican issues and ideologies that triumphed in presidential elections. Many basically conservative districts, especially in the South, that had long since gone over to the GOP at the presidential level continued to support local Democrats who distanced themselves from the liberalism of the national party by ignoring national issues and emphasizing constituency service and pork barrel politics at the local level.

Local talk radio undermined this strategy. Through talk radio programs Republicans were able to bring national political issues and ideologies into local communities and congressional districts. Often the hosts of radio interview and discussion programs sought to link local politicians to national stories and to inform audiences of the positions their representatives had taken in Washington. By bringing national issues into local races, these programs made it much more difficult for Democratic congressional candidates to insulate themselves from national political forces. This in turn made it less likely that districts that voted Republican at the presidential level would support Democratic congressional representatives. Nationalization of political issues played an important role in bringing about the GOP's dramatic victory.

THE REPUBLICANS UNDER GINGRICH: FROM TRIUMPH TO FAILURE

Ironically, the new activist cadres that helped carry the GOP to success in the 1994 congressional races played a role in bringing about the Republican defeat in the 1996 presidential elections. In some measure, Republicans came to confront a dilemma similar to the one traditionally faced by the Democrats. For three decades Democratic presidential prospects were undermined by the liberal positions needed to satisfy its activist cadres. After 1994 the militance needed to satisfy its new conservative activists now began to complicate Republican presidential prospects.

The Republican party of the 1990s—what might be called the Gingrich-era GOP—differed significantly from the Republican coalition assembled by Ronald Reagan and his lieutenants in the late 1970s and early 1980s.

GOP Organization and Mobilization

First, in terms of organization and mobilization, Reaganism had involved the mobilization of disparate conservative constituencies through the development and communication of ideas via the mass media. Indeed, Reagan was dubbed the Great Communicator because of his capacity to articulate themes and issues that would appeal to various groups that had reasons to oppose the established regime. Thus, a host of new issues—tax reduction, increased military spending, economic and financial deregulation, restrictions on abortion, limitations on the power of labor unions, and the reintroduction of prayer in the public schools—were used to appeal for the votes and support of members of the business community, suburban middle-class taxpayers, rural evangelical Protestants, and urban working-class Catholics.

But while the Reagan Republicans appealed to all these groups, they did little to organize any of them. Reaganism was very much a media phenomenon, relying upon a small number of activists and possessing little organizational presence at the grass roots. With some notable exceptions (e.g., the Moral Majority), most of the groups formed during the Reagan era to advance conservative causes were little more than staff-directed, direct-mail organizations based in Washington. In some respects, grassroots conservatism actually suffered during the Reagan era, as thousands of local activists were drawn to Washington to work in the administration. By the late 1980s even the Moral Majority had lost most of its local chapters.[6]

Gingrich Republicanism, on the other hand, involved a very substantial measure of grassroots organization. Reagan Republicanism consisted of activists at the center connected by television and direct mail to the periphery. This form of mobilization had only a limited impact upon Congress, once the initial surge of popular support for Ronald Reagan diminished. It also had virtually no influence on state and local governments. The Reagan revolution did not penetrate far from the nation's capital.

By contrast, the forces constituting the Republican coalition of the 1990s were organized at the state, county, and local levels in almost all regions of the nation. Unlike the Reaganites, the Gingrich Republicans had the capacity to bring pressure to bear on members of Congress as well as on state and local officials. For example, the Christian Coalition, successor to the Moral Majority, has nearly two million active members organized in local chapters in every state. Twenty of the state chapters have full-time staff, and fifteen have annual budgets over two hundred thousand dollars.[7] The National Taxpayers Union has several hundred local chapters. The National Federation of Independent Business has hundreds of active local chapters throughout the nation, particularly in the Midwest and Southeast. Associations dedicated to defending "property rights" are organized at the local level throughout the West. Right-to-life groups are organized in virtually every congressional district. Even proponents of the exotic principle of home schooling are organized through the Home School Legal Defense Association (HSLDA), which has seventy-five regional chapters that in turn are linked to more than three thousand local support groups.

Much of this organizational complexity emerged after Reagan left office. Thousands of conservative activists who had gone to Washington to work in his administration returned to their homes still eager to be involved in Republican politics. These former officials, who formed what came to be called the Reagan Diaspora, played a leading role in organizing conservative groups at the local level. For example, lawyers who formerly worked for the Reagan administration are responsible for establishing most of the several dozen conservative public interest law centers currently active in the United States. Similarly, members of the Reagan Diaspora have been active in establishing conservative policy organizations, forums, centers, and associations, as well as local chapters of national conservative organizations. This has helped produce an explosion in conservative groups at the state and local levels.[8]

These local conservative organizations were energized by the political struggles that took place between 1989 and 1994. Fights over environmental regulation stimulated organization and activity on the part of property rights groups throughout the West, including the organization of armed "citizens' militia," whose members have been implicated in some episodes of political violence in recent years. Disputes regarding the Family Medical Leave Act during the Bush presidency and fights over the employer mandates of the Clinton health care reform proposals drew hundreds of thousands of small-business owners into the political arena under the auspices of the NFIB. Employer mandates would have required employers to pay much of the cost of their employees' health care coverage, and this outraged most owners of small businesses. In its struggle against employer mandates, the NFIB organized meetings and community forums around the country, and its members conducted an active campaign of letters, telephone calls, and faxes to members of Congress arguing that small business would be ruined by the requirement. During the debates over the Clinton administration's health care proposal, the NFIB's membership rolls grew at the expense of business organizations, such as the U.S. Chamber of Commerce, that sought to reach accommodations with the administration.[9]

Similarly, battles over the restrictions on gun ownership in the Clinton administration's 1993 crime bill helped the NRA energize local gun owner groups throughout the country. The struggle over a proposed amendment to the 1993 education bill that would have placed additional restrictions on home schooling helped the HSLDA enroll thousands of active new members in its regional and local chapters. After an intense campaign it succeeded both in defeating the amendment and in enhancing the political awareness and activism of its formerly quiescent members. Of course, the ongoing struggles over abortion and school prayer have helped the Christian Coalition, the Family Research Council, and other organizations constituting the Christian right to expand the membership rolls of their state and local organizations. Antiabortion forces, in particular, are organized at the local level throughout the nation and are prepared to participate in political campaigns and legislative battles.

The development of local conservative organizations allied with the GOP has been greatly facilitated by the emergence of conservative communications media throughout the United States. As was noted above, the most important element of these media is conservative talk radio—discussion programs run by conservative commentators, often featuring conservative politicians and activists as guests and inviting listener commentary via the telephone. Some talk radio programs are nationally syndicated. The most important of the nationally syndicated radio hosts of course is Rush Limbaugh, whose program is heard on more than six hundred local radio stations. His syndicated television program is seen on more than two hundred local TV stations. Other national commentators include former Republican operatives Oliver North and G. Gordon Liddy as well as James Dobson, whose program, *Focus on the Family,* reaches nearly five million listeners every week and discusses social issues from a conservative Christian perspective. These programs, along with Pat Robertson's Christian Broadcasting Network, focus on national issues and endeavor to present a conservative and Republican perspective on national events.

These nationally syndicated radio and television programs helped the Gingrich Republicans to circumvent the antagonism of the established national news media and to promote their ideas on the national level. The emergence of local conservative talk radio programs in nearly every media market in the nation has been even more important in stimulating grassroots activism. Such programs broadcast in large markets (e.g., programs run by Bob Grant in New York and Michael Reagan in Los Angeles), as well as in smaller cities (e.g., the programs of Blanquita Cullum in Richmond, Kirby McClure in Seattle, Ron Smith in Baltimore, and Ray Appleton in Fresno). Rural areas in the Midwest are reached by such programs as Jerry Hughes's *Washington on Trial* on the People's Radio Network.

Local and regional talk radio programs focus on the activities of grassroots groups and often invite local conservative activists to appear as guests. These programs can be extremely effective in mobilizing support for local electoral and lobbying efforts as well as in encouraging local groups to participate in national campaigns. To foster such political mobilization, the House Republican Conference faxes daily news updates to hundreds of local radio hosts, who in turn urge their listeners to call or write local and national legislators about such issues as lobby reform, welfare reform, and balancing the federal budget.

In addition, local antiabortion and property rights protests are publicized on talk radio, as are the meeting times and places for grassroots conservative organizations. Talk radio has been such an effective communications network for the conservative movement in recent years that the Democrats have singled it out for attack. For example, in the aftermath of the bombing of the Oklahoma City Federal Building in 1995, Bill Clinton asserted that conservative talk radio hosts were responsible for inspiring violence against government facilities and officials.

This extensive organization of the periphery meant that Gingrich-era conservatives were not only able to bring pressure to bear upon the national government but also became a real presence in the corridors of state capitols, county seats, and city halls. For instance, spurred by conservative groups and conservative radio programs, legislators in all fifty states have introduced property rights legislation. Eighteen states have already enacted laws requiring a "takings impact analysis," before any new government regulation affecting property can go into effect.[10] Such legislation is designed to diminish the ability of state and local governments to enact land use restrictions for environmental or planning purposes. In a similar vein, seventeen states, pressed by local conservative groups, have recently enacted legislation protecting or expanding the rights of gun owners.[11]

Gingrich Republicanism: Class Composition

The class composition of Gingrich Republicanism also differed from that of Reaganism. The class character of Reaganism was similar to more traditional Republicanism, despite its populist rhetoric and appeals to blue-collar voters. The Reaganite coalition was essentially an alliance between the industrial and financial communities and the middle class. This alliance was cemented by the programs that formed the heart of Reaganism: The Reaganite tax cuts helped middle- and upper-class taxpayers, increased military spending and the Reagan administration's antiunion posture benefited industrial corporations, and its extensive program of deregulation served the interests of the financial community. The Reaganites, to be sure, wooed social conservatives through expressions of opposition to abortion, support for school prayer, and the like. But social conservatives were not included in the administration's inner councils, and the Reaganites made little effort to enact or implement social programs advocated by these conservatives.

The Gingrich coalition, by contrast, had something of a populist flavor. Of course big business, the financial community, and taxpayers with above-average incomes had scarcely been drummed out of the Republican party in the Gingrich era. In fact, a number of conservative causes were promoted by coalitions that included both conservative ideologues and corporate interests. For example, reforming tort law had been supported by insurance companies and major corporations, seeking to protect themselves from huge liability awards. These interests were in turn allied with conservative ideologues and activists, who sought to strike a blow against both the tort lawyers in private practice, who had become an important Democrat constituency, and the array of liberal public interest groups for which civil litigation had become a key political strategy and a major means of financing their activities.

Similarly, the property rights movement included real estate, logging, and mining interests seeking relief from land use and environmental restrictions, as well as landowners, largely in the West, demanding compensation for, or protection from, federal and state regulations that affect the value of their holdings.

Indeed, in some cases the views of major corporate interests had been the principal base for Republican legislative proposals during the 1990s. For example, lobbyists for petrochemical companies actually drafted Republican environmental proposals, while lobbyists for the United Parcel Service played a major role in formulating the House GOP position on occupational safety.[12]

Nevertheless, Gingrich Republicanism reached somewhat farther down both the class structure and the corporate ladder than did Reaganism and that distinction has had a lasting impact. Because they are now organized and mobilized, local lower-middle-class conservative groups that displayed little or no weight during the Reagan period have the capacity to exercise substantial political influence today. During the Reagan era, for instance, Republicans in Washington, D.C., had never heard of the home schoolers, a decidedly downscale group, whose headquarters are in Purcellville, Virginia. But nowadays this political force is well organized as the HSLDA and can mobilize its local chapters through Christian talk radio. No less significant a Republican than House Majority Leader Dick Armey is in regular contact with the HSLDA and endeavors to accommodate its views on education policy.

In a similar vein, small business is a far more important component of the Republican coalition today than it was during the Reagan period. The coming to power of Gingrichism was a triumph for Main Street business and for the NFIB, which has become a major force in the Republican coalition. NFIB President Jack Faris commented, "We are fortunate to have a pro-small business Congress willing to give [our issues] serious consideration."[13]

In the 104th Congress Republicans endeavored to enact major elements of the NFIB legislative agenda. These included increased income tax deductibility for the health insurance premiums of the self-employed; a substantial increase in personal exemptions from estate taxes; a large increase in the immediate tax deductibility of small-business equipment purchases; a targeted tax cut for those investing in small businesses; the elimination of gender and race preferences from small business loan guarantee programs; reduction in the growth of employer Medicare payroll taxes; and the Occupational Safety and Health Administration Reform Act, which would limit the ability of OSHA to impose penalties upon employers it deems to have violated federal safety standards.

The NFIB has also been active at the state level. In New York it secured inclusion in Governor George Pataki's 1996 budget of cuts in the worker compensation and unemployment insurance programs. Small-business lobbyists argued that these programs limit the creation of new jobs in the state. In New Hampshire small business has sought a constitutional change to require a legislative supermajority of 60 percent before any increase in state taxes can be imposed. In Arizona the NFIB played an important role in securing a substantial reduction in the state's property taxes on small businesses, as well as in other taxes affecting small-business owners.

This increased importance in the GOP of Main Street, relative to Wall Street, has come about because small business is now extensively organized and fully mobilized. Many of the seventy-three House Republican freshmen in the 104th Congress had small-business backgrounds and were drawn into politics during the struggles of the past seven years over family leave, employer health care mandates, and OSHA regulations. At the present time local NFIB chapters are providing small-business owners with formal training seminars in campaign management, fund-raising, press relations, voter mobilization, and lobbying to enhance their political effectiveness and draw more of them into the political arena.[14]

Gingrich Republicanism: Goals and Methods

Finally, Gingrich-era Republicanism involved a more ambitious set of goals and more radical methods than did Reaganite Republicanism. The goals pursued by the Reagan revolution were actually modest. Initially the Reagan administration employed what might be called a fiscal strategy to halt the expansion of existing federal social programs and to prevent the enactment of any new social programs. Substantial tax cuts, embodied in the 1981 Tax Reform Act, reduced the revenues flowing to the U.S. Treasury, and this limited the resources available for federal expenditure programs. At the same time the increase in military outlays meant that the funds available for both existing domestic programs and for any new social policies would be severely constrained.

However, after a bitter struggle with its Democratic foes, the Reagan administration in 1982 reached an accommodation with its opponents. The White House and Congress allowed the U.S. deficit to increase sufficiently to enable the federal government to finance its new military priorities as well as established domestic programs. Indeed, the rate at which expenditures on social programs *increased* during the Reagan years scarcely differed from the growth rate of social spending during the preceding administrations. This accommodation, which President Reagan's first budget director, David Stockman, in 1986 termed "the triumph of politics," was largely responsible for the enormous U.S. debt that accumulated during the Reagan presidency.

After the 1982 accommodation Reaganism became little more than an effort to prevent the creation of *new* social programs financed by the U.S. Treasury. In this limited sense the Reaganites were successful. Not a single new domestic social spending program was enacted during President Reagan's eight years in office.

By the late 1980s, however, congressional Democrats had devised a means of at least partially circumventing the fiscal constraints on the creation of new social programs. Programs such as the Americans with Disabilities Act, family leave, and the Clinton administration's proposal to reform the nation's health care system called for benefits that would be paid for by employers and other private institutions rather than by the U.S. Treasury. In this way, new social programs could be established despite the federal government's lack of new funds. These programs, moreover, could be expanded through litigation. Litigation, much of it initiated by liberal public interest groups affiliated with the Democratic coalition, enabled liberals and Democrats to extend the benefits available to their constituencies without needing to secure congressional approval of new tax and spending programs. Under a number of statutory citizen enforcement provisions, moreover, many public interest groups—including Defenders of Wildlife, Ralph Nader's Public Interest Research Group, the Disability Rights Litigation and Defense Fund, and a score of others—were able to secure a substantial portion of their own funding from the fees and damages awarded to successful public interest litigants.

After the 1994 elections Republicans sought to undo this compromise by slashing funding for existing social programs as well as enacting a number of other programs, under the rubric of the "Contract with America," that threatened to strike directly at the institutions and programs through which liberal Democrats exercise power. We shall examine some of the details of this effort in subsequent chapters. What is important in the present context is that the militance of the new Republican coalition led directly to the GOP's crushing defeat in the climactic 1995–1996 battle over the federal budget. Congressional Republicans were determined to bring about substantial cuts in the growth of government spending. This plan posed a mortal threat to Democratic domestic agencies and programs and engendered fierce Democratic resistance. As Republicans had anticipated, President Clinton refused to accept GOP budget proposals, allowing the federal government's spending authority to lapse in the closing weeks of 1995. During a similar face-off between President Bush and a Democratic Congress in 1990, Bush had eventually compromised with the Democrats on a new tax and spending package in order to avert a partial shutdown of the federal government. This compromise had infuriated Republican conservatives and was a factor in Bush's 1992 defeat.

Led by House Speaker Newt Gingrich, Republicans were determined not to repeat what they saw as Bush's great error. The GOP was convinced that if it held firm, President Clinton would be the one to give in to prevent federal agencies from shutting their doors when the federal government's spending authority lapsed. Republicans calculated that a government shutdown would work to their advantage by demonstrating to millions of Americans that life would go on as always with much of the federal government closed. This of course was precisely the point Republicans had sought to make since the era of Ronald Reagan.

After the White House and congressional Republicans failed to reach agreement on a new budget, the federal government was shut down twice: once in November 1995 and again for a twenty-one-day period beginning December 1995 and not ending until January 6, 1996. Nearly eight hundred thousand federal workers were furloughed, though with a promise of back pay after the crisis ended. Hundreds of thousands of individuals working for private firms under federal government contracts were also furloughed, but with little chance of ever collecting back pay. The media and public response to the budget crisis shocked Republicans. Instead of leading to a realization that the nation could get along with a smaller government, as Republicans had anticipated, the budget crisis seemed to turn the public against the GOP.

The Republicans' basic problem was that instead of focusing on the principle of a balanced budget during the crisis, the national media devoted virtually all their attention to the human side of the budget impasse. The GOP's uncompromising and militant stance gave the national media ample opportunity to portray the Republicans as a group of radicals intent upon destroying the government. "We were so heady after capturing both houses of Congress in 1994," said former Republican National Committee Chairman Frank Fahrenkopf. "We tried to reverse 40 years in two years."[15]

Every evening television stories told of federal workers unable to make mortgage payments or to buy Christmas presents for their children as the holidays approached.[16] Speaker Gingrich was widely caricatured as "the Gingrich who stole Christmas." Poll after poll showed a dramatic drop in popular support for the Republicans in the wake of the government shutdown. The public blamed the GOP for causing an unnecessary crisis through its intransigence.[17]

In January 1996 the GOP surrendered. "People realize that the strategy of shutting the government down didn't work and that we lost the PR battle and Clinton gained everything from it," said GOP freshman Ray LaHood of Illinois. "We need to move on."[18] Republicans agreed to reopen the government and, subsequently, reached a budget agreement with President Clinton that achieved few of their initial goals.[19]

The Aftermath of Defeat

The GOP budget debacle weakened Newt Gingrich and the Republican congressional leadership. Disgruntled Republicans nearly ousted Gingrich from the Speakership. President Clinton, however, received a new political life. After the 1994 elections Clinton had brought his longtime political adviser Richard Morris into the White House to help improve the president's image. Dick Morris developed a strategy he dubbed triangulation. This strategy called for Clinton to move sharply to the political right to occupy a middle ground between liberal congressional Democrats and conservative congressional Republicans. Under Morris's influence, Clinton advocated a series of tax cut initiatives referred to as the "middle-class bill of rights," called for tough measures on crime, embraced the idea of voluntary school prayer, spoke against sex and violence on television, dropped much of his opposition to Republican welfare reform proposals (leading him to sign a bill he had opposed), and advocated "family values" in a series of public addresses.

Clinton's shift to the right outraged many of his liberal advisers, including his deputy chief of staff, Harold Ickes, and senior adviser, George Stephanopoulos. The Morris strategy, however, was calculated to rob the Republicans of their most potent issues in the 1996 elections.[20] The 1995–1996 budget battle played into Morris's hands by allowing him to portray Clinton as a moderate, eager to find room for compromise, while congressional Republicans were pilloried as militant extremists by the national media. "The most important event of 1995," said Democratic pollster Geoff Garin, "was that the Republicans vacated the center in a radical way, and President Clinton was very smart and very effective in filling the vacuum and occupying the center in American politics."[21] Later Morris was forced to resign after the publication of a series of newspaper stories revealed that the architect of Clinton's move to the center and family values campaign had a close relationship with a Washington prostitute. Clinton, on the other hand, was able to raise tens of millions of dollars and to display the same vigorous and articulate campaign style that had carried him to victory in 1992.

A third consequence of the 1995–1996 budget battle was the character of Bob Dole's 1996 presidential campaign. The GOP's ignominious defeat in the budget battle convinced Dole that militancy and radicalism in the struggle against the Democrats were the route to failure and that his own more moderate and cautious instincts were the correct ones. It was Dole who organized the series of compromises that ended the budget stalemate and Dole who urged congressional Republicans to attempt to shed their radical image by moderating their rhetoric and positions. Dole was already widely seen as the front-runner for the 1996 Republican presidential nomination, and he now saw his presidential chances undermined by the GOP's disastrous budget confrontation with President Clinton. His effort to undo the damage of this defeat shaped his entire 1996 campaign.

First, of course, Dole had to win the Republican nomination, and this proved more difficult than many analysts had anticipated. Of the 1996 Republican hopefuls, only Texas Senator Phil Gramm seemed a real threat to Dole, and Gramm proved to be a lackluster campaigner who was never able to generate much support even in his home region. Dole, on the other hand, boasted a lengthy and illustrious political career and unmatched ability as a fund-raiser. He entered the GOP presidential primaries with the support of most important Republican leaders and access to substantial financial support.

Nevertheless, Dole stumbled badly in the early contests held in February. He barely eked out a victory in the Iowa caucuses and then suffered a humiliating defeat in the February 20 New Hampshire primary at the hands of conservative radio commentator Patrick Buchanan, with former Tennessee Governor Lamar Alexander running a close third. The next week publishing heir Malcolm ("Steve") Forbes won the Arizona and Delaware primaries, though Dole carried the Dakotas. Beginning with the March 2 South Carolina primary, however, Dole's organization, contacts, and support began to assert themselves. Dole carried South Carolina by a wide margin, despite Buchanan's efforts to take advantage of the conservatism of the state's Republican voters. Dole then swept to victory in Georgia, New York, Colorado, and Maryland, and he won seven primaries on March 12 alone. All the Republican contenders but Buchanan withdrew from the race, in effect handing Dole the Republican nomination months before the GOP's August convention.

During the months before the convention and at the convention itself, Dole's strategy continued to be shaped by the perceived need to project a moderate image. On May 15, 1996, Dole startled political observers by resigning from the Senate to devote his full attention to the race for the White House. The major purpose of this move was to distance himself from the increasingly unpopular congressional Republicans, especially House Speaker Newt Gingrich.[22] At the convention Dole refused to cede any points to Buchanan and his militantly conservative followers, with the exception of a few platform planks that Dole promptly repudiated, claiming to have no interest in even reading them. Dole arranged to have the convention's major opening speech delivered by General Colin Powell, a symbol of the Republican party's moderate wing. Finally, Dole named Jack Kemp as his vice presidential running mate. Though Dole had no personal love for Kemp, he viewed the former housing secretary as an individual who would give the ticket a decidedly moderate image. Kemp was one of the few Republicans known as advocates of affirmative action and was well regarded by the liberal Washington press corps.

Dole's theme of moderation also governed his choice of campaign issues. His major issue was a pledge to cut personal income taxes by 15 percent. This was viewed as a position around which most Republicans could rally and that would not frighten or offend independents and Democrats. Dole determinedly avoided divisive racial and social issues, ignored the congressional GOP's policy agenda, and even refused—until the second presidential debate and the waning days of the campaign—to discuss Clinton's various ethical problems. Attacking the president's ethics was seen as inconsistent with the image of moderation Dole sought to project.

Thus, Dole's entire 1996 campaign was shaped by an effort to distinguish himself from the image of GOP radicalism that had developed as a result of the budget crisis. Of course this Dole strategy proved to be electorally futile. Given Clinton's triangulation, Dole seemed to offer uncommitted voters little reason to support him over a sitting president. Moreover, the conservative GOP loyalists whose activism had swept Republicans to power in 1994 virtually ignored a presidential race that seemed to jettison all the principles they thought worth fighting for.[23] In the last days of the campaign Dole made some halting references to affirmative action, gun control, welfare, and immigration. This, however, was too little and too late.[24] Many conservative activists chose to sit out the presidential election. "Those who focus on economics alone lose," said Gary Bauer, president of the Family Research Council, a conservative religious group. Bauer said Dole's decision to avoid moral issues cost him the support of social conservatives and, as a result, the election.[25] Unable to woo independents, and offering lit-

tle reason to hard-core Republican activists to take an interest in
the election, Dole went down to defeat.

In this way the ghost of the GOP's great victory in 1994 returned to doom Republican efforts in 1996, leading Clinton's advisers to call the 1994 election a "blessing in disguise."[26] Ironically,
while Dole was being held to account for the misdeeds of the Republican 104th Congress, voters were busy reelecting almost all the
members of that Congress. Because of the higher levels of voter
turnout and media attention involved, the Republican party's activist cadres are less important in a congressional election held
during a presidential year than in a low-turnout off-year race. Now,
however, the GOP had benefited from the effects of incumbency.
Moreover, while President Clinton raised enormous amounts of
money in 1996, most of it was spent on his race in the form of soft
money expenditures by Democratic party organizations. The Republicans, by contrast, spent the bulk of their funds to make certain that they retained control of Congress. Bob Dole was sacrificed
to this greater good. In the 2000 election, which we shall discuss
more fully in Chapter 6, Republicans were able to retain control of
the House of Representatives and to take control of the White
House, despite losing the popular presidential vote. The Senate
was evenly divided, though with Vice President Cheney casting tie-
breaking votes, the GOP retained nominal control of the upper
chamber. In May 2001, Senator James Jeffords defected from the
GOP, swinging control over to the Democrats. These events
seemed tailor-made for continuing governmental stalemate and
struggle.

The Politics of Stalemate

In the 1990s the Democrats and Republicans appeared to have
traded places. For three decades the GOP dominated the arena of
presidential elections while Democrats controlled Congress. In the
1990s the Democrats won two successive presidential elections
while the GOP came to control Congress. The two parties found

themselves facing a similar dilemma. Winning congressional races requires the enthusiastic work of activist ideologues willing to engage in grassroots electioneering. At the same time a political party in which activist ideologues are important will be hard pressed to win national presidential elections. Its candidates will be seen as either too radical by the general electorate or too moderate by the party's activist cadres. Under these conditions, inconclusive elections and divided government are likely to be the norm in American politics.

In some measure this dilemma, like many other aspects of American electoral politics, is a product of America's weak political parties and low levels of political participation. First, in the era of strong party machines the parties' activist cadres were motivated less by ideology and more by patronage and other forms of material incentives. Whatever their flaws, the old-fashioned party precinct workers who got out the vote for congressional and local candidates never posed problems for their parties' presidential tickets.

Second, one of the reasons that relatively small numbers of committed activists are so important in congressional and local races is that turnout in these contests is so low. Barely one-third of eligible voters participate in congressional contests, and in some local elections turnout drops to less than half this meager percentage. In such a low-turnout environment, activist cadres are extremely important. Where there are few voters, a small number of party workers can contact, and perhaps influence, a sizable fraction of those who go to the polls. If voter turnout in congressional and local races approached the levels manifested in presidential elections, the influence of party workers would be reduced and congressional and local election results would be more likely to resemble national presidential outcomes.

Under present electoral conditions, however, the chance of inconclusive outcomes and divided government remains high. This in turn increases the likelihood that political combat outside the electoral arena will continue to grow in importance.

3

The Democrats
and the
Domestic State

THE DEMOCRATS AND REPUBLICANS have in recent decades established links with different segments of the nation's governmental apparatus. The Democrats have entrenched themselves in Congress, federal social service, labor and regulatory agencies, and government bureaucracies and nonprofit organizations on the state and local levels that help administer national social programs. The Democrats' base has its roots in the events of the 1930s and 1960s and, reinforced by the party's hold on Congress, has become so well established that it can withstand Republican control of the White House. Together these developments have transformed the Democrats from a political force based on local party machines into one grounded in Congress and the domestic state.

The Republicans, as we shall see in subsequent chapters, have sought to entrench themselves in the White House, the national security apparatus, sectors of the economy that benefit from military spending, and those segments of American society whose income, autonomy, or values are threatened by the welfare and regulatory state built by the Democrats. This competitive entrenchment by the Republicans and Democrats has to a considerable extent replaced mass electoral mobilization as a means of securing power in the United States today and helps explain how high levels of partisan conflict can coexist with low rates of voting participation in contemporary American politics.

FORMS OF DEMOCRATIC ENTRENCHMENT

Since the 1930s Democratic presidents and Congresses have secured the enactment of a large number of social and regulatory programs. To administer these programs, they created or expanded such agencies as Health and Human Services (HHS), the Department of Labor (DOL), and the Environmental Protection Agency (EPA). These bureaucracies are linked by grants-in-aid to public agencies and nonprofit organizations at the state and local levels and through these to the Democratic party's mass base.[1] This entire complex is tied to Democrats in Congress, who affirm the worth of federal social and regulatory programs and defend the authority and budgets of the agencies responsible for their administration.

There are three ways in which federal social and regulatory agencies serve as centers of influence for the Democrats even when the White House is controlled by the Republicans. First, individuals who work in agencies such as HHS—and their counterparts in the state, local, and nonprofit sectors—are likely to have Democratic loyalties.[2] When agencies that provide such benefits as health care and welfare hire employees, they quite properly seek and attract individuals who by personal belief and training are committed to these organizations' goals, and a commitment to the public sector is more likely to be found among Democrats than Republicans. The Democrats' defense of social programs and expenditures has over time reproduced and reinforced the attachment of public employees to that party. In turn, the millions of Americans who work in domestic public sector occupations are an important source of votes and campaign support for the Democrats. The majority of them—over 60 percent in 1984—vote Democratic.[3] In addition, individuals who are active in Democratic campaigns are drawn heavily from state and local governments, universities, and other nonprofit institutions.

Second, federal domestic programs and agencies enable the Democrats to establish links with groups and forces throughout the nation. These bureaucratic networks have largely supplanted party organizations as the instruments through which Democrats in Washington are tied to a popular base. Since the New Deal era the Democratic party has channeled benefits to a plethora of interests.[4] The beneficiaries of this largess of course have reason to reward the Democrats with their political support. For the past half century Democrats have thus been able to win strong backing from unionized workers and ethnic minorities—and even some middle-class homeowners, professionals, and members of the business community. Generally, the more dependent members of a group are on federal domestic spending programs, the more likely they are to vote Democratic. In the 1988 presidential election, for example, 62 percent of voters with annual family incomes under $12,500 supported Dukakis, whereas only 37 percent of voters with incomes above $50,000 did so.[5]

Finally, the Democratic party's entrenchment in domestic agencies provides Democrats in Congress with administrative capabilities that endure even when they lose control of the presidency. The career employees of federal social and regulatory agencies have an enduring commitment to public sector programs championed by the Democrats; these employees work with Democrats in Congress to maintain and protect such programs. The support of these agency employees enables the Democrats to retain substantial influence over the implementation of major areas of public policy and to play a significant role in the nation's governance even when a Republican occupies the White House.

With the support of congressional Democrats, agencies that administer federal social and regulatory programs often resist efforts by Republican presidents to redirect or limit their activities. For example, when the Reagan administration attempted to reorient EPA policies, it encountered stiff opposition from members of the agency's staff. Agency employees leaked information to Congress and the media, leaks that led to a series of congressional investigations and ultimately resulted in the ouster of Anne Burford Gorsuch, Reagan's EPA chief. As a result of this controversy, Reagan was compelled to appoint a new administrator, William Ruckelshaus, who was seen as likely to return the agency to its former course.

ORIGINS OF DEMOCRATIC ENTRENCHMENT: THE NEW DEAL

Democrats' links to federal social welfare and regulatory agencies date from the 1930s, when President Franklin Roosevelt sought to institutionalize the New Deal. By establishing a base in agencies of the national government, New Deal liberals undertook not only to counter the influence of the conservative machine politicians and southern oligarchs who formerly dominated the party but also to strengthen the Democrats in their competition with the Republicans. New Deal liberals thus began the process through which the Democrats became a party grounded in governmental bureaucracies rather than local organizations.

The multitude of new agencies—the famous alphabet agencies—created to administer New Deal programs initially were viewed as temporary and were located outside the regular governmental structure. But in the mid-1930s Roosevelt moved to make them permanent features of the American governmental system. Chronologically and politically, Roosevelt's effort belonged to the second phase of the New Deal, the phase extending from the Wagner Act and Social Security Act of 1935, through the Reorganization Act of 1937, to the congressional purge of 1938. The

Reorganization Act was an effort to institutionalize the programs of FDR's first term by creating two new cabinet departments (to administer the public welfare and public works programs that had been enacted between 1933 and 1936) and by granting the president the authority to integrate other New Deal programs into the existing departmental structure.[6]

The reforms of 1935–1938 also helped institutionalize the power of the Democrats by establishing direct links between the administration and a mass constituency. These links were accomplished by the National Labor Relations Act, which established procedures for organizing workers into unions, and the Social Security Act, which established a bureaucracy to provide benefits to Americans in times of need. Such assistance had formerly been provided, if at all, only by political machines.

Significantly, under amendments to the Social Security Act adopted in 1939, the Social Security Board required states to establish merit systems for the employees who administered the program on the state and local level; this requirement led to the creation of the first civil service systems in most states of the Union.[7] The New Dealers sought through this requirement to ensure that control of the program would not be seized by whatever political forces happened to be dominant locally. New Dealers wanted the flow of these new benefits to be controlled from the center so that the political advantages of the program would accrue to the national Democratic administration that enacted it.

Roosevelt also undertook through his 1937 executive reorganization bill to extend White House control over the entire federal administrative apparatus, but he was not entirely successful. FDR's reorganization plan sought to expand the White House staff, create a central planning agency in the executive office, and place all administrative agencies, including the independent regulatory commissions, under one of the cabinet departments.

Opponents of the New Deal resisted Roosevelt's efforts to centralize in the White House control over the executive branch. FDR was forced to accept a compromise: Executive agencies retained a measure of independence, and Congress continued to exercise significant influence over the bureaucracy. Executive agencies were therefore left free to cultivate their own political alliances with interest groups and members of Congress. Ironically, it was the defeat of Roosevelt's efforts to strengthen White House control over the bureaucracy that made it possible for congressional Democrats in the 1970s and 1980s to retain substantial influence over administrative agencies in the face of Republican dominance of the presidency.

Administrative Entrenchment and Party Decline

Roosevelt's moves toward centralization began the transformation of the Democrats from a party dependent on an extensive network of political clubs and organizations to one grounded in administrative institutions. After the 1930s the Democrats relied increasingly on administrative rather than party channels to establish links with their constituencies, to recruit and retain the loyalty of party activists, and to implement their party's programs. Eventually the Democrats became so firmly entrenched in segments of the national administrative apparatus and its state and local counterparts that even loss of control of the White House was not sufficient to dislodge them.

Roosevelt was determined to entrench his followers in the national governmental apparatus because in many states and localities the Democratic party machinery was in the hands of his factional rivals and in others it was too weak to be politically useful to him. By strengthening bureaucratic institutions, and tying them closely to his cause, FDR sought to create a national apparatus through which he could mobilize political support and govern.[8]

On the state and local levels, FDR's endeavor to centralize and control the national government was supported by middle-class liberals, who had a particular interest in substituting bureaucratic for partisan modes of organization. New Deal liberals wanted the government to play an active role in society, and bureaucracies are better suited than patronage machines to perform tasks requiring technical proficiency. By replacing patronage practices with personnel systems based on competitive examinations, bureaucratization would also skew the distribution of public jobs to the advantage of the public sector professionals—teachers, social workers, and so on—who were an important element of the liberal constituency.[9]

Roosevelt's efforts generated major struggles, on state and local levels, between political forces committed to the national administration and incumbent Democratic leaders. Conflicts occurred in some states while FDR was still in the White House; in other states they did not erupt until fifteen or twenty years after his death.[10] The timing and character of these struggles for power depended upon the stance that local party leaders took toward the national administration and the techniques the leaders employed to maintain their power.

Where incumbent machine politicians supported the New Deal (as in Chicago and Pittsburgh), FDR was perfectly willing to distribute the patronage generated by New Deal programs through local party machines.[11] Where the incumbent Democratic leadership was hostile to the national administration and commanded a broadly based, patronage-oriented party machine (such as Tammany Hall in New York City), the president's followers organized through third-party movements or reform clubs (such as the American Labor party and later the Democratic reform movement in New York).[12] Finally, where the local Democratic leadership was hostile or indifferent to the New Deal and did not command a mass-based party organization (as in Michigan and Minnesota), Roosevelt loyalists were able with little difficulty to take over the Democratic caucus structure by allying with labor unions and farm organizations that had benefited from New Deal programs.[13] In these states, factional struggles within the Democratic party took the form of a straight ideological conflict between New Deal liberals and conservative Democrats.

By the 1960s these struggles had given the Democrats an

institutionally heterogeneous structure. Traditional patronage-oriented party organizations remained important in many states and localities, particularly in the Northeast and lower Midwest.[14] Labor unions continued to play an important role in party affairs.[15] At the same time a number of federal, state, and local bureaucracies had come to be major Democratic party bastions.

THE 1960s AND 1970s

During the 1960s and 1970s traditional party organizations were almost completely obliterated, labor unions were weakened, and the Democratic party became more fully dependent on its base of power in the domestic state. The efforts of a coalition of middle-class liberals and blacks to enhance their influence in American government and politics were largely responsible for this shift. To this end they abandoned accommodations in which they had formerly participated and allies with whom they formerly had been associated in the realms of civil rights and social policy, national security policy, and regulatory policy. In addition, they sought to rewrite the rules of the Democratic party and to alter the administrative procedures of the federal government so as to increase their own influence.

Civil Rights and Social Policy

One of the major accommodations underlying the New Deal coalition involved civil rights. Southern votes were crucial to the Democratic party's fortunes in the 1930s and 1940s, and therefore Roosevelt had avoided challenging the southern caste system. The emergence of a vigorous black civil rights movement in the 1950s and 1960s, however, made it impossible to ignore the issue of race any longer. Northern Democratic liberals were sympathetic to the plight of blacks and, at the same time, found in the issue of civil rights a means of discrediting their opponents within the Democratic party—initially southern conservatives and subsequently working-class ethnics in the North. A similar mix of considerations underlay the urban programs of the New Frontier and Great Society.

As a number of scholars have noted, the major urban programs of the New Frontier and Great Society were drafted not in response to demands from their presumed beneficiaries—black slum dwellers—but rather on the initiative of presidentially appointed task forces.[16] The members of these task forces were mainly "professional reformers": academics, foundation officials, senior civil servants, representatives of professional associations, and so forth.[17] Presidents Kennedy and Johnson were receptive to proposals of this sort if for no other reason than to retain the support of this important element of the party's national constituency.

Middle-class liberals were considerably less influential on the local level. In many large cities after World War II a stable accommodation had been achieved among party politicians, businessmen, union leaders, newspaper publishers, middle-income homeowners, and the ethnic working classes. Writing in the early 1960s, Robert Salisbury described this pattern as "the new convergence of power," and these forces roughly converged around a program of urban renewal in the central business district for the business community and construction unions, low taxes for homeowners, and secure jobs in the municipal civil service for the lower middle class and upwardly mobile members of the working class.[18] Upper-middle-class professionals had some influence over municipal agencies, although their influence was constrained by the desire of mayors to keep taxes low and of municipal employees to control their own work routines and determine the standards that would govern the hiring, promotion, and firing of civil servants.

Upper-middle-class liberals wanted to increase their influence over municipal agencies; to this end they sought to use the access they enjoyed to the Kennedy and Johnson administrations to circumvent the local convergence of power. The presidential task forces that drafted New Frontier and Great Society legislation argued that municipal bureaucracies did not command the resources, the talent, or the initiative that were necessary to solve the "urban crisis." To deal with this problem, they proposed to extend federal grants-in-aid to local governments to support "innovative" programs.

To obtain these federal grants, cities found it necessary to establish independent agencies that would be controlled by local counterparts of the Washington officials who dispensed this money, to have existing municipal departments contract with consulting firms, or to hire administrators who shared the outlook or knew the vocabulary of the dispensers of federal grants. The "grantsmen" who were most successful in obtaining federal funds naturally were those whose educational backgrounds, social origins, and institutional affiliations were similar to those of the federal grant givers and who proposed to spend federal monies for purposes their Washington counterparts favored. In other words, the federal grant-in-aid programs initiated by the Kennedy and Johnson administrations allowed upper-middle-class professionals and their political allies, by using their access to the White House, to extend their influence over the policies, programs, and hiring practices of municipal agencies. Federal grants-in-aid to state and local governments expanded dramatically during the 1960s and 1970s.

Blacks were important allies in the liberals' battle for control of these agencies. Liberals denounced municipal bureaucracies as "insensitive" and "unresponsive" to the needs of the black community. Blacks had strong reasons to join this attack: The mechanisms of community participation that were attached to Great Society programs provided them with channels through which they could both influence the way municipal departments distributed their benefits and obtain access to the patronage controlled by federally funded community action agencies, model cities boards, neighborhood service centers, and community development corporations. These mechanisms of community participation, furthermore, legitimized federal intervention in local affairs and provided an institutional framework through which blacks could be organized to provide local political support for these programs.[19]

National Security Policy

Factional struggles within the Democratic party intensified after Lyndon B. Johnson escalated the war in Vietnam. Vietnam turned upper-middle-class liberal Democrats against the White House and transformed the struggle for influence at the periphery of the political system into an all-out battle for control at the center. In the late 1960s liberals launched a full-scale attack on the national security establishment. They strongly disapproved of how American military power was being used and argued that the funds spent on weapons could better be used to meet pressing domestic needs. Of course such a reordering of national priorities would also direct the flow of federal funds toward government agencies over which liberals exercised influence—and away from the political forces they now opposed.

Opponents of American military and national security policy began to criticize sharply practices that previously had aroused little journalistic attention or public opposition: the Pentagon's tolerance of cost overruns in weapons procurement contracts; the public relations campaigns and lobbying efforts of the Pentagon; the hiring of retired military officers by defense contractors; the failure of Congress to monitor the activities of the CIA and other intelligence agencies. Liberals sought to subject the military-industrial complex to stricter external control and to limit the role it had come to play in the nation's life during the Cold War years.

By attacking these practices, liberals were attempting to disrupt the set of compromises that Presidents Roosevelt and Harry Truman had arranged during World War II and the Cold War, a foreign policy consensus in which liberals at the time had been enthusiastic participants. The construction of a permanent military apparatus in the 1940s and 1950s made it possible to give all the major actors in American politics a stake in national security policies. Members of Congress were given access to a huge pork barrel, which incumbents could use to enhance their political security.[20] National defense made it politically possible for public expenditures to be maintained at a level that kept unemployment reasonably low, wages reasonably high, and labor reasonably happy. Moreover, through the procurement of weapons and supplies, those elements of the American business community that had been most strongly identified with the isolationist wing of the Republican party were reconciled to internationalism and big government.

The post-Vietnam attack on the national security sector was quite successful, and defense spending as a percentage of the gross national product (GNP) dropped sharply through the 1970s. Especially after the 1979 Soviet invasion of Afghanistan, however, conservative Republicans were able to charge that their opponents had dangerously weakened the nation's defenses and in this way to rally support for a major military buildup. The Republicans were able to cultivate support in regions of the country—the South and West—and among interests in the business community with a stake in defense spending.

The New Regulation

The 1960s and 1970s witnessed a major expansion of the regulatory activities of the federal government. Liberal consumer advocates, environmentalists, and their supporters in Congress asserted that existing regulatory agencies had been captured by business; they proposed major reforms that promised both to protect the public better and to enhance their own political influence.[21]

These consumer advocates and environmentalists undertook to alter the procedures and practices of regulatory agencies so that the agencies would serve broader public interests rather than the interests of business. In particular, these activists sought to limit the interchange of personnel between agencies and the interests they regulated; the cocoon of minimum rates, entry restrictions, public subsidies, and tax benefits that had been placed around the transportation and energy sectors of the economy; and the mutually beneficial relationships that had developed among executive agencies, congressional committees, and private interests. Such groups as Common Cause, Ralph Nader's Public Citizen, and the Natural

Resources Defense Council attempted to end these practices and increase their own influence in the regulatory process by sponsoring sunshine laws, by subjecting regulatory agencies to close judicial supervision, and by providing for the representation of public interest groups in the administrative process.

In addition, consumer and environmental activists insisted that the federal government undertake major new programs to deal with such problems as air and water pollution, product safety, and health hazards associated with food and drugs. Between 1966 and 1976 these activists were able to secure the enactment of dozens of new regulatory statutes, greatly expanding the federal government's role in the economy. In contrast with the typical New Deal regulatory program that encompassed a single industrial sector, such as trucking or airlines, the "new regulation" of the 1960s and 1970s affected firms throughout the economy. To administer these programs, Congress created a number of new federal regulatory agencies such as the EPA, the Consumer Product Safety Commission, and OSHA.[22] These agencies and the congressional committees that oversee and protect them subsequently became major Democratic bastions with substantial influence over the domestic economy.

Party and Administrative Reform

During the 1960s liberal political forces also significantly changed the structure and practices of the Democratic party.[23] The party reforms enacted after the antiwar candidates were defeated at the 1968 Democratic National Convention were the most comprehensive since the Progressive Era. Chief among them were rules requiring that delegations to future national conventions be composed of blacks, women, and youths in a "reasonable relationship to their presence in the population of the state." Other important reforms encouraged states to select convention delegations through primary elections or open caucus procedures and discouraged the slate-making efforts of party organizations. Groups such as Common Cause also sponsored reforms in the area of campaign finance, including public subsidies to presidential candidates, limitations on individual contributions, and public disclosure of the names of contributors.

Through these reforms, liberals weakened the position of their major competitors within the Democratic camp—urban politicians, labor and business leaders—and enhanced the importance of middle-class issue-oriented activists and racial minorities.[24] Moreover, the political reforms of the 1960s and 1970s all but destroyed what remained of local party organizations. This left the Democrats more fully dependent upon their bastions within the domestic state.

In addition to party reform, liberal Democrats sought to secure a number of major reforms in governmental and bureaucratic organization. They modified the public personnel system, which had been built around competitive examinations and a career civil service, by advocating various mechanisms of affirmative action and by delegating many public tasks to nongovernmental institutions whose employees were not career civil servants. Prior to these reforms, the New Dealers had drawn support from a middle class and an upwardly mobile working class whose members could expect to secure civil service jobs through competitive examinations; Democratic liberals in the 1960s and 1970s sought to win the support of blacks who had been excluded from public jobs by such examinations and of an upper middle class that had little interest in moving slowly up the ladder in career civil service systems. The former would benefit from affirmative action programs, and the latter stood to gain if public responsibilities were delegated and public monies were allocated to the institutions with which they were affiliated: nonprofit social service agencies, legal service clinics, public interest law firms, and so forth.

After their break with the Johnson administration, and after the defeats in the 1968 and 1972 presidential elections, liberal Democrats lost the access to the presidency they previously had enjoyed. Consequently, they opposed reforms that would increase presidential control over the executive branch, such as those proposed by the Ash Council on management reform in 1970 or the ones President Nixon sought to implement by fiat in 1973. They hoped instead to reduce the powers of the presidency and to increase the influence within the administrative process of the institutions with which they were allied or to which they enjoyed access.

Liberal political forces also used their access to national news media to influence the behavior of executive agencies through investigative reporting and Naderite exposés. Similarly, environmental, consumer, and civil rights groups attempted to subject administrative agencies to tighter court supervision; these groups commanded considerable legal talent, and the federal judiciary in the 1960s and 1970s loosened requirements for standing, narrowed the scope of the doctrine of political questions, and enriched the range of remedies it was prepared to consider in class action suits.[25] Finally, after decades of seeking to limit the powers of Congress, Democrats in the 1970s sought to expand Congress's power over the administration—especially in the areas of budgeting, investigations, and executive privilege—because of the access they enjoyed to that body.

For the very reason that these efforts to reorder national priorities and alter government processes were part of a struggle for political power in the United States, they sparked major conflicts. It may seem paradoxical, then, that the political turbulence of the 1960s and 1970s was accompanied by a marked decline in voter turnout rates. The explanation for this apparent paradox is that the liberal Democrats' strategies of bureaucratic warfare during this period served as a substitute for party building. Rather than build mass organizations and mobilize voters, Democrats sought to entrench themselves in major segments of the domestic state. This provided an opening that Richard Nixon, Ronald Reagan, and George Bush later exploited.

BUREAUCRATIC ENTRENCHMENT VERSUS VOTER MOBILIZATION

During the 1960s and 1970s a coalition of liberals and blacks within the Democratic party took the initiative in expanding federal social and regulatory programs and reforming governmental procedures. These efforts were in part related to factional conflicts among Democrats and were at times resisted by other elements of the party, such as southern conservatives, organized labor, and old-line urban politicians.

During the Reagan-Bush era, however, such factional divisions were less evident. In response to the threat that a resurgent GOP presented to them all, the major components of the Democratic party strove to overcome their differences and to unite in defense of those domestic programs and agencies they all could support. In recent budget battles, congressional Democrats have displayed unusual unity in opposing White House efforts to cut domestic expenditures and maintain spending on the military. Indeed, in recent years Democrats in the House and Senate have taken the extraordinary step of delegating to the congressional party leadership the authority to negotiate a budget agreement with the White House and then have lined up solidly behind the resulting revenue and expenditure decisions.[26] This dramatic reversal of the trend of increasing decentralization in Congress is also reflected in roll call votes. Over the course of the 1980s, Democrats displayed increasing cohesion in roll call voting in the House of Representatives. Party voting in the Senate followed a similar path.

Congressional Democrats have united in defense of domestic programs and agencies because these have become central bastions of the party. Persons affiliated with federal domestic agencies, and with the state and municipal bureaucracies and nonprofit organizations linked to them, vote disproportionately for the Democrats and provide the party with a major portion of its activists. In addition, federal social and regulatory agencies are notable centers of resistance to Republican efforts to shape national policy. Finally, domestic programs and agencies, in conjunction with the party's control of Congress, provide the Democrats with a continuing governing capacity despite their diminishing ability to mobilize votes in the arena of presidential elections.

Federal spending (adjusted for inflation) on social programs defended by the Democrats has continued to rise over the past quarter century despite declining Democratic vote mobilization in presidential elections. Thus, the Democrats have become increasingly entrenched in social and regulatory agencies of the domestic state at the same time that the party's capacity to mobilize large numbers of voters has declined.

Because federal domestic programs and agencies have become such important Democratic bastions, the Republicans laid siege to them during the 1980s.

During the 1980s the Reagan and Bush administrations were, for the most part, able to prevent Congress from enacting new domestic spending programs. The enormous federal deficits of this era allowed Republicans to argue that the nation could not afford new domestic spending programs. Democrats, however, found a way to expand the domestic state that did not require Congress to pass and the president to sign bills requiring new federal expenditures. Instead of seeking new spending in the face of presidential opposition, the Democrats concentrated on persuading Congress and the courts that the claims of their various constituency groups were *rights* worthy of government protection. Political activists who asserted they were speaking for groups being denied their rights then devoted their efforts to obtaining favorable rulings from the federal courts and from administrative agencies. In the 1980s among the claims recognized as rights worthy of government protection were those asserted by, or on behalf of, the disabled, the elderly, consumers, various ethnic and racial minorities, resident aliens, and prison inmates. In some instances, realization of these rights was paid for by private sector firms or government agencies compelled by the courts, for example, to subsidize the employment of handicapped persons or to provide family leave to workers with new babies. In this way Democrats were able to expand the reach of the domestic state even though Republican presidents were able to prevent the enactment of new domestic spending programs.

After Clinton's victory in 1992 gave the Democrats control of the White House for the first time in twelve years, the new administration moved to entrench further the liberal wing of the Democratic party in the domestic state. The most important such programs of the Clinton administration were in the fields of economic policy, health care, and political reform.

In economic policy President Clinton introduced a package of tax increases and spending cuts that the White House projected would reduce the nation's projected budget deficit by some five hundred billion dollars in five years. The burden of the tax increases would be borne chiefly by wealthier taxpayers, although virtually all but the poorest Americans would see some increase in their taxes. A middle-class tax cut, which Clinton had proposed during the campaign, was dropped. A tax on energy was to provide substantial new revenues. Also, the president proposed a sixteen-billion-dollar economic stimulus package containing new spending for a variety of domestic programs.

In the area of health policy the president asserted that the escalating cost of medical care amounted to a national social and economic crisis. To meet this problem, Clinton created a five hundred-person task force under the leadership of his wife, Hillary Rodham Clinton, which developed a proposal for a complete overhaul of the nation's health care system. Although the deliberations, and even the membership, of the task force were secret, it soon became known that the administration favored some form of managed competition. In such a system the federal government would oversee the creation of large groups of health care purchasers who would contract with health care providers for a complete package of medical services. All Americans would receive a basic package of health insurance. The annual costs of the program to the federal government, estimated between fifty billion and one hundred billion dollars, would be funded primarily by new payroll taxes.

As for political reform, Clinton proposed changes in campaign spending rules, limiting private contributions and providing public funding for congressional campaigns; amending the Hatch Act to permit federal civil servants to play a larger role in the political process; and prohibiting lobbyists from making campaign contributions to national legislative or executive officials if they had lobbied these officials within the previous twelve months. Finally, the president sought legislation stipulating that companies employing lobbyists not be allowed to deduct lobbying costs from their federal taxes as a business expense, thereby making it more costly for firms to employ lobbyists.

Taken together, the major elements of Clinton's program can be seen as an effort to expand the power of liberal Democrats in American national politics. Clinton's economic package entailed significant tax increases and cuts in military spending. Under the rubric of "investment," it channeled additional revenues into Democratic social programs and agencies that had faced restrictive funding during the years of Republican rule from 1980 to 1992. In the name of deficit reduction, Clinton actually proposed to increase domestic spending.

Clinton's health care reform proposals would have created an extensive set of new government agencies and institutions enabling Democratic legislators and executive officials to extend their influence over a sector constituting nearly 15 percent of the national economy. Politically, health care promised to achieve for the Clintonians what Social Security had accomplished for the New Dealers: It would provide millions of voters with an ongoing reason to support the Democratic party, while giving the Democrats a means to manage a major sector of the economy. Indeed, in his nationally televised speech before a joint session of Congress, Clinton sought to identify his health care program, which he called health security, with Social Security retirement benefits.

Finally, Clinton's proposed changes in campaign spending rules would have generally worked to the advantage of his political allies, including liberal public interest groups and incumbent Democratic representatives and senators. Reform of the Hatch Act promised to permit the overwhelmingly Democratic federal civil service to play a larger role in the political process.

After a protracted political struggle, Clinton's health care and energy tax proposals were defeated. Following the GOP's capture of both houses of Congress in 1994, the president was in no position to introduce major new proposals. In 1997 and 1998, however, with the congressional Republican leadership weakened by factional fighting, Clinton introduced several initiatives designed to expand the agencies of the domestic state. Two of the most important of these proposals involved Medicare and child care. Under Clinton's Medicare proposal, individuals as young as fifty-five would be allowed to buy into the Medicare program by paying a four-hundred-dollar per month premium if they lost their jobs, while individuals between the ages of sixty-two and sixty-five would be permitted to obtain Medicare coverage for three hundred dollars per month. Medicare is currently limited to those over sixty-five. Clinton's proposal would of course increase the reach and scope of the Medicare program, expanding a bureaucracy allied with the Democrats and providing the Democratic party with additional control over the nation's health care system. All this at a time when the fiscal viability of the Medicare system is open to serious question.

Clinton's child care proposal called for some twenty-one billion dollars in new spending and tax credits to increase the availability of child care for working families. Spending was to be financed by the tobacco industry under the terms of the proposed settlement of a host of lawsuits against the major tobacco companies. Again, Clinton hoped to expand the size of the domestic state and the reach of social agencies affiliated with the Democratic party. The president understood that programs aimed at helping children were difficult for the GOP to oppose. Hence children could be the key to overcoming Republican opposition to new domestic programs. This strategy had been successful in 1997, when Congress approved a twenty-billion-dollar children's health initiative and increased funding for education. Congressional Republicans nevertheless greeted the president's proposals with skepticism. Republicans worked to block the tobacco settlement as a way of defeating Clinton's proposals without overtly opposing social services for children. The defeat of the tobacco settlement would cut off funding for Clinton's projects.

The continuing importance of the institutions of the domestic state to the Democrats was evident during the first year of George W. Bush's administration when they waged fierce rearguard actions to block presidential appointments to what had been considered Democratic bastions. For example, when Bush sought to name Peter Kirsanow, a black Republican labor lawyer, to the U.S. Civil Rights Commission, the chair of the commission, Mary Francis Berry, refused to acknolwedge the new member and brought action in the federal courts to forestall his appointment. In a similar vein, Senate Democrats endeavored to prevent the naming of Eugene Scalia, son of Justice Antonin Scalia, as solicitor of the U.S. Labor Department. In these and other battles over appointments, Democrats demonstrated that they would resist the GOP's efforts to take control of domestic agencies long regarded as the domain of the Democratic party.

4

The Republican Offensive

AFTER WINNING CONTROL of the presidency in 1980, the Republicans launched the first phase of an effort to undermine Democratic strongholds and to create a constellation of institutions, policies, and political forces to solidify their power. The principal weapons the GOP deployed against its opponents were domestic spending cuts, tax reductions, and deregulation. These weapons have weakened important institutional bastions of the Democratic party and disrupted the social groups and forces upon which it depended for support. At the same time, through national security, monetary, and fiscal policy, the Republicans undertook to reorganize social forces and establish mechanisms of governance to maintain their own rule. These Republican efforts were partially successful. The GOP was able to control the White House for twelve successive years. During these years the Republicans disrupted a number of key Democratic constituencies and at least temporarily weakened a number of important institutions linked to the Democrats.

Republican efforts suffered a serious setback when Democrat Bill Clinton won the 1992 presidential election. The GOP, however, regrouped its forces and, in 1994, took control of both houses of Congress for the first time in decades. From this new position of power Republicans launched what might be called Phase 2 of their attack upon Democratic political bastions.

Of course these disparate strategies were not components of some master plan that the Republicans devised prior to gaining power. Rather, they emerged in the course of conflicts both within the GOP and between the White House and institutions controlled by the Democrats. The Republicans' political weapons have been shaped not only by the victories they have achieved but also by the compromises the GOP has been compelled to make and the defeats it has suffered in these struggles.

THE GOP'S PHASE 1: DISRUPTING DEMOCRATIC INSTITUTIONS

Beginning in 1981, the Republicans worked to weaken social service and regulatory agencies in which the Democrats were entrenched. The Reagan and Bush administrations promoted tax reductions, domestic spending cuts, and efforts at deregulation to limit these agencies' powers. These Republican policies reduced the extractive, distributive, and regulatory capabilities of institutions over which the Democrats exercised influence. This diminished the Democrats' ability to achieve their policy objectives, overcome divisions in their coalition, and provide benefits to groups allied with the party.

In 1981 the Reagan administration sponsored legislation that substantially cut individual and corporate income tax rates and indexed these rates to inflation. Congressional Democrats responded to the administration's bill by introducing a proposal of their own.

A bidding war ensued, and the tax bill that was enacted reduced revenues more sharply than the White House had planned. Coupled with the administration's military buildup and inability to secure reductions in domestic spending as drastic as it had proposed, these tax cuts produced the enormous budget deficits of the 1980s. The federal government's annual deficit increased from approximately sixty billion dollars at the end of the Carter administration to a peak of more than two hundred billion dollars during the Reagan presidency. Annual deficits began to decline from that peak in the late 1980s, although the decline was largely a result of surpluses in the Social Security trust fund.

Five years later, in the 1986 Tax Reform Act, tax rates were further reduced, and numerous loopholes—deductions, exemptions, and tax preferences—were eliminated from the federal tax code. By closing the loopholes for influential groups that had made nominally high income tax rates politically feasible, the 1986 Tax Reform Act made it more difficult for Congress to restore any of the lost revenues. Thus, when seeking to reduce the budget deficit at the beginning of the Bush administration, Congress was only able to consider increasing those taxes that produced little in the way of revenue, such as those on alcohol, gasoline, and tobacco.

These restrictions on the extractive capacities of Congress impaired that institution's distributive capabilities. Because the federal government was strapped for revenues, funding levels for domestic programs came under pressure, and it was all but impossible for congressional Democrats to enact new social programs, despite demands that more be done to cope with such problems as the AIDS epidemic and homelessness.[1]

Republican tax policies also exacerbated cleavages within the Democratic party. During the New Deal and postwar decades, many groups made claims on the federal treasury; their claims were accommodated through logrolling arrangements that characteristically were negotiated by the Democratic leadership of Congress. These arrangements entailed a steady growth of the public sector through a process of budgetary incrementalism, as Aaron Wildavsky then called it.[2] This pattern of policy making depended on a steady expansion of public revenues, which was achieved—without the political conflict that would have resulted from repeated increases in nominal tax rates—by allowing inflation to increase real rates of federal income taxation steadily through what came to be called bracket creep.

By slashing federal tax rates and introducing indexation to prevent bracket creep, the Republicans at least temporarily undermined the fiscal foundations of the New Deal pattern of accommodations among the beneficiaries of federal expenditure programs. The enormous deficit created by Republican fiscal policies exerted constant pressure on the funding levels of domestic programs. To protect their favorite programs in this fiscal environment, lobbyists representing such groups as farmers, organized labor, senior citizens, advocates of welfare spending, and local government officials were compelled to engage in zero-sum conflict, in contrast with the positive-sum politics of the New Deal and postwar systems. One group's gain now became another group's loss.[3] This state of affairs placed strains on the Democratic coalition.

The 1989 outcry over catastrophic health insurance for the elderly illustrates how Reaganite fiscal policies altered the political environment in which Congress operated. To avoid an increase in either tax rates or the deficit, Congress found it necessary to impose the costs of the new coverage on the program's beneficiaries. This generated a firestorm of protest among the elderly, compelling Congress to curtail the program. Thus, members of Congress discovered that under the Republican fiscal regime the enactment of new spending measures was no longer a sure means of winning political support.

After gaining control of the White House in the 1980s, the Republicans also undertook to restrict the regulatory capabilities of the federal government. They promoted deregulation in the transportation, energy, banking, and financial sectors of the economy, and they curtailed enforcement of environmental, health, safety, consumer, and antitrust laws. Regulatory agencies were consequently less able to intervene against business on behalf of groups disadvantaged by market processes. For example, financial deregulation and the relaxation of antitrust enforcement in the 1980s left labor and other Democratic constituencies with little protection against the threat to their interests posed by the largest wave of corporate reorganizations—hostile takeovers, leveraged buyouts, plant closings—since the days of J. P. Morgan.

Deregulation also eroded the accommodations between business and labor that had been fashioned by the Democrats. During the New Deal period the federal government established or extended a regime of regulation over numerous sectors of the American economy. Characteristically these regulations restricted price competition among firms within the regulated industry and, in some cases, erected barriers to the entry of new firms. To the extent that firms within such industries could pass added costs to their customers without fear of being undersold by competitors, they lost an incentive to control their labor costs. Union-management relations in most regulated industries were consequently more cooperative than adversarial in character. Rather than fight each other over wages and work rules, unions and employers entered the political arena as allies to defend and extend the regulatory regime and to secure direct or indirect public subsidies for their industries.

Asserting that these business-labor accommodations served "special interests" at the expense of the "public interest," an unlikely coalition of conservatives and liberal consumer advocates secured a substantial measure of deregulation during the late 1970s.[4] Through deregulation, conservatives hoped to get business to break its alliance with organized labor. Consumer advocates, for their part, were happy to weaken the labor unions and business interests that had been their rivals for influence within the Democratic party.

In the face of the threats that Reaganism posed to them both, liberals and labor rekindled their coalition in the 1980s. Increasingly, organized labor supported liberal causes, such as the nuclear freeze and comparable worth, that it would formerly have disdained.

Liberals, for their part, began to see merit in a number of causes supported by organized labor, such as protectionism, and lost their enthusiasm for deregulation.

The Republicans, though, continued to press for deregulation, and with good reason. Particularly in airlines, telecommunications, and trucking, deregulation allowed nonunion firms to undersell the established giants in their industry. Established firms were compelled to demand givebacks from their unions to lower their own labor costs, and alliances between business and labor were disrupted.

REORGANIZING POLITICAL FORCES

By undermining the governing capacities of institutions over which the Democrats exercised influence, the Republicans also weakened the Democrats' social base. They destabilized some of the major political forces upon which the Democrats depended and reorganized them under Republican auspices.

Most observers assume that politicians must deal with whatever groups they find in society, but it is important to note that political leaders are not limited to working with some predefined constellation of forces. At times politicians can destroy established centers of power, reorganize interests, and even call new groups into being. Leaders can attempt to reorganize the constellation of interests central to the political process in several ways. They may be able to transform the political identities of established groups, create new political forces by dividing existing groups, or construct new interests by uniting previously disparate elements. In these ways the Republicans worked to reshape the political attachments of business executives, middle-class suburbanites, blue-collar ethnics, and white southerners.

Reunifying Business

In the 1980s the Republicans sought to unify the business community under their auspices. After World War II the Democrats had come to terms with many segments of big business: internationally competitive firms that benefited from free trade policies, firms in capital-intensive industries that found it relatively easy to make concessions to organized labor, and defense contractors who benefited from a foreign policy of internationalism.[5] However, proprietors of smaller firms that were not involved in international markets often found Democratic labor and social programs onerous, and they characteristically aligned themselves with the Republican party. This breach between Wall Street and Main Street undermined the political potency of American business.

During the 1970s the accord between big business and the Democratic party was severely strained by two developments that the Republicans sought to exploit. The erosion of America's position in the world economy caused many business leaders to reject the high labor costs and taxes associated with the Democrats that they had previously accepted. Also, Democratic support for environmental, consumer, and other new regulatory programs further alienated many of the party's allies in the business community. In his 1980 presidential campaign Ronald Reagan appealed for the support of business by indicating that he would trim costly social programs, weaken the influence of organized labor, and relax the environmental rules and other forms of regulation that had been sponsored by Democratic politicians during the 1960s and 1970s. Moreover, Reagan offered the thousands of firms that stood to benefit from military contracts substantial increases in defense spending.

Enacted into law, these policies helped reunify American business and attach it to the Republican party,[6] where it remained until Bill Clinton's probusiness policies lured some segments of the business community back into the Democratic fold. Even before Clinton, Reaganite budget and trade deficits produced a conflict between what may be termed the traditionalist and supply-side camps within the Republican party. The traditionalists asserted that the nation's first economic priority was to reduce the budget deficit—through budget cuts and, if necessary, tax increases. The supply-siders were prepared to accept continuing deficits in order to protect tax cuts and to avoid reductions in defense spending.[7]

The conflict between traditionalists and supply-siders had two sources. The first was a difference in economic and political perspectives. Traditionalist Republicans feared that continuing huge deficits could wreck the economy and hence their party's electoral fortunes. Supply-siders asserted that the deficit posed no immediate threat to the economy, and they feared that steps taken to cut the deficit—such as raising taxes—could severely damage Republican electoral prospects.

The second source of disagreement between traditionalists and supply-siders was the conflict between two sets of economic interests in the Republican party. Large budget and trade deficits hurt sectors of the economy that produced goods in the United States for export (e.g., agriculture) and faced competition in the American market from goods produced abroad (such as steel). Large budget deficits also exerted upward pressure on interest rates, hurting local banks and thrift institutions. Together, these interests were the mainstays of the traditionalist camp.

Other sectors of American business (notably, domestic importers of goods produced by foreign manufacturers), however, benefited from Reagan's economic policies. Firms in the service sector were not severely affected by interest rates or the trade deficit, but they prospered as a result of the macroeconomic stimulus provided by budget deficits.

In the battle for the 1988 Republican presidential nomination, George Bush was the leader of the supply-side forces and Senator Robert Dole spoke for the traditionalists. But once Bush wrapped up the nomination, all segments of the business community united behind his candidacy. However uneasy some business executives might have been over budget deficits, they were even more distrustful of a Democratic party whose leading representatives then called for the enactment of plant-closing legislation, higher levels of social service spending, and increased taxes on the wealthy.

From Beneficiaries to Taxpayers

Middle-income suburbanites were a second group to which the Republicans appealed. The GOP attempted to convince these voters to regard themselves less as beneficiaries of federal expenditure programs than as taxpayers. After World War II many suburbanites were integrated into the political process and linked to the Democratic party by federal programs that subsidized mortgages, built arterial highways, and expanded access to higher education. By placating the poor and reducing working-class militancy, Democratic welfare and labor programs also promoted social peace. In exchange for the benefits they received, members of the middle class gave their support to the various expenditure programs through which the Democratic party channeled public funds to its other constituency groups: crop subsidies for farmers, maritime subsidies for the shipping industry, and so on. This system of interest group liberalism enabled the Democrats to accommodate the claims of a host of disparate groups in their electoral coalition.[8]

During the 1960s and 1970s many benefits that middle-income Americans had come to expect from federal programs and policies were sharply curtailed. For example, rising mortgage interest rates increased housing costs, affirmative action programs seemed to threaten the middle class's privileged access to higher education, social peace was disrupted by urban violence and riots, and above all, double-digit inflation during the late 1970s eroded the middle class's real income and standard of living. The curtailment of these benefits undermined the political basis of the loyalty that many middle-income individuals had shown to the Democrats. This provided the GOP with an opportunity to win their support.[9]

In wooing suburbanites, the GOP chose not to promise new federal benefits although, to be sure, it did not seek to repeal existing middle-class benefit programs. Instead it sought to link these individuals to the Republican camp in their capacity as taxpayers. In 1980 Reagan declared tax relief to be a central political issue. The Republicans argued that taxation was linked to inflation and blamed high rates of inflation on Democratic tax and spending policies. Indeed, Reagan called inflation the "cruelest tax of all."

After Reagan's 1980 election his administration cooperated with Federal Reserve Board Chairman Paul Volcker in a relentless attack on inflation.[10] The Reagan-Volcker war on inflation was successful, albeit at the cost of a severe recession and high rates of unemployment for blue-collar workers. At the same time the Reagan administration provided middle- and upper-income groups with a sizable reduction in federal income tax rates. Reagan's warning to middle-income voters that the Democrats wanted to take their tax cuts away was a crucial element of his successful 1984 campaign against Democratic presidential candidate Walter Mondale. This theme was echoed by George Bush in 1988. Bush promised to oppose any efforts to raise federal income tax rates and heaped scorn on Michael Dukakis's proposal to step up collection of delinquent federal taxes. Bush derided what he characterized as a Democratic plan to put an Internal Revenue Service auditor into every taxpayer's home.

In the 1980s the Republican party was successful in convincing middle-income Americans to focus on taxes. In 1976 only 2 percent of middle-class voters identified taxes and spending as important national problems; by 1984, 23 percent of voters with above-average incomes did so. Of these voters, 67 percent cast their ballots for the Republican presidential candidate.[11]

Republicans appealed to members of the middle class as taxpayers rather than as beneficiaries of spending programs chiefly because they hoped to erode middle-income support for domestic expenditures in general. Transforming middle-class Americans into taxpayers not only linked them to the Republican party but also helped undermine the entire apparatus of interest group liberalism through which the Democrats maintained their various constituencies' allegiances. This helped disorganize the Democrats' political base.

Republican tax policies also served to divide a politically important middle-class group—college-educated professionals—that had given substantial support to the Democrats during the 1960s and 1970s. Socially this group is heterogeneous, ranging from ill-paid social workers to lavishly compensated attorneys. The group is so heterogeneous that sociologists have debated whether it is meaningful to speak of this "new class" as a coherent social and political force.[12] But groups are constituted in the political realm, and in the 1960s and 1970s political entrepreneurs were able to mobilize large numbers of professionals on behalf of such liberal causes as environmentalism and opposition to the Vietnam War.

The Republicans attempted to divide this new class by shifting the political debate to the issues of tax and budget cuts. The 1981 tax cut was promoted as a means of stimulating the private sector. The tax reform package that Reagan made the centerpiece of his second administration was especially beneficial to professionals with high salaries. Professionals in a position to take advantage of these new opportunities—namely, those who worked in the private sector—were attracted into the Republican party.

Republican reductions in federal domestic expenditures, however, restricted opportunities for professionals who worked in the public and nonprofit sectors. The Republicans were not altogether unhappy to see schoolteachers, social workers, and university professors try to defend their interests by becoming increasingly active in Democratic party politics. The more committed the Democrats became to the cause of boosting domestic expenditures, the more likely it was that taxpayers, business executives, and private sector professionals would flock to the Republican party.

This Republican strategy was quite successful. College graduates working in public sector occupations gave the Republicans only 40 percent of their votes in the 1984 presidential election. On the other hand, college graduates in the private sector supported the GOP by the overwhelming margin of 68 percent to 32 percent for the Democrats.

From Workers to Patriots

The GOP also sought to appeal to blue-collar voters. During the New Deal era, members of urban ethnic groups had been integrated into politics in their capacity as workers, through organizations informally affiliated with the national Democratic party: trade unions, political machines, and urban service bureaucracies. These institutions provided members of urban ethnic groups with public and private employment at relatively high wages, with social services, and with preferential access to locally administered federal programs. At the same time trade unions and urban machines and bureaucracies functioned as the local institutional foundations of the national Democratic party, mobilizing urban voters to support Democratic candidates.[13]

The Republicans weakened the links between the Democrats and blue-collar workers by attacking these institutions. They undermined organized labor by encouraging employers to engage in antiunion practices; indeed, the Reagan administration set an example by destroying the Professional Air Traffic Controllers Organization when the group conducted a strike in 1981.[14] The Republicans also appointed officials who were hostile to organized labor to the National Labor Relations Board (an agency formerly controlled by labor sympathizers). Moreover, as discussed above, the Reagan and Bush administrations supported policies of deregulation that provided business firms with a strong incentive to rid themselves of their unions. The Republican commitment to free trade also allowed foreign goods to flood American markets, increasing unemployment in heavily unionized industries and reducing labor's bargaining power. As a result of these policies, union membership dropped sharply during the 1980s.

The Republicans attacked urban political machines and national and municipal service bureaucracies mainly through domestic spending reductions. The programs whose budgets suffered most under Reagan and Bush were precisely those that once provided local governments with substantial funds, such as revenue sharing and the Comprehensive Employment and Training Act (CETA). The tax reform package whose enactment was secured by the Reagan administration in 1986 reduced the deductability of local sales taxes (thereby heightening taxpayers' resistance to rate increases) and restricted the ability of local governments to issue tax-free revenue bonds. These changes in the tax code further diminished the resources available to municipal governments. The Justice Department also attacked urban machines and bureaucracies by launching a series of investigations into municipal government corruption; these investigations primarily targeted large cities controlled by the Democrats.[15]

The attack on labor unions, political machines, and social service agencies diminished the ability of these institutions to provide benefits to blue-collar voters; thus, this group's links to the Democratic party were undermined, and Republicans seized an opportunity to capture the support of a previously staunch Democratic constituency.

The Republicans' appeal to this constituency was hindered in one important way. In their capacity as workers, many urban ethnic voters were hurt by Republican economic and tax programs, which mainly served the interests of the upper middle class and segments of the business community. Instead of trying to appeal to members of urban ethnic groups on economic grounds, the Republicans therefore attempted to secure and institutionalize their support on three other bases. First, they sought to link urban ethnics to the GOP on the basis of their moral and religious convictions. The Republicans politicized these concerns by focusing on so-called family issues—above all, the issue of abortion. In this endeavor they sought to make use of Roman Catholic churches, which rally the faithful against proabortion candidates.[16] The importance of this political focus became evident during the 1984 presidential election. White working-class voters who belonged to trade unions but did not regularly attend a church gave Reagan only 46 percent of their vote. By contrast, among white working-class voters who attended a church regularly but did not belong to a union, the Republicans received 67 percent of the vote.

The Republicans attempted to mobilize blue-collar voters with patriotic as well as moral appeals. In this effort they were at times able to harness the national media, an institution whose editorial pages and televised commentary frequently were hostile to Republican policies. Reagan and Bush created news events filled with patriotic symbols that the media could neither attack nor ignore. In addition, where the risks of failure were low, Republican administrations used military force abroad not only to demonstrate America's resolve to foreigners but also to reinforce national pride among Americans. The 1984 Grenada invasion and the 1986 bombing of Libya exemplify this strategy. During the 1988 presidential campaign, Bush sought to make political use of patriotic sentiments by charging that his Democratic rival, Massachusetts Governor Michael Dukakis, had demonstrated a lack of respect for the American flag when he vetoed a Massachusetts bill that mandated the daily recitation of the pledge of allegiance in public schools.

Finally, the Republicans made use of race-related issues to seek support from blue-collar whites. The Reagan and Bush administrations opposed affirmative action and school busing plans and promoted efforts to narrow the rights that the liberal Warren Court granted to persons accused of crimes. In his 1988 presidential campaign, Bush made a major issue of the Willie Horton case. Horton, a black man, had been convicted of murder and sentenced to life imprisonment without parole. Under a program supported by Governor Dukakis, Massachusetts prison authorities granted Horton a weekend furlough. While on furlough, Horton fled the state and raped a white woman in Maryland. Groups supporting the Bush campaign repeatedly broadcast television ads displaying a picture of Horton and asserting that Dukakis was soft on crime.

From Southerners to Evangelicals

Southern whites were the fourth constituency that the Republicans strove to add to their camp. For a century after the Civil War, white southerners had participated in politics through the Democratic party, which had defended the southern caste system. These voters were linked to the Democrats not simply by their racial attitudes but also by local political institutions that were connected

with the party—county commissions, sheriffs, voting registrars—
and that guaranteed white political power by excluding blacks
from participation in government and politics.[17]

The civil rights revolution—in particular the Voting Rights
Act of 1965—destroyed the institutional foundations of the traditional southern Democratic regime. Local governmental institutions were prevented from maintaining white privilege at the
expense of black political subordination. The disruption of this
system gave Republicans an opportunity to win the support of
southern whites. The GOP stance on affirmative action, busing,
and the rights of defendants in criminal trials helped them win
support among white southerners as well as northern blue-collar
voters. The GOP also appealed to southerners on the basis of their
religious orientations. By focusing on the issue of abortion, Republicans politicized the moral concerns of white southerners. They
made use of fundamentalist Protestant churches, a prominent feature of the southern landscape, to forge institutional links between
southern whites and the Republican party. Republicans in effect
made these churches organizational components of their party. For
example, funds and technical support were often provided to conservative Protestant churches for voter registration activities. As a
result of these efforts, many southern whites were integrated into
politics through their evangelical religious affiliations. This helped
give the Republicans a firm social base in the white South for the
first time in the party's history.

As in the case of urban ethnics, who are mainly Roman
Catholic, the moral issue that Republicans used most effectively to
appeal to white southerners was abortion. Indeed, Republicans
used the question of abortion to promote an alliance between evangelical southern Protestants and conservative Catholics and to attach both to the Republican party. Political mobilization around
the right-to-life issue was initiated by Richard Viguerie, Paul
Weyrich, Howard Phillips, and other conservative Republican activists. Seeking to take advantage of the furor caused by the
Supreme Court's prochoice decision in *Roe v. Wade,* these politicians

convinced Catholic political activists and evangelical Protestant leaders that they had common interests and worked with these leaders to arouse public opposition to abortion. The right-to-life issue helped unite politically, under Republican auspices, two religious groups that had been bitter opponents through much of American history.[18]

The Republicans also used foreign policy and military issues to mobilize support among southerners. Military bases and defense plants play a major role in the economy of many southern states. Republican support and Democratic opposition to a military buildup during the 1980s tied many southern workers, business executives, and local communities to the GOP. Defense spending was thus the material foundation for the GOP's patriotic appeals that so successfully wooed support in the white South.

CONSTRUCTING MECHANISMS OF GOVERNANCE

While the Democrats entrenched themselves primarily in the social service and regulatory agencies of the domestic state, the Republicans relied more heavily on two other mechanisms of governance. These were the military and national security apparatus and monetary and fiscal policy.

The National Security Apparatus

Beginning in the 1980s, the Republicans undertook to enhance the size and power of America's military and national security apparatus and to use it as an instrument for governing and perpetuating their party's power. Toward this end the Reagan administration sponsored the largest peacetime military buildup in the nation's history.[19] Annual military expenditures in constant 1982 dollars were increased by more than 40 percent, from $171 billion at the end of the Carter administration to $242 billion by the middle of President Reagan's second term. Liberal opposition in Congress limited further increases to the annual rate of inflation. But the enormous military buildup of the first Reagan administration had enlarged the base upon which even these modest changes in spending were calculated.

When the Democrats returned to the White House in 1993, they attacked the military and national security sectors. President Clinton proposed substantial cuts in defense spending. Moreover, Clinton and some congressional Democrats sharply criticized the military for closing its eyes to the sexual abuse of women in the ranks and for prohibiting the recruitment and retention of gay and lesbian personnel.

Indeed, the congressional investigation of the Tailhook affair and the entire conflict regarding homosexuals in the military may be seen as efforts by Democrats to stigmatize and delegitimize an institution that had become an important Republican bastion. In October 1993 Clinton's navy secretary, John Dalton, cited sexual harassment at the Tailhook Association convention both in demanding the resignation of the Chief of Naval Operations (CNO) and in instituting disciplinary proceedings against a dozen admirals and marine generals.

This attempted decapitation of the navy's chain of command (the secretary of defense ultimately refused to fire the CNO) was announced just one day after the Pentagon had indicated that it would delay implementing the "don't ask, don't tell" compromise concerning gays and lesbians in the military that it had worked out with the Clinton administration. The Pentagon attributed this delay to the technical difficulty of informing base commanders about the new regulations. But the actions on both sides can be seen as an escalation in the struggle between the Clinton administration and the military establishment. An earlier episode had been the scathing public criticism of the commander in chief by an air force major general, for which the general was only mildly rebuked by his superiors and advised to take early retirement.

Other incidents bespoke the hostility between the military and the Clinton administration. For example, when General Colin Powell, the chairman of the Joint Chiefs of Staff, introduced former Republican Defense Secretary Dick Cheney at a Pentagon function in 1993, he saluted and called Cheney Boss. The entire room, filled with military officers, erupted into loud and sustained cheering at this suggestion that the wrong people were now in power. This was not an unusual incident: Republican officials tend to develop close relationships with military personnel as officers rise through the ranks. Republican defense secretaries typically recruit their assistants from the military rather than from civilian institutions (Colin Powell, for example, had served as assistant to Secretary of Defense Caspar Weinberger); they also rely heavily on the Pentagon's joint staff (the uniformed staff of the Joint Chiefs) for policy planning. In contrast, Democratic secretaries of defense recruit their assistants mainly from congressional staffs and university faculties. These civilian officials regard the joint staff with suspicion. The military brass in turn is disdainful of a group it calls the faculty club.

Just as the officials of domestic agencies, such as the Environmental Protection Agency, appealed to Democrats and liberal Republicans in Congress for support when they came under attack in the 1980s, so the military sought the support of congressional Republicans and conservative Democrats in its conflicts with the Clinton administration.

Within the first months of the Clinton presidency, the military launched a counterattack against the "faculty club." Acting on a complaint from career officers, the Pentagon's inspector general charged that Assistant Secretary of Defense–designate Graham Allison had twice broken government ethics rules during the period that he served as a consultant to the secretary of defense while he was awaiting Senate confirmation of his permanent appointment. The inspector general's report alleged that Allison, a former dean of Harvard's Kennedy School of Government, had arranged for his Harvard colleague Robert Blackwill to receive a Pentagon consulting contract. The report further charged that Allison had subsequently met with the Russian defense attaché in Washington to encourage the Russian government to make a donation to Harvard University that would guarantee the inclusion of Russians in a military exchange program organized by Blackwill. Career officers claimed, moreover, that Blackwill had used the position secured for him by Allison to lobby for federal funding of yet another Harvard program. These charges evidently infuriated conservative members of the Senate Armed Services Committee and threatened Allison's confirmation.[20]

Within a year of Clinton's taking office, this bureaucratic warfare led him to fire his first defense secretary, Les Aspin, just as leaks to their congressional allies by bureaucrats in the Environmental Protection Agency had compelled President Reagan to dismiss his initial EPA administrator, Anne Gorsuch Burford, whose conservative policies were vehemently opposed by her subordinates. The military's triumph over the White House was so complete that at the televised announcement of Aspin's replacement by Admiral Bobby Inman, Clinton found it necessary to stand in silence as Inman told the press that his interview with the president left him with a "comfort level" concerning Clinton's service as commander in chief sufficient to accept the president's offer to appoint him secretary of defense. Ultimately Inman withdrew his name for personal reasons, but Clinton was compelled to replace him with an appointee, William Perry, deemed equally acceptable to the Republicans. In his second term, Clinton appointed William Cohen, a former Republican senator, to head the Department of Defense, in a sense acknowledging that this governmental institution belongs to the GOP.

The dramatic expansion of national security activities included in President George W. Bush's war on terrorism has given the GOP new opportunities to strengthen the sector of the state with which it is most closely affiliated. Not only does the war on terrorism require increases in military spending, it also entails the militarization of a number of domestic institutions needed for "homeland defense." How these new possibilities will be realized remains to be seen, but it is worth noting that former Pennsylvania governor Tom Ridge, the president's homeland security director, refused when asked to testify before Congress—citing executive privilege. This refusal indicates that the administration is determined not to allow its political foes access to its emergent new homeland security domain.

Monetary and Fiscal Policy

The complex of Republican policies described in this chapter was sustained by a fiscal regime that was one of the most notable features of the contemporary American political economy.[21] Central to this regime were the enormous budget and trade deficits of the Reagan-Bush years. The budget deficit resulted from the tax reductions and military spending increases of the first Reagan administration and from Congress's opposition to further domestic spending cuts. In conjunction with the restrictive monetary policies the Federal Reserve pursued in its fight against inflation, the budget deficit led to sharp increases in real interest rates and the value of the American dollar in the early 1980s. These increases greatly reduced American exports and encouraged a flood of foreign imports into the United States. During the second Reagan administration, coordinated central bank intervention led the dollar to fall, but by that time foreign manufacturers had established such a solid position in the American market that the nation's trade deficit continued to grow.

Despite the economic risks they posed, these deficits provided the Republicans with important political benefits and opportunities. The budget deficit made it difficult for politicians to appeal for votes with new public expenditure programs and impeded the Democrats' efforts to reconstruct their political base. More important, the twin deficits functioned as a novel revenue collection apparatus that, at least in the short run, enabled the Republicans to finance government expenditures without raising taxes and alienating their political constituency.

This apparatus worked as follows. The Reagan administration's fiscal policies encouraged Americans to purchase foreign—especially Japanese and German—goods. At the same time America's high interest rates and political stability encouraged foreign bankers—notably the Japanese—to purchase U.S. Treasury securities with the profits their nation's manufacturers made in the United States. Thus, during the 1980s what might be called autodollars came to be recycled by Japanese banks, much as petrodollars had been recycled by American banks in the 1970s. These autodollars, invested in U.S. government securities, were used to help finance the American budget deficit.[22] In essence, Japanese industrialists and bankers served as revenue agents for the Republican administration. American voters demonstrated in 1980, in 1984, and again in 1988 that they opposed increased taxation, but as consumers they willingly—indeed, enthusiastically—handed over billions of dollars for this purpose whenever they purchased Japanese and other foreign-made goods.

The costs of this revenue system were borne by unemployed American workers in the industrial sector and by American manufacturers who failed to restructure their firms to meet foreign competition. The benefits of the system flowed to groups with which the Republicans were allied. Military spending benefited the defense industry and its thousands of subcontractors. The fiscal stimulus of the deficit boosted corporate profits. High-income professionals received substantial tax cuts, access to foreign goods at low prices, and high rates of return on their savings.

This fiscal regime came under attack during the 1980s, as Democrats and some Republicans argued that the growing budget and trade deficits were destroying the American economy and threatening America's place in the world. Concern about the deficit led to the 1990 budget crisis that wrecked George Bush's presidency. In 1992 the issue of the deficit was used very successfully by Ross Perot to launch a major third-party presidential bid. In a series of televised infomercials, Perot increased public concern about the deficit while further undermining Bush's chances for reelection.

After Bill Clinton's victory in 1992 the deficit continued to hamper Democratic efforts to increase levels of domestic social spending. Clinton's 1993 budget, for example, which called for substantial new domestic spending programs, was defeated by a coalition of Republicans and conservative Democrats who feared it would increase the deficit. Congressional "deficit hawks" continually pushed for spending cuts during the early and mid-1990s to erase what had come to be seen as America's major economic problem.

By 1998 expansion of the domestic economy had all but erased the current deficit, though leaving a substantial national debt. President Clinton moved to take advantage of this new opportunity to propose a substantial expansion of social spending in the realms of child care and health care. Republicans attacked the Clinton initiative as fiscally irresponsible.

Thus, by the end of the 1990s the political significance of the deficit seemed to be eroding. It is significant, however, that for nearly two decades this element of Republican fiscal policy substantially undermined efforts by Democrats to serve their party's constituencies and strengthen the institutions with which the party was associated. Thus, taken together, the fiscal, monetary, and national security policies of the Reagan and Bush administrations strengthened the institutional bastions and governing capacities of the Republicans and threatened those of the Democrats.

THE REPUBLICAN OFFENSIVE: PHASE 2

What might be called Phase 2 of the Republican offensive against Democratic bastions of power came after the 1994 national elections had given the GOP control of both houses of Congress for the first time in nearly fifty years. Even before the election, Republican leader Newt Gingrich had persuaded nearly all Republican congressional candidates to sign the "Contract with America." The contract, which Republicans pledged to support if they won control of Congress, called for a variety of tax cuts as well as such popular political reforms as term limits and a balanced budget amendment. The contract was part of the GOP's effort to nationalize the election, as well as a first step by the Republican leadership to impose party discipline on their new troops. New Republican members of Congress who failed to follow the leadership's dictates could be accused of breaking their pledge to the American people.

At the same time that he was compelling Republicans to sign this contract, Gingrich told a group of lobbyists that after Republicans took control of Congress, the GOP would launch legislative investigations to look into wrongdoing in the executive branch. Just as Democratic Congresses had used their power to investigate Republican presidents, so a Republican Congress would use its power to investigate the conduct of the Clinton presidency.

In the first days of the 104th Congress, Gingrich moved quickly to consolidate his power and put forth his initial legislative agenda. Gingrich's first move was to reorganize the House in a way that would eradicate any vestiges of Democratic influence, streamline the chamber's operations, and significantly expand the power of the Speaker.[23] The new Speaker showed little inclination to compromise with the Democrats and began his term by placing strict limits on Democratic representation on major House committees.

Gingrich began his "housecleaning" by breaching the time-honored seniority rule and appointing committee chairs who were likely to be energetic and loyal. At his behest, the Republican leadership selected Henry Hyde of Illinois rather than the more senior committee Republican, Carlos Moorhead of California, to chair the House Judiciary Committee. Similarly, Gingrich named the fifth-ranking Republican on the House Appropriations Committee, Bob Livingston of Louisiana, to chair that important panel. Thomas Bliley of Virginia, the second-ranking Republican on the Energy and Commerce Committee (renamed Commerce), was given the chair over the most senior GOP member. In addition, three freshmen, Tom Davis (Virginia), David McIntosh (Indiana), and Linda Smith (Washington), were slated to head congressional subcommittees.[24] In each of these cases, Republican leaders were determined to appoint an active committee chair who would push hard for the leadership's program, even if that meant violating tradition.

In addition to overriding seniority in their appointment of committee chairs, Gingrich and the Republican leaders moved to reorganize partially the committee system itself. Three House committees—Post Office, District of Columbia, and Merchant

Marine and Fisheries—were eliminated, and their functions transferred to other committees. Nominally these committees were eliminated to streamline House operations. Political considerations also played a role, however; the three committees were closely linked to traditionally Democratic constituencies.

The Republican leadership also diminished the size of most committees and eliminated 25 of the House's 115 subcommittees. Both these changes were moves to increase the power of committee chairs and, ultimately, of the Speaker who appointed them.

In a more symbolic move, the Republicans renamed a number of committees and made minor changes in their jurisdictions. For example, the Education and Labor Committee was renamed Economic and Educational Opportunities to emphasize a new, free market orientation. Similarly, Government Operations was renamed Government Reform and Oversight to emphasize its focus on improving, rather than merely supervising, the work of the government.

Next, the new Republican House leadership eliminated the budgets, staffs, and offices of all House caucuses (formally known as Legislative Service Organizations, or LSOs). Several of the most effective LSOs, including the Black Caucus, the Hispanic Caucus, and the Women's Caucus, were closely tied to the Democratic party. One LSO, the Democratic Study Group, had employed eighteen full-time analysts to help congressional Democrats evaluate proposed and pending legislation. Congress had been spending roughly four million dollars per year to support caucus activities.

Republicans also moved to fire hundreds of Democratic committee staffers. Most did not even receive severance pay.[25] At the same time Republicans planned sharp cuts in the budgets and staffs of three of the four congressional staff agencies: the General Accounting Office, the Library of Congress, and the Congressional Budget Office. The fourth, the Office of Technology Assessment, was disbanded altogether. Although these agencies were officially nonpartisan, Republicans believed that they had become too closely identified with the Democrats who had ruled Congress for decades.

Once Republicans purged the remaining staff agencies of zealous Democratic supporters, they began to rebuild them with a more Republican cast. The staff agencies were too useful to Congress to be permanently weakened.

With the support of the Republican leadership and, indeed, much of the Republican House delegation, Gingrich then moved to reduce the influence of committee chairs by limiting them to three consecutive two-year terms; ending the practice of proxy voting, which allowed chairs to control committee votes without the full participation of committee members; and eliminating the practice of multiple referral, which allowed several committee chairs to claim jurisdiction over one bill. Reducing the power of the committee chairs would almost inevitably enhance the power of the Speaker and the majority leadership, who would now have more control over the appointment of chairs and the referral of bills to committees.

Finally, Gingrich moved to change the House rules to make it more difficult to vote tax increases and less difficult to cut spending. He proposed that a three-fifths vote be required to pass any piece of legislation that included an income tax increase. At the same time he suggested new procedures that would make it much easier for members to offer so-called limitation amendments to propose cuts in spending bills.

Taken together, these changes were designed to centralize power and prepare the Congress to do battle with the Democrats. After completing its reorganization of the House of Representatives, the GOP launched a major assault upon the institution, programs, and procedures that had strengthened their Democratic opponents. First, Republicans adopted a budget resolution calling for a balanced budget within seven years. Since the GOP also proposed to increase military spending and to reduce federal taxes by more than $245 billion within the same period, the Republican budget would have required substantial reductions in the rate at which spending for existing federal domestic programs increased. The GOP proposal would even have limited the growth of such previously untouchable programs as Medicare. The budget proposed by congressional Republicans in November 1995, indeed, called for reductions in projected Medicare spending of $270 billion over the next seven years, reductions in projected Medicaid spending totaling $163 billion, and reductions in projected welfare spending of $82 billion.

In addition, Republicans attacked the federal social and regulatory agencies that the GOP had long seen as institutional bastions of the Democratic party. The weapons forged for this attack were regulatory reform and the devolution of federal administrative responsibilities to the states. The Republicans also called for the elimination of more than three hundred federal programs and agencies, including the Corporation for Public Broadcasting, the Department of Commerce, and the Legal Services Corporation.

The regulatory reform proposals backed by the Republicans would have required federal agencies to justify any proposed health, safety, or environmental regulation through cost-benefit analyses. Such a requirement would have made it considerably more difficult for federal agencies to adopt and enforce rules and regulations that imposed significant costs on either the private sector or state and local governments. Cost-benefit analyses are time-consuming and seldom are fully conclusive. An agency required to prove definitively that a proposed rule was economically justified would find itself involved in years of administrative procedures and court challenges before the rule could be adopted. Such "reforms" thus would have made it considerably more difficult and time-consuming for public officials to enact and implement new regulations and hence would have greatly weakened federal regulatory agencies. The very purpose of environmental regulations, for example, is to prevent purely economic concerns from prevailing over other values. More generally, this requirement would have shifted the burden of proof from interests opposed to a regulation to the agency proposing it.

Another weapon forged by the GOP to attack federal administrative agencies was devolution. Republicans proposed to convert most public assistance programs (e.g., Aid to Families with Dependent Children [AFDC] and Medicaid) from federal entitlement programs into block grants to the states. Each state would receive a designated sum to be spent as it saw fit within guidelines established by the Congress. For instance, under GOP proposals, federal expenditures on Medicaid would have gone to the state governments as block grants. State governments would enjoy considerable latitude in designing programs of medical assistance to the poor and in determining eligibility requirements. (States would be required, however, to cover children and low-income pregnant women.) In the case of welfare the bill, approved by Congress but vetoed by President Clinton in January 1996, would have given state governments more extensive authority over their public assistance, food stamp, and child care programs than the bill Clinton eventually signed.

These Republican proposals represented an effort to transfer power from the executive agencies of the federal government to Congress. Most analyses of devolution regard it chiefly as an effort to transfer power from Washington to the states. But of equal or greater importance is the impact devolution would have on the relative power of institutions within the national government. Congressional Republicans proposed to strip federal administrative agencies of much of their authority over Medicaid and various welfare programs. The Republicans were not, however, proposing to strip Congress of any of its power. Congress would remain perfectly free to establish rules and spending priorities as it chose. In effect, under devolution, Congress would be using state, rather than federal, agencies to administer its programs. Republicans regard federal social and regulatory agencies as closely linked to the liberal wing of the Democratic party. On the other hand, many state administrative agencies, especially in the South and Southwest, are more closely attuned to Republican and conservative views on welfare. Devolution was intended to provide congressional Republicans with an administrative mechanism more sympathetic to such GOP proposals as work requirements, time limits for cash benefits, restrictions on aid to unwed teenage mothers—proposals opposed and likely to be subverted by the employees of federal social service agencies.

Moreover, to the extent that devolution actually transferred discretion to the states, its effect would be to place decisions concerning welfare policies in a very different political environment from that in Washington, D.C. As Margaret Weir notes, in most states the dominant political forces are coalitions of rural and suburban interests. The urban forces and liberal public interest groups that are influential in Washington are far less important in most state capitals.[26] The states, moreover, are compelled to compete with one another for business investment and are under constant pressure to hold down taxes and social spending. For these reasons, the decisions of state governments regarding Medicaid and other social programs are likely to be less generous than federal policies.

At the same time that they attacked federal regulatory agencies, Republicans used their control of Congress to endeavor to strike at the liberal public interest groups that have become central to the Democratic party. The two most important weapons in this assault were lobby regulation and tort reform. During the course of the 104th Congress, Republicans proposed restrictions on the lobbying efforts of tax-exempt, charitable, and not-for-profit groups that received federal grants or contracts. The GOP also proposed restrictions on efforts by federal agencies to mobilize public support for (or opposition to) legislation pending in Congress.

The first of these Republican initiatives was designed to undermine liberal public interest groups that receive federal funding and at the same time actively lobby on behalf of liberal causes. For example, Planned Parenthood receives roughly one-third of its $462 million annual budget from federal grants and Medicaid reimbursements; it also lobbies vigorously against federal and state restrictions on abortion rights.[27] Similarly, the American Association of Retired Persons (AARP) receives millions of dollars in federal contracts to administer programs for the elderly, while spending money to lobby for the expansion of federal social programs, including those from which it benefits.

As for the second Republican initiative, restrictions on the lobbying activities of federal agencies were designed to prevent domestic social and regulatory agencies—such as HHS, HUD, and the EPA—from using federal funds to mobilize the liberal forces upon which these agencies rely to support their programs and budgetary requests. Over the past thirty years this has become a common tactic. Threatened with spending or program cuts, federal social agencies will bring pressure to bear on Congress by mobilizing the public interest groups that have stakes in these programs. For example, the Children's Defense Fund, a group whose membership consists primarily of social workers, is often mobilized by HHS to campaign against reductions in social spending. The lobby reform bill passed by Congress in December 1995 contained restrictions on lobbying by not-for-profit groups, called 501(c)4 organizations for the portion of the tax code that defines their privileges and obligations. Some of these groups—notably the AARP—vowed to continue their lobbying activities by forming special affiliates that would not be barred from lobbying under the new law.

Finally, congressional Republicans sought to enact tort reform legislation. Tort reform had two purposes: protecting business interests and fighting against liberal public interest groups. A number of liberal groups use litigation as a political weapon. Also, as noted earlier, litigation had become a significant source of funding for some advocacy groups. Litigation became especially important for liberal public interest groups after the Reagan administration's fiscal policy had limited the availability of funds for new federal social programs. The opening salvo in the GOP tort reform effort was the bill passed by Congress in December 1995, vetoed by President Clinton, and subsequently enacted over the president's veto. This bill placed limits on the ability of shareholders to sue corporate executives whose predictions of increased stock prices failed to materialize.

As we shall see in Chapter 5, Phase 2 of the great Republican offensive culminated in a bruising battle between Congress and President Clinton in which most of the GOP's efforts were defeated. The major, albeit somewhat tentative, Republican success came in the area of welfare reform in which Clinton was forced to agree to a bill replacing AFDC with state-run programs. Despite this success, the GOP's legislative momentum was blunted. Even after Republicans retained control of Congress in the 1996 national elections, their fragmented leadership seemed to lack ideas and to be reluctant to engage the Democrats in new legislative battles. Republicans instead contented themselves with launching ferocious attacks against the White House in the form of legislative investigations and inquiries by special prosecutors. While the Republicans had been unable to implement their own agenda, they were not about to allow President Clinton to promote any alternative plan of governance.

5

Institutional Combat

As the Democratic and Republican parties have developed bastions in different institutions and sectors of American government, the character of American politics has been transformed. Intense institutional struggles have increasingly come to supplant electoral competition as the central focus of politics in the United States. Conflicts over the budget and trade deficits, foreign and defense policy, judicial power and social policy that have raged during the Reagan, Bush, and Clinton years can only be understood in light of these struggles.

Deficits and Institutional Combat

The budget and tax cuts enacted during the Reagan presidency, as we have seen, were crucial to the Republican party's effort to expand its own influence and weaken political forces and governmental institutions controlled by its opponents. Spending cuts diminished the flow of resources to groups and forces with close ties to the Democrats. Tax cuts generated enormous budget and trade deficits. The economic dislocations caused by these deficits weakened two other institutions linked to the Democrats: labor unions in import-sensitive industries and municipal governments in the nation's industrial belt.

Equally important, the Reagan tax cuts served to restrict the distributive and extractive capacities of Congress. The enormous budget deficits resulting from the 1981 tax cuts limited Congress's ability to enact new spending programs because such programs would further exacerbate the deficit problem. The 1986 Tax Reform Act at least temporarily reduced the extractive capacities of Congress, by eliminating many of the exemptions, deductions, and preferences that in prior decades had made high nominal tax rates politically acceptable.

The Republicans' attack on Congress and other institutions affiliated with the Democrats was initially successful. Congress was unable to enact a single major new domestic spending program during the first six years of Reagan's presidency. After the Democrats had regained control of the Senate in 1987, some new legislation was enacted, but Congress was able to establish only programs that imposed no additional burdens on the U.S. Treasury. For example, the costs of the 1988 statute requiring employers to provide prior notification of plant closings fell upon private business firms rather than the federal government. And the catastrophic health care legislation enacted in 1988 was financed by premium increases and surcharges borne by Medicare recipients, rather than by new budgetary outlays.

Deadlock between Congress and the president over methods of coping with the deficit reduced Congress's ability to play a leading role in macroeconomic management.[1] The deadlock prevented fiscal policy—over which Congress exercises ultimate authority—from being adjusted in light of changing economic conditions and greatly increased the significance of monetary and exchange rate policies. These policies are controlled by agencies that are directly or indirectly subject to administration influence: the Federal Reserve and the Treasury Department. With White House support, the Federal Reserve squeezed inflation from the economy by raising real interest rates. High real interest rates also helped attract the huge foreign purchases of U.S. government securities that are necessary to fund the budget deficit.

During the mid-1980s congressional Democrats mounted a two-pronged assault on this Republican fiscal system by attacking the budget and trade deficits. Congressional Democrats and Republicans unhappy with the budget deficit united in December 1985 to secure the enactment of the Gramm-Rudman-Hollings deficit reduction act. The act set deficit targets for balancing the budget over a period of five years and mandated across-the-board cuts in defense and domestic programs if the targets were not met. Calculating that the president would not willingly reduce military spending, the Democrats saw Gramm-Rudman-Hollings as a way to compel Reagan to accept tax increases. Republicans who were concerned with the adverse impact of the deficit on key sectors of the economy (traditionalists, as we have named them) were prepared to accept either tax increases or spending cuts to reduce the budget deficit. Some Republicans, including Senator Phil Gramm, supported the bill as a way to compel Congress to accept further domestic spending cuts and prevent their political opponents from capitalizing on the deficit issue.

The second weapon the Democrats deployed against the Republican fiscal system was protectionism. By blocking the flow of foreign imports into the United States, the Democrats hoped to protect the jobs of workers in heavily unionized manufacturing industries.[2] Protectionism would also reduce foreign purchases of U.S. Treasury securities and limit the administration's ability to rely on this means of funding the budget deficit.

The administration responded to this threat by joining the nation's major trading partners (Japan, Germany, Great Britain, and France, the other members of the so-called Group of Five) in the Plaza agreement of September 1985. In an effort to stimulate American exports, the Group of Five undertook to drive down the value of the American dollar. Over the next two years the dollar fell by nearly one-half against both the Japanese yen and the German mark, but the United States continued to run an enormous trade deficit. Moreover, the declining dollar threatened to revive domestic inflation, and America's foreign creditors were appalled to see the value of their holdings in dollar-denominated securities shrink.[3]

As the value of the dollar continued to fall, foreign private investors became reluctant to purchase additional U.S. Treasury notes and bonds; their reluctance threatened the administration's ability to fund the American budget deficit. Therefore, in the Louvre Accords of 1987, the United States and the other leading industrial nations agreed to stabilize the value of the dollar. Japan and Germany agreed to reduce their interest rates and pursue expansionary fiscal policies. The United States promised to raise its interest rates and reduce its budget deficits, thus strengthening the dollar. The three nations hoped that these coordinated policies would improve the U.S. trade deficit by increasing the market for American goods in Germany and Japan, while reducing German and Japanese exports to the United States.[4]

Following the Louvre Accords, the United States did increase its interest rates. However, disagreements emerged over the extent to which the major participants had fulfilled their other commitments. The Germans and Japanese asserted that the Americans had not sufficiently reduced the U.S. budget deficit, whereas the Americans claimed that the other two, especially Germany, had not sufficiently stimulated their domestic economies.

In the fall of 1987 rising interest rates and the U.S. trade deficit's failure to improve weakened the American stock market. Investor confidence was also shaken by the continuing conflict between the United States and its trading partners over implementation of the Louvre Accords. The conflict came to a head in mid-October, when Treasury Secretary James Baker threatened to allow the dollar to resume its fall unless Germany cut its interest rates. Investors feared that a further decline in the value of the dollar would prompt foreigners to abandon the American stock and bond markets. These fears sparked the stock market collapse of October 19, 1987.

In the wake of the crash, both the administration and Congress came under increased pressure to reduce the budget deficit. However, the White House remained firmly opposed to significant tax increases or cuts in military spending, and congressional Democrats opposed any substantial cuts in domestic spending. Negotiations between the White House and Congress following the crash thus produced little more than token deficit reductions.

As discussed above, the Bush administration engaged in a protracted struggle with Congress over deficit reduction in 1990. Congressional Democrats insisted that the administration agree to new revenue programs, while President Bush insisted that he would accept no new taxes. Bush eventually surrendered—at the cost of his presidency—and a budget that included tax increases was enacted in 1991. This budget also contained a formula for reduction of the deficit over a period of several years. Under the terms of one element of the budget formula, no new spending programs could be enacted without equal cuts in existing spending programs or the enactment of new taxes to cover any cost increases. The administration saw this provision as a mechanism that would block Democratic efforts to create new social programs while Democrats hoped that the overall package of revenue enhancements would gradually reduce the deficit and pave the way for new domestic spending.

Despite the deficit, congressional Democrats did find one way to create new social programs. This was through the creation of new rights, such as the rights of the disabled under the Americans with Disabilities Act (ADA) and the rights of new parents under family leave legislation. These new rights provided defined constituency groups with a package of benefits whose costs were borne by business rather than by the deficit-crippled federal treasury. The cost, for example, of making a workplace suitable for handicapped employees fell upon the employer rather than on the public. Moreover, by defining the benefits awarded to the disabled as rights rather than mere benefits, Congress opened the way for the courts to interpret and expand these new programs without any need for further action on its part. In recent years the courts have shown a willingness to interpret rights in an expansive way, and Congress hoped that in the years to come they would find that additional rights were implied by the initial rights and so expand ADA and the other programs. A number of advocacy groups prepared for campaigns of litigation designed to begin this process of rights expansion.

After his election in 1992 Bill Clinton sought to circumvent the deficit by introducing a new package of social programs under the rubric of "investment." Clinton claimed that spending on education, crime prevention, health care, and community services should be understood as a form of investment in the nation's future rather than merely a form of current expenditure. At the same time he introduced a new tax program, the BTU or energy tax, to alleviate some of the costs of these new programs in accordance with the terms of the 1991 budget compromise. His effort was defeated by Congress, and as noted above, the deficit continued to restrict the possibility for new Democratic programs until 1998, when as a result of three years of sustained economic growth, increased tax revenues all but eliminated the federal deficit.

THE NATIONAL SECURITY APPARATUS AND INSTITUTIONAL COMBAT

Just as they sought to make political use of fiscal policy, the Republicans in recent decades used the military and national security apparatus as a political weapon.

After World War II there had been a bipartisan consensus in the United States on questions of foreign and military policy.[5]

Democrats and Republicans agreed on the need to maintain powerful military forces and a capacity for covert intelligence operations. The leaders of both parties were prepared to deploy these forces to contain the Soviet Union and its allies and to fight left-wing insurgent movements. The Vietnam War destroyed this consensus. Antiwar forces gained influence within the Democratic party and were able to impose limits on both military expenditures and American intervention in Third World conflicts. Reagan Republicans regarded Democratic "neoisolationism" as a danger to the nation and as an opportunity for their party's political gain.

The Reagan defense buildup of the 1980s sought to attach social forces with a stake in defense programs to the GOP and created a governing apparatus that supplanted institutions of the domestic state linked to the Democrats. The Reagan administration adopted policies of military Keynesianism to stimulate the economy, used military procurement as a form of industrial policy, and maintained funding for Veterans Administration social programs while attempting to slash drastically spending on welfare programs administered by domestic agencies. Reagan and Bush also sought to reassert their prerogative to deploy American military force abroad, to conduct covert intelligence operations, and to support guerrilla movements fighting Soviet-backed regimes. Thus, without seeking the prior approval of Congress, the Reagan administration sent troops to invade Grenada and aircraft to bomb Libya. American ground troops were sent to intervene in Lebanon in 1982, and American naval forces were sent into action in the Persian Gulf in 1988. Large quantities of American arms were supplied to pro-Western forces in Angola and Afghanistan. The Reagan administration rebuilt the CIA's capacity to engage in covert operations by greatly expanding its budget and personnel and by attempting to circumvent congressional scrutiny of intelligence operations, particularly in Central America, where the White House hoped to undermine the Sandinista regime in Nicaragua.

Gradually this use of military forces by the White House established precedents for still more substantial uses of these forces.

In 1989 the Bush administration launched a large-scale invasion of Panama, culminating in the arrest of Panamanian President Manuel Noriega. In 1990 President Bush assembled a huge military force to attack Iraq. Bush, to be sure, obtained congressional authorization for the use of force against Iraq, but he was prepared to proceed even without such approval. In 1992 Bush sent American forces into Somalia while in 1993 President Clinton sent troops to Haiti. Later Clinton sent a large peacekeeping force to Bosnia. In 1998 President Clinton assembled air and sea power to attack Iraq. By this time the principle that presidents have the authority to use American military forces was no longer debated though of course questions about the wisdom of using force were always raised. Thus, Reagan and Bush effectively eroded the constraints on using military forces established in the wake of the Vietnam War.

The Reagan and Bush administrations also made efforts to develop alliances with foreign governments that could help them to achieve political goals that would be unattainable through America's own governmental institutions. The most important of these alliances was a tacit one with the government of Japan. Despite protectionist pressures, the White House kept America's borders open to a flood of Japanese goods. In turn the Japanese government helped fund the American budget deficit by purchasing U.S. Treasury securities through its central bank and encouraged private Japanese financial institutions to do the same. This alliance with Japan permitted both the Reagan and Bush administrations to maintain high levels of military spending without raising taxes.

The White House also entered into joint ventures with the leaders of Israel and Saudi Arabia. The Reagan administration and the Israelis cooperated in channeling arms to Iran. The administration also sold advanced weapons to Saudi Arabia, and the Saudi royal family helped finance the Nicaraguan contra forces. In both instances arrangements with a foreign government were used by the White House to circumvent congressional opposition.

A number of these Republican ventures were successful. President Reagan oversaw the largest peacetime military buildup in the nation's history. Military spending provided major segments of industry and regions of the country with a continuing stake in the success of the Republicans and helped fuel the longest period of economic expansion in the postwar period. Reagan also demonstrated that it was possible, despite the trauma of Vietnam, for a politician to increase his popularity at home by using American forces abroad.

Congressional Democrats sought to block the Republicans' use of the national security apparatus as a political weapon. Liberal Democrats resisted the president's military buildup, arguing that Reaganite military policies, especially the Strategic Defense Initiative ("Star Wars"), would provoke an arms race with the Soviets and serve more to diminish than to enhance American security. Democrats asserted that the nation's security would be better served by arms control agreements, and they demanded that the administration pursue serious negotiations with the Soviet Union to achieve reductions in nuclear and conventional forces. To this end Democrats gave their support to what became the largest peace movement since the end of the Vietnam War and to its key proposal, the nuclear freeze.[6] Though the freeze proposal ultimately failed, arms control was a central issue for the Democrats throughout the Reagan administration. Arms control also promised to reduce the Republicans' ability to derive political benefits from military spending and to make more money available for domestic programs.

Not long after the defeat of the nuclear freeze proposal, congressional Democrats found a new way to attack the Republican military buildup. They charged that waste and fraud were rampant in the military procurement process and suggested that much of the money being appropriated for defense was actually lining the pockets of unscrupulous defense contractors.[7] In televised testimony, witnesses displayed toilet seats, coffeepots, and hammers for which defense contractors had billed the American taxpayer hundreds or even thousands of dollars.[8] This attack was equivalent to the conservatives' crusades against welfare fraud, an effort to discredit a major spending program by focusing on the abuses that inevitably accompany it. The campaign against waste and fraud in military procurement helped undermine support for the Reagan buildup and, with the pressure of the growing federal budget deficit, permitted Congress to hold defense spending increases to the rate of inflation after Reagan's first term. The Democrats continued their attack on military spending during the Bush presidency, forcing cutbacks in costly weapons systems, such as the B-2 stealth bomber.

In addition to attacking the administration's military buildup, liberal Democrats sought to turn veterans' programs to their own political advantage. Liberals created organizations of Vietnam veterans that were separate from the leading veterans' groups, the American Legion and the Veterans of Foreign Wars. Traditional veterans' groups served the conservative cause by extolling the American military and supporting a strong defense; the new Vietnam veterans' group portrayed soldiers who served in Southeast Asia as victims of American military policy. Rather than glorify the American military establishment, they emphasized the suffering the military imposed even on its own soldiers—for example, by exposing them to the toxic herbicide Agent Orange. These liberal veterans' groups sought to gain access to the resources of the Department of Veterans Affairs, for example, by demanding that it fund programs for the treatment of posttraumatic stress disorder, a condition they asserted was common among Vietnam veterans.[9]

Congressional Democrats worked to block Reagan's efforts to deploy military forces abroad and to further his policy goals through U.S. alliances with foreign governments. Reagan's opponents tried to compel him to end U.S. military involvement in Lebanon and criticized him for failing to use the procedures outlined in the War Powers Act to secure congressional approval for the deployment of American forces elsewhere.[10] Moreover, congressional Democrats attacked the administration's alliances with foreign dictators. For example, Congress played a key role in the sequence of events that led to the ouster of Philippine dictator Ferdinand Marcos, an ally of successive American administrations. As noted above, the administration's opponents also used protectionism to attack the alliance with Japan upon which the Republican fiscal regime depended.

Finally, congressional Democrats attacked the administration's Nicaragua policy by compelling the CIA to stop mining harbors, by insisting that the agency withdraw a training manual that advocated the assassination of Sandinista cadres, and by publicizing charges that the contras were engaged in drug smuggling and routinely violated human rights. The Democrats ultimately were able to restrict Reagan's aid to the contras by enacting a series of amendments—the Boland amendments—to foreign military assistance bills.

The Iran-Contra Affair

In the face of congressional Democratic opposition to administration policy in Nicaragua, conservative forces within the Reagan administration built an alternative intelligence apparatus attached to the National Security Council. This apparatus enabled them to conduct covert operations (such as aid to the contras) that Congress had refused to approve, as well as activities (such as the sale of weapons to Iran) that Congress would certainly not countenance.

The network was managed by CIA Director William Casey, Marine Colonel Oliver North, and retired Air Force General Richard Secord. When the network was discovered, critics in Congress called it a "state within the state." The characterization is not inappropriate; that covert system had some of the administrative, extractive, and coercive capacities of a governmental intelligence agency. The network was able to conduct covert operations because it was staffed by retired military officers and CIA operatives and had ties to foreign intelligence officials and arms merchants. Lacking access to tax revenues, the network was financed by gifts from foreign governments, contributions from wealthy American conservatives, and the profits from weapons sales to Iran. Depending on how one chooses to characterize its relationship with the anti-Sandinista forces—to which it provided political and military guidance as well as financial support—the network might be said to have had coercive capacities as well.[11]

The existence of the covert network was revealed at the end of 1986 in what came to be called the Iran-contra affair. The eruption of the Iran-contra scandal did more than destroy this intelligence network. It disrupted and embarrassed the entire Reagan administration and strengthened institutions that compete with the presidency. The difficulties the administration experienced cannot simply be attributed to its committing a major blunder in selling arms to Iran in exchange for the release of American hostages and diverting some of the proceeds from those sales to the contras. Scandals such as the Iran-contra affair must be understood as political events. Politically damaging revelations are a *consequence* of investigators' efforts to uncover facts that will embarrass an administration politically as much as they are a *source* of that administration's difficulties. After all, prior to November 1986 there were press reports that Israel was shipping arms to Iran and that Oliver North was helping the contras secure weapons, but neither the media nor Congress tried to discover the source of these arms. To account for the challenge that the Iran-contra affair posed to the Reagan presidency, one must look to changes within political constituencies and to institutional factors.

As for changes within political constituencies, two developments weakened the coalition Reagan had constructed and energized the institutions through which his opponents operated. First, the Democrats regained control of the U.S. Senate in the midterm elections of 1986. (The great benefits of incumbency in House elections had helped the Democrats retain control of that chamber despite the GOP landslides in the 1980 and 1984 presidential elections.) The Democrats' success in 1986 emboldened the president's opponents in Congress. Their success also emboldened the press, which until then had treated the Reagan administration gingerly for fear of alienating its middle-class audience.

The second development that contributed to the administration's rapid loss of support as the Iran-contra affair unfolded was the emergence of a rift between the White House and elements of the nation's foreign policy establishment. Many members of that establishment were upset by the White House's behavior during and after the October 1986 Reykjavik summit—actions that had strained the Atlantic alliance. Foreign policy elites were appalled by revelations of the extent to which the White House had conducted sensitive operations in the Mideast and Central America through the Casey-North-Secord network. They denounced the "cowboys" in the White House for constructing this covert network, supported the State Department's virtual declaration of independence after the Iran-contra scandal erupted, and joined in the attack on the Reagan administration.[12]

The administration was also weakened by the very way in which the Iranian weapons deal was conducted. The administration used a covert network of retired military officers and arms merchants to deal with Iran because its policy was opposed by the State and Defense departments and would certainly have provoked a hostile reaction in Congress. The expedient of using this network was ultimately self-defeating, however, because after the weapons deal was revealed and the president came under attack, that network was not powerful enough to sustain him. Reagan could not rely on it to maintain his Iranian initiative (which he continued to insist was a good idea), nor was that network linked to powerful social forces to which he could turn for political support.

The administration's opponents, by contrast, were able to use the formidable iron triangle of institutions—Congress, the national news media, and the federal judiciary—that had triumphed over the White House in the Watergate affair. The extent to which this nexus became institutionalized is striking: After the diversion of funds to the contras was revealed, it was universally assumed that Congress should conduct televised hearings and the judiciary should appoint an independent counsel to investigate and prosecute the officials involved in the episode. In contrast with

President Nixon, Ronald Reagan recognized that it would be fruitless to assert claims of executive privilege, and he turned over all documents requested by the congressional investigators, including his personal diaries.

Nevertheless, in the Iran-contra investigation Congress did not score as complete a victory over the White House as it had in the Watergate affair. Following the precedent of Watergate, congressional Democrats searched for evidence of direct presidential involvement in criminal activity—a "smoking gun." They thus focused the hearings on the illegal diversion of funds to the contras more than on the sale of weapons to Iran. Their tactic, however, ultimately blunted the impact of the entire congressional investigation.

In his televised testimony Colonel North skillfully portrayed the contras as freedom fighters and generated far more public sympathy for his actions than would have been possible if he had been compelled to defend the sale of weapons to Ayatollah Khomeini's government. The outpouring of public support for North intimidated the Democrats and encouraged Republicans on the committee to depict the entire investigation as an exercise in partisan politics.[13] When North's superior, former National Security Adviser John Poindexter, asserted that he had neither informed the president of nor secured presidential approval for the fund diversion, the force of the congressional investigation was dissipated.

The blunting of the congressional investigation reduced the effectiveness of the probe conducted by independent counsel Lawrence Walsh. In the Watergate case it was Congress that uncovered the key sources of evidence—the White House tapes—and stood ready to impeach President Nixon if he failed to turn these over to Special Prosecutor Archibald Cox. In the Iran-contra case, Congress provided no such help to the independent counsel, and the administration was able to refuse to release many classified documents for use at North's trial.

The Reagan administration was not destroyed by Congress in the Iran-contra imbroglio as the Nixon administration had been in the Watergate affair. Nevertheless, it was weakened. Reagan was compelled to appoint a national security adviser, a director of central intelligence, and a White House chief of staff acceptable to the opposition in Congress. He was also compelled to appoint a presidential panel, the Tower Commission, to look into White House management of foreign affairs and to endure a good deal of ridicule when the commission issued a final report describing his lackadaisical "management style."

In the wake of the Iran-contra affair, Reagan also was unable to advance his conservative agenda any further. Indeed, he found it possible to take major initiatives—notably in arms control—only when these coincided with the agenda of his liberal opponents. The Reagan administration's negotiations with the Soviets did lead to the signing of a significant arms control agreement, the 1988 treaty banning intermediate-range nuclear missiles in Europe. Ironically, this foreign policy success restored Reagan's personal popularity and contributed to Bush's Republican victory in the 1988 presidential election.[14] Though the Republicans were able to overcome the potential electoral damage of the Iran-contra affair, it did end their use of the National Security Council to circumvent congressional influence over foreign policy.

THE COURTS AND INSTITUTIONAL COMBAT

The federal judiciary has become another major focus of institutional conflict in contemporary American politics. During the past two decades congressional Democrats and the White House have been locked in a struggle over both the scope of judicial power and who will control the courts. Moreover, the judiciary is not only an object of institutional struggles but also a major participant in them.

An alliance between the federal courts and liberal political forces emerged during the postwar decades.[15] The judiciary took up causes of concern to liberals, most important, the defense of civil rights and civil liberties. Liberals, for their part, supported the federal judiciary's efforts to expand its jurisdiction, and they defended it when it came under attack by conservatives. This helped the courts substantially expand their role and power.

Since the 1960s the Supreme Court has relaxed the rules governing justiciability—the conditions under which courts will hear a case—to increase greatly the range of issues with which the federal judiciary can deal. For example, the Court has liberalized the doctrine of standing to permit taxpayers' suits in which First Amendment issues are involved. It has amended the Federal Rules of Civil Procedure to facilitate class action suits. Claims that might have been rejected as *de minimis* if asserted individually can now be aggregated against a common defendant. In recent years Republicans have been able to prevent liberal forces from using class actions in certain limited types of cases. For example, in 1996 Congress prohibited the courts from hearing class actions brought by advocates for immigrants against the Immigration and Naturalization Service (INS) and by Legal Services lawyers on behalf of indigents. In general, however, class litigation remains a powerful political tool.

The Supreme Court has also effectively rescinded the abstention doctrine, which called for federal judges to decline to hear cases that rested on questions of state law not yet resolved by the state courts. The Court has relaxed the rules governing determinations of mootness and, for all intents and purposes, has done away with the political questions doctrine, which functioned as a limit on judicial activism. The liberalization of rules governing justiciability has given a wider range of litigants access to the courts, has rendered a broader range of issues subject to judicial settlement, and so has greatly increased the reach of the courts in American life. Subsequently, the creation of new rights, enforceable by the courts, further expanded judicial power. Taken together, these changes help explain the enormous growth over the past three decades in the number of cases handled by the federal judiciary.

The federal courts have also come to exercise new powers by expanding the range of remedies and forms of relief they are prepared to employ. Rather than simply ruling that a government agency has

violated a plaintiff's rights and ordering that agency to devise remedies, the courts now issue detailed decrees, setting forth the manner in which the agency must thereafter conduct its business. Suits
challenging conditions in state prisons, for example, have produced
a host of detailed judicial orders that specify living space, recre-
ational programs, and counseling services that must be provided to
all prisoners and that order states to appropriate the necessary funds.
Increasingly, judges have also made use of special masters, under the
control of the court, to take charge of the day-to-day operations of
such institutional defendants as the Boston school system and the
Alabama state prison system. The federal judiciary thus can now
provide litigants with remedies that historically were available only
through the executive and legislative branches.[16]

In the 1960s and 1970s the most important beneficiaries of
these new judicial powers were liberal forces that made litigation
a major weapon in their arsenal. Civil rights groups, through federal court suits, launched successful assaults on southern school
systems, state and local governments, and legislative districting
schemes; these groups could not possibly have altered such institutions in the electoral arena. Environmental groups used the
courts to block the construction of highways, dams, and other public projects that not only threatened to damage the environment
but also provided money and other resources to their political rivals. Women's groups were able to overturn state laws restricting
abortion as well as statutes discriminating against women in the
labor market.

Congress helped liberal interest groups make use of the federal
courts for these purposes. "Citizen suit" provisions of a number of
regulatory statutes enacted during the 1970s gave public interest
groups the right to bring suits challenging the decisions of executive agencies in environmental cases. Congress also authorized public interest groups to serve as "private attorneys general" and to
finance their activities by collecting legal fees and expenses from
their opponents—generally business firms or government agencies—in such suits.

During the 1960s the Supreme Court supported Congress in its struggles with the White House. It refused to permit the Nixon administration to block publication of the *Pentagon Papers*. It ordered the president to turn over the Watergate tapes to the special prosecutor. During the Reagan administration the Court, in reviewing the constitutionality of the Ethics in Government Act, upheld the designation of special prosecutors as instruments for investigating misconduct in the executive branch.

In the 1970s and 1980s conservatives reacted to the alliance between liberals and the courts by attempting to restrict the power of the federal judiciary. For example, when the Republicans gained control of the Senate in 1981, North Carolina Senator Jesse Helms introduced legislation seeking to strip the Supreme Court of its jurisdiction over a number of matters of concern to the new right. That same year the Reagan administration announced a policy of nonacquiescence that would limit the courts' ability to interfere with the administration's effort to purge some 490,000 recipients from the Social Security disability rolls. Under this policy the Social Security Administration would obey lower federal court orders to reinstate a particular individual who had been dropped from the rolls but would not recognize such an order as precedent in any other case. The administration issued assurances that it would recognize U.S. Supreme Court decisions as precedent, but because it planned to avoid appealing adverse rulings to the Supreme Court, there would be no such precedents.

In these and other instances, liberal Democrats took the lead in defending the power and prerogatives of the courts. The Helms court-stripping legislation was defeated in 1981. In 1984 Congress adopted the Social Security Disability Reform Act, which required the administration to accept lower court rulings as precedent in the federal judicial circuit in which they were made. Under further pressure from congressional hearings, the administration in 1985 was forced to abandon the policy of nonacquiescence entirely.[17]

The expansion of judicial power during the 1960s and 1970s increased the stakes involved in the judicial appointment process.

This in turn led to two decades of harsh struggles over judicial selection. Both Presidents Nixon and Reagan sought to appoint conservative jurists to the federal bench in an effort to curb the liberals' ability to exercise influence through the federal judiciary. During his six years in office Nixon appointed four justices, including Chief Justice Warren Burger and Associate Justice William Rehnquist, to the Supreme Court. Liberal Democrats sought to block Nixon's efforts to create a conservative majority on the High Court and succeeded in defeating the confirmation of two other conservative jurists, Clement Haynsworth and G. Harrold Carswell. The two remaining justices appointed by Nixon, Harry A. Blackmun and Lewis F. Powell, proved to be moderates who were not intent on reversing the Court's direction.

The Reagan administration attempted to ensure that appointees to all levels of the federal bench—district and circuit courts as well as the Supreme Court—were committed conservatives. The administration made a particular effort to appoint conservative legal scholars to federal appeals courts. These scholars included Robert Bork and Ralph K. Winter of Yale; Antonin Scalia, Richard Posner, and Frank Easterbrook of the University of Chicago; Douglas Ginsburg of Harvard; John Noonan of Berkeley; and J. Harvie Wilkinson of the University of Virginia. Through such appointments, the White House hoped to foster an intellectual revolution on the bench and enhance the impact of conservative principles on American jurisprudence.

In the case of the Supreme Court, Reagan appointed Sandra Day O'Connor, a moderate conservative, and Antonin Scalia, whom the president had previously named to the circuit court. After a bitter confirmation battle in the Senate, Reagan also was able to elevate William Rehnquist to chief justice. Reagan's efforts to place archconservative Judge Robert Bork on the High Court, however, encountered fierce resistance. Liberal groups organized fund-raising drives and sponsored television advertising in the largest public campaign of the nation's history to defeat a judicial nominee. The administration's opponents on the Senate Judiciary Committee sought to discredit Bork in nationally televised hearings. Rather than examine the nominee's professional competence and ethics, which previously had been seen as the Senate's proper role, they asked him to defend his writings, questioned his philosophy, and sought to ascertain how he would decide major issues likely to face the Court. In the end they rejected the Bork nomination.

Conservative Judge Douglas Ginsburg, whom Reagan nominated in Bork's place, was compelled to withdraw his name from consideration when reporters revealed that while on the faculty of the Harvard Law School he had been seen smoking marijuana. Reagan then named Judge Anthony Kennedy to fill the Court's vacant position. Prodded by members of the Senate Judiciary Committee, Kennedy was compelled to give assurances at his confirmation hearings that he was not intent on overturning Supreme Court precedents. On the strength of these assurances, Kennedy was unanimously confirmed.

George Bush appointed two more conservatives to the Court. In 1990 he appointed David Souter, a federal appeals judge from New Hampshire, and in 1991 he appointed Clarence Thomas, a prominent black conservative, to replace liberal Justice Thurgood Marshall. Thomas's nomination sparked one of the most bitter struggles in recent American political history. During his lengthy confirmation hearing, Anita Hill, a University of Oklahoma law professor, testified that Thomas had sexually harassed her when she worked for him at the Equal Employment Opportunity Commission and, previously, at the Department of Education. At the end of the controversial hearing, Thomas was confirmed by the Senate by the narrow vote of fifty-two to forty-eight. Reagan and Bush's appointments to the Supreme Court gave it a much more conservative cast than it had at any time since the New Deal.

In a series of five to four decisions in 1989, President Reagan's appointees were able to swing the Court to a more conservative position on civil rights and abortion. In the area of civil rights the case of *Wards Cove v. Atonio* shifted the burden of proof from employers to employees in hiring and promotion discrimination suits. (This decision was subsequently reversed by Congress in the 1991 Civil Rights Act.)[18] In 1993, the Library of Congress made public the papers of the late Justice Thurgood Marshall, long a champion of the civil rights cause. Marshall's papers reveal not only his disappointment at the Court's change of direction but also the key role played by President Reagan's appointees in bringing about this change.[19]

The Rehnquist Court's key abortion decision came in the case of *Webster v. Reproductive Health Services.* Justice Marshall's papers reveal that the Court actually came very close to overturning *Roe.* Rehnquist's early drafts of the decision would have effectively overturned *Roe.* He was able to win the support of only three other justices, Scalia, Kennedy, and White, for this course of action. A fourth justice, Sandra Day O'Connor, wavered for several weeks. Had O'Connor joined Rehnquist, of course the chief justice would have had the five votes needed for a majority. Ultimately O'Connor decided not to support overturning *Roe,* and Rehnquist was forced to write a narrower ruling, which nevertheless opened the way for new state regulation of abortion. Subsequently, the Court upheld state laws requiring parental notification before an abortion could be performed on a woman under the age of eighteen.[20]

In addition to these areas, the Rehnquist Court eased restriction on the use of capital punishment, allowing states to execute mentally retarded murderers and murderers who were as young as sixteen at the time of their crimes.[21]

After 1990 the Court made a number of decisions in the areas of civil rights, abortion, property rights, and criminal procedure that indicated a shift to the political right under the influence of the Reagan and Bush appointees. For example, in the case of *Board of Education of Oklahoma City v. Dowell* the Court restricted the use of judicially mandated busing plans to achieve school integration.[22] In the case of *Rust v. Sullivan* the Court held that employees of federally financed family planning programs could be forbidden to discuss abortion with their clients.[23] In *Arizona v. Fulminante* the Court found that the use of a coerced confession in a trial did not automatically invalidate a conviction.[24] In *Lucas v. South Carolina Coastal Council* the Court gave a sympathetic hearing to a property owner's claim that state restrictions on land development constituted a seizure of property without compensation in violation of the Constitution's Fifth Amendment.[25] In the 1993 case of *Shaw v. Reno* the Court placed limits upon the "benign gerrymandering" of legislative district boundaries that is used to increase the representation of racial minorities.[26]

Efforts by Reagan and Bush to reshape the federal judiciary, however, were not fully successful. Often in American history, judges have surprised and disappointed the presidents who named them to the bench, and the Reagan and Bush appointees were no exception. Justice Souter has been far less conservative than Republicans hoped. Justices O'Connor and Kennedy have disappointed conservatives by opposing limitations on abortion.

In the important 1992 case of *Planned Parenthood of Southeastern Pennsylvania v. Casey* the Court upheld state regulations requiring that women seeking abortions wait twenty-four hours after being provided with the information about the process and also requiring parental consent for minors.[27] Yet it reaffirmed the constitutional right to an abortion established by *Roe v. Wade.* Indeed, in their unusual joint opinion, Justices O'Connor, Kennedy, and Souter expressed irritation at the White House for its ceaseless pressure on the Court to strike down *Roe v. Wade.*[28] These three justices believed that this pressure represented a threat to the institutional integrity of the Supreme Court.

With a combined total of twelve years in office, Republican Presidents Reagan and Bush were also able to exercise a good deal of influence on the composition of the federal district and appellate courts. By the end of Bush's term he and Reagan together had appointed nearly half of all federal judges. Thus, whatever impact Reagan and Bush ultimately have on the Supreme Court, their appointments will continue to influence the temperament and behavior of the district and circuit courts for years to come. After his election in 1992, President Bill Clinton sought to appoint more liberal judges to these courts. He named a number of women and minorities to the district and circuit benches. However, the president moved so slowly to fill vacancies that his impact on the lower federal courts has been less than liberals had hoped.[29] Clinton's efforts of course were hindered by the fact that Republicans have controlled the Senate Judiciary Committee during most of his presidency. This fact forced Clinton to be cautious in his nominations. The White House canceled plans to nominate several liberals after determining that they had no chance of winning Senate confirmation. Still other Clinton nominees, such as liberal Pennsylvania Judge Messiah Jackson, were bottled up in committee by Republicans who feared their ideology and activism.

Bill Clinton's election in 1992 and reelection in 1996 seemed to reduce the possibility of much further rightward movement on the part of the Court. During Clinton's first year in office, Justice Byron White, the conservative bloc's lone Democrat, announced his desire to retire from the bench. After a long search the president nominated a federal appeals court judge, Ruth Bader Ginsburg, a moderate liberal, to succeed White. She had a long record of support for abortion rights and women's rights. However, as a federal appeals court judge she often sided with the government in criminal cases and did not hesitate to vote against affirmative action plans she deemed to be too broad.

During her first term on the Court, Ginsburg was most frequently aligned with Souter and generally strengthened the Court's moderate center,[30] especially cases dealing with the issues of religious exercise and abortion.

In 1994 President Clinton had another opportunity to alter the balance of the Court when he named Federal Appeals Court Judge Stephen Breyer to succeed retiring Justice Harry Blackmun. But Breyer was generally viewed as another judicial moderate, unlikely to change the Court's direction.

Since 1994, led by Chief Justice Rehnquist and Justices Scalia and Thomas, who were often joined by Justices O'Connor and Kennedy, the Court continued on a conservative course in most areas, issuing rulings that placed limits on affirmative action, school desegregation, voting rights, the separation of church and state, and the power of the national government. In *Adarand Constructors v. Pena* the Court ruled that federal programs that award preferences to people on the basis of race are presumed to be unconstitutional unless they are "narrowly tailored" to achieve a "compelling national interest." This decision cast doubt on the constitutionality of all federal programs that classify people on the basis of race. In the case of *Missouri v. Jenkins* the Court rescinded a school desegregation plan that it had earlier approved, indicating that it would no longer support ambitious efforts by lower courts to integrate public schools forcibly. The Court has continued to place limits upon efforts to use the Voting Rights Act to increase minority representation. In the case of *Johnson v. DeGrandy* it held that states were not required to create as many black or minority districts as might be theoretically possible. They were required only to ensure that minority representation was "roughly proportional" to the state's minority population. In *Holder v. Hall* the Court ruled that the Voting Rights Act could not be used to challenge the size of a governing body—in this case, a single-member county commission—to accommodate minority representation.[31] In the case of *Miller v. Johnson* the Court struck down yet another redistricting plan that had purposely created minority-dominated election districts in the state of Georgia. In invalidating the Georgia plan, the Court ruled that the use of race as a "predominant factor" in drawing district lines was presumptively unconstitutional. Although the Court left open the possibility that race could be *one* of the factors taken into account in a redistricting plan, its ruling opened the way for challenges to recently created "majority-minority" districts in at least twelve states.[32] Similarly, in *Bush v. Vera* the Court ruled that three Texas congressional districts with black or Hispanic majorities were unconstitutional because state officials put too much emphasis on race in drawing boundaries. "Voters," said the Court, "are more than mere racial statistics." In *Shaw v. Hunt* the Court struck down a North Carolina black majority voting district for similar reasons. Most recently, in the 1997 case of *Abrams v. Johnson,* the Court upheld a new Georgia congressional district map that eliminated two of the state's three majority-black districts.[33]

Another area in which the Supreme Court moved in a conservative direction in recent years involved the First Amendment's establishment clause, which established a "wall of separation" between church and state. In the 1995 case of *Rosenberger v. University of Virginia* the Court seemed to open a new breach in the wall between church and state when it ruled that the university had violated the free speech rights of a Christian student group by refusing to provide student activity funds for the group's magazine, although other student groups had been given funds for their publications. In the 1997 case of *Agostini v. Felton* the Court again breached the wall between church and state, ruling that states could pay public school teachers to offer remedial courses at religious schools.[34]

Several of the Court's recent decisions also unexpectedly reopened the question of the relationship between the federal government and the states. In its five to four decision in *U.S. v. Lopez,* striking down a federal law banning the possession of a gun near a school, the Court signaled that it would no longer interpret Congress's authority to regulate commerce as broadly as it had for the previous sixty years. Another significant decision involving the relationship between the federal government and state governments was the 1997 case *Printz v. United States* (joined with *Mack v. United States*), in which the Court struck down a key provision of the Brady Bill, enacted by Congress in 1993 to regulate gun sales. Under the terms of the act, state and local law enforcement officers were required to conduct background checks on prospective gun purchasers. The Court held that the federal government cannot require states to administer or enforce federal regulatory programs. Since the states bear administrative responsibility for a variety of other federal programs, this decision could have far-reaching consequences. Finally, in another major ruling from the 1996–1997 term, in *City of Boerne v. Flores,* the Court sought to limit the extent of congressional power.[35]

As presented to the Court, the *Flores* case revolved around the constitutionality of the 1993 Religious Freedom Restoration Act. This act had been adopted by Congress in an effort to nullify the Supreme Court's decision in the 1990 case of *Employment Division v. Smith.*[36] In the *Smith* case the Court had ruled that the First Amendment guarantee of free exercise of religion did not give members of a Native American group the right to violate Oregon's narcotics laws by using illegal drugs in their religious rituals. The Court said there was no religious exemption from laws that applied generally to everyone and were not used to discriminate against religion. Pressured by a broad coalition of religious groups, Congress declared in the Religious Freedom Restoration Act that state governments could not restrict or burden religious observance without demonstrating a "compelling need" to do so. Even if the need was compelling, the state must use the "least restrictive means available" to achieve its purposes. This act was hailed by religious organizations, and after its passage was used to prevent states from prohibiting prison inmates from wearing religious jewelry, to keep church-run soup kitchens open in neighborhoods that did not want them, to protect the Amish from being required to put orange warning signs on their buggies, and to undermine a host of other state regulations that affected religious practice.

In the *Flores* case a church had sought to invoke the Religious Freedom Restoration Act to challenge the city's refusal to allow it to enlarge its building in a neighborhood zoned for historic preservation. The city, in response, challenged the constitutionality of the act. In its six to three decision, written by Justice Kennedy, the Supreme Court sided with states' rights over unrestricted religious exercise. It ruled that Congress had gone too far in restricting the power of the states to enact regulations they deemed necessary for the protection of the public health, safety, or welfare. Many observers also saw the *Flores* decision, overturning what amounted to a congressional effort to nullify a Supreme Court decision, as an effort to demonstrate the power of the Court vis-à-vis Congress and the executive branch. As an indication of the complexity of the issues involved in the case, the majority in *Flores* included the Court's three most conservative members, Rehnquist, Thomas, and Scalia, as well as two of its most liberal justices, Ginsburg and Stevens.

Two other important 1997 decisions also dealt with matters of congressional and presidential power. In *Raines v. Byrd* the Court refused to hear a challenge by several members of Congress to the president's new line-item veto power. Since the Court did not directly rule on the constitutionality of the line-item veto power, it remained in place. The Court did deal the presidency a blow, however, when it unanimously ruled in *Clinton v. Jones* that the Constitution does not grant presidents immunity from civil suits stemming from their private unofficial conduct. This decision freed Paula Jones, a former Arkansas state employee, to continue her sexual harassment suit against the president.[37]

In 1998 the Court stripped President Clinton of his newly won line-item veto power. In the case of *Clinton v. New York,* the Court held that the line-item veto violated the constitutionally mandated separation of powers. While affirmative action decisions have disappointed liberals, in the areas of free speech, gay rights, and women's rights the High Court has angered some conservatives. In the Court's most important recent free speech case, *Reno v. American Civil Liberties Union,* the Communications Decency Act, a federal law restricting indecent material on the Internet, was struck down as a violation of free speech.[38] In the 1996 case of *United States v. Virginia* the Court ruled that the Virginia Military Institute's exclusion of women constituted a violation of the constitutional guarantee of equal protection. And in the case of *Romer v. Evans* the Court declared that states may not prohibit local governments from writing ordinances that protect homosexuals from discrimination.[39] In these decisions the Court appeared to be making a distinction between affirmative action—or positive governmental action on behalf of a minority group—and equal protection, meaning equality before the law. Liberals argue that equal protection is not enough to vindicate the rights of minorities that have long suffered from discriminatory treatment. The current Supreme Court majority, however, does not appear to accept this view.

Thus, while the 1992 and 1996 elections had seemed to offer new possibilities for the expansion of judicial liberalism, by 1997 the Court's more conservative justices—Rehnquist, Scalia, and Thomas—appeared to have increased their influence. The political struggles of the 1980s and 1990s amply illustrate the importance of who sits on the Supreme Court. Is abortion a fundamental right or a criminal activity? How much separation must there be between church and state? Does the use of the Voting Rights Act to increase minority representation constitute a violation of the rights of whites? The answers to these and many other questions cannot be found in the words of the Constitution. They must be located instead in the hearts of the judges who interpret that text. Hence judicial appointments will continue to be an arena of intense conflict.

During his first year in office, President George W. Bush did not have an opportunity to make a Supreme Court appointment. Nevertheless, Democrats served notice that judicial nominees would recieve sharp scrutiny. In April 2002, Senate Democrats blocked the nomination of Mississippi district court judge Thomas Pickering to a position on the federal court of appeals. Pickering's opponents charged that the judge had a history of racial bias. In another court-related battle, Senate Democrats refused to move through the nomination of Eugene Scalia, son of Supreme Court Justice Antonin Scalia, for the position of U.S. Labor Department solicitor. Democratic opposition to the younger Scalia was widely understood to represent an attack against the arch-conservative Justice Scalia who had helped put Bush in office. Bush responded by appointing the younger Scalia while Congress was in recess.

SOCIAL POLICY AND INSTITUTIONAL COMBAT

As noted earlier, entrenchment in the agencies of the domestic state has been a key strategy for the Democratic party since the

New Deal. Through expansive social programs, the Democrats were able to construct an institutional base and to forge ties to major constituency groups. In the first year of his presidency Bill Clinton proposed an enormous expansion of the Democrats' domestic realm through the vehicle of health care reform. The president's proposed regime of managed competition could have given the Democrats control over 15 percent of the nation's economy and made virtually every American a beneficiary of Democratic largess. Health care reform had the potential to play an even more important role in promoting the fortunes of the Democratic party than Social Security had played sixty years earlier.

Clinton's health care reform effort alarmed Republicans. Some Republican strategists like William Kristol, who had served as chief of staff for former Vice President Dan Quayle, worked feverishly to mobilize GOP opposition to Clinton's proposal. Health care reform was ultimately defeated more by the efforts of a coalition of corporate interests than by the Republican party. The seriousness of the threat posed by Clinton's initiative, however, convinced many Republicans that Clinton was an extremely dangerous adversary and prompted the GOP to mount an all-out campaign against him. Adding to the ferocity of the GOP's attack, of course, was the rage of some social conservatives in the Republican camp over Clinton's stands on such issues as abortion and gays in the military.

As noted in Chapter 1, in 1993 and 1994 Republicans levied numerous charges of misconduct on the part of the president and his wife. While they were able to embarrass and harass Clinton, Republicans were unable to do serious harm to the administration during this period. By winning control of both houses of Congress in 1994, however, Republicans took command of Congress's own investigative processes and the machinery needed to secure the appointment of independent counsels to probe the White House. Now headed by Republicans, congressional committees immediately launched investigations of Clinton's conduct during his years as governor of Arkansas. Subsequently, congressional committees probed the president's involvement in what reporters called the Travelgate and Filegate affairs. After the 1996 elections once again left Republicans in command of Congress, congressional committees investigated allegations of illegal fund-raising practices on the part of Clinton and Vice President Al Gore.

At the same time, of course, congressional Republicans secured the appointment of several independent counsels to search for wrongdoing by Clinton and his associates. As noted earlier, the most important of these prosecutors, Kenneth Starr, was able to extend the scope of his investigation from his initial jurisdiction—Whitewater—to include eventually the firing of White House travel office personnel, allegations concerning White House abuse of FBI files, and allegations that the president had an affair with a White House intern and later both perjured himself and suborned perjury on the part of the intern to prevent disclosure of his inappropriate conduct.

Clinton and his allies responded aggressively to every attack, ultimately developing a complex defensive posture that frequently seemed to stymie the president's foes. One element of Clinton's defensive strategy was stonewalling, a strategy of denying everything and withholding information for as long as possible. In a number of instances, for example, the White House claimed to be unable to find subpoenaed records and documents only to have them turn up after media and public attention had turned to other matters.

A second element in Clinton's defensive strategy was the countercharge, in which the White House sought to investigate, embarrass, and discredit the president's various adversaries and accusers. For example, detectives connected to the president's attorneys were sent to seek damaging information about Paula Corbin Jones, the plaintiff in the sexual harassment suit against the president. Subsequently, some of this information was leaked to the press. In a similar vein, a major Washington detective agency was retained by the president's attorneys to investigate the backgrounds of members of Kenneth Starr's staff to ascertain if any aspect of any Starr staffer's record could be used to discredit the special counsel's probe.[40] This effort came on the heels of a determined Clinton media campaign charging that Starr was part of a right-wing conspiracy against the president rather than a disinterested public official. In June 1998 Clinton supporters accused the independent counsel's office of leaking confidential information about the Lewinsky investigation to the media. Starr admitted providing some reporters with "background" data but denied disclosing sensitive material. The president's attorneys demanded investigations by the federal court and the bar association into what they deemed Starr's breach of ethics. Thus the White House sought to turn an ethics investigation against the chief ethics investigator.[41]

A third defensive tactic was the leak and counterleak. This entailed White House leaks of damaging information about Clinton's adversaries accompanied by vehement charges that prosecutors were improperly leaking information harmful to the president. Leak and counterleak are, of course, a standard Washington strategy used by nearly all the president's friends and foes.[42]

A fourth Clinton defensive tactic was the joint defense agreement. This involved arrangements for a coordinated defense strategy between the president's lawyers and attorneys for various White House staff members like the president's secretary, Betty Currie, who had been subpoenaed by the independent counsel for information about the president. Joint defense agreements were designed to diminish the possibility that a staff member would agree to disclose information that might hurt the president.

A fifth strategy involves claims of presidential privilege. The idea of executive privilege as a shield allowing the president to refuse to provide information to Congress and the courts was discredited during the Nixon era. President Clinton, however, has sought to broaden the scope of attorney-client privilege in order to prevent his adversaries from being able to question some of his closest advisers. The administration has also sought to use the claim of privilege to prevent Starr from questioning members of the Secret Service about what they might have seen while guarding the president. In 1998, however, federal district and appellate courts ruled that Secret Service agents could be compelled to testify before the grand jury looking into Clinton's conduct.

A final Clinton strategy is the institutionalization of damage control. In January 1998 the White House established a formal damage control center at the Democratic National Committee (DNC) to coordinate strategies, disseminate information, respond to charges, and generally seek to protect the president from new revelations and accusations.[43] This DNC office is probably the first institutionalized response to the RIP (revelation, investigation, prosecution) weapon that has become so prominent in American politics in recent decades.

Taken together, these tactics probably represent the most sustained, vigorous, and complex effort made by any American politician to thwart a determined RIP attack on the part of his adversaries. Significantly, however, just as Clinton's efforts in the realm of social policy were responsible for sparking the GOP's campaign against him, so the president's social policy positions played a major role in bolstering his defense. The president was able to withstand the forces marshaled against him not only because of his clever political tactics but also because groups and forces that supported his positions in the realm of social policy generally stood by him in the face of the GOP's onslaught.

One such force was the Democratic party. Throughout the various congressional investigations and independent counsel probes, not a single prominent Democratic politician or interest group connected to the Democratic party spoke against the president, until Clinton's admissions of sexual misconduct in August 1998 forced several Democrats to distance themselves from him. Though some Capitol Hill Democrats had personal reservations about him, most supported his domestic agenda and believed that the destruction of his administration would open the gates for a renewed Republican effort to undermine the domestic social institutions fashioned by the Democratic party over the past sixty-five years. It should be recalled that Republican defections badly damaged the Nixon administration in the Watergate affair and the Reagan ad-

ministration during the Iran-contra probe. Clinton was not compelled to contend with such a problem.

A second important group that was reluctant to destroy Clinton was the national press. Obviously newspaper and television accounts of the sometimes sensational charges against Clinton in the
Monica Lewinsky case were the source of many of the president's
problems. Many journalists, however, also wrote stories questioning
the propriety of the "media frenzy" and "rush to judgment" surrounding the scandal. Most, albeit not all, reporters are liberal and
Democratic in their political orientation, and most support the president's domestic agenda. As was not true in Nixon's Watergate imbroglio, when push came to shove, few reporters actually wanted to
see Clinton destroyed. For example, speaking on *The McLaughlin
Group,* veteran Washington correspondent Eleanor Clift lamented
that the Starr investigation of Clinton posed a threat to abortion
rights.[44]

A third important group committed to Clinton's social policies that stood by the president during his travail was the
women's movement. The president stood accused of sexual harassment, of having an affair with a young intern, and of various
marital infidelities. While women's groups had vehemently attacked other politicians accused of sexual improprieties, not a
single spokesperson for any major women's group spoke against
President Clinton or in support of any of the women mentioned
in connection with him. The obvious reason is that Clinton was
a staunch proponent of abortion rights, of federal funding for
child care, and of the appointment of women to high political offices. As a result, women's groups were prepared to ignore
allegations made against Clinton much as they had always disre-
garded similar allegations made about Massachusetts Senator Ted
Kennedy, another ally of women's causes. The stance taken by
women's groups was extremely significant for Clinton. In political debate, just as African Americans are the most important ar-
biters of what is or is not racist, women's groups are important
judges of what does or does not constitute an affront to women.

Had women's groups attacked the president, as they had attacked Supreme Court nominee Clarence Thomas or Oregon Senator Bob Packwood, they might have done serious damage to his standing in the polls and relationship with Congress. The silence of women's groups served the president's interests and paved the way for Hillary Rodham Clinton's furious defense of her husband before national television cameras. The silence of the women's movement left the president's staunchest defender as the only avowed feminist to speak out on the Lewinsky affair. Thus, ironically, a president accused of sexual harassment and other offenses against women was, in an important political sense, able to secure the blessing of the feminist movement.

Despite Clinton's vigorous defense against revelations and investigations, the Republican attack did damage the administration and undermine White House efforts to promote the president's domestic agenda. White House staffers seemed more concerned with subpoenas and legal expenses than with the business of government. At the same time several domestic cabinet departments had to contend with special counsels investigating the activities of their top executives. Whether or not the GOP was ultimately able to destroy Clinton through a tactic of RIP, a sustained political attack left the administration unable to focus on policy issues. After retaining control of Congress in 1996, Republicans promised to use their investigative powers to harass Clinton for the remainder of his presidency. "Clinton will be debilitated," predicted the former Bush White House counsel C. Boyden Gray.[45] To a very substantial extent, Gray was right.

Republicans on the Defensive

Clinton's efforts to expand the Democratic party's domain in the realm of domestic social policy sparked enormous struggles with the GOP. Republican efforts to undermine Democratic social programs also touched off major political conflicts. As discussed in Chapter 4, on the heels of their capture of both houses of Congress in 1994, Republicans introduced welfare reform, lobby reform, tort reform, and regulatory reform legislation designed to attack Democratic domestic programs and agencies.

These GOP efforts engendered enormous struggles with congressional Democrats and between congressional leaders and the Clinton White House. Though Republicans scored some successes, notably in the area of welfare reform, the end result was defeat for the GOP. Democrats fiercely resisted every Republican effort to undermine the groups, procedures, and institutions through which the Democratic party had exercised power for decades. GOP regulatory reform proposals were defeated by a Democratic Senate filibuster. Republican tort reform proposals were vetoed by President Clinton. Further lobby reforms were blocked after a bitter battle in which ethics complaints were filed against the major House sponsor of lobby reform, Representative David McIntosh (R.-Ind.). Nan Aron, head of the Alliance for Justice, charged that McIntosh had falsely accused her group of using taxpayer dollars to subsidize lobbying efforts. The complaint against McIntosh was filed by Representative Louise Slaughter (D.-N.Y.) and was endorsed by Aron and Ralph Nader. The Alliance for Justice lobbies on behalf of liberal causes and played an important role in campaigning against the judicial nominees of Presidents Reagan and Bush. Several of the alliance's constituent groups receive federal funds, though Aron denies that any of this money is used for lobbying.[46]

The GOP's lone, and very tentative, success came in the realm of welfare reform. The bill passed by Congress and signed into law by President Clinton in August 1996 ended the federal entitlement to welfare and replaced AFDC, the nation's basic cash welfare program, with state-run programs supported by federal grants from a $16.4 billion annual fund. States were given wide discretion in determining welfare eligibility but were prohibited from using block grant funds for adults who had received welfare for more than five years.[47]

President Clinton signed the welfare reform bill, over the vehement objections of liberal Democrats, in order to avoid handing the GOP a potent campaign issue for the 1996 presidential election. His action led three liberal welfare officials, including long-time Clinton friend Acting Assistant Secretary of Health and Human Services Peter Edelman to resign in protest.[48] Clinton, however, signaled to liberals that if reelected, he would attempt to undo the GOP's apparent success. At the Democratic National Convention First Lady Hillary Rodham Clinton said, "Much of my thinking about welfare reform rests on my belief that my husband will do as he said he will do, which is to fix those parts of the bill that are unfair, that the Republicans put in." Subsequently, the administration worked to block a number of welfare changes instituted by the state of Wisconsin. This seemed to be an effort to undermine the concept of increased state discretion embodied in the new law.[49] At the same time the administration encouraged liberal Democratic advocacy groups to launch an all-out attack in the courts against the new welfare law.[50]

The GOP's most crushing defeat, as we saw in Chapter 5, came in the climactic 1995–1996 battle over the federal budget. While Republicans reeled under media criticism for shutting down the government, the White House launched a series of television commercials accusing the GOP of seeking to cut Medicare. Republicans unaccountably failed to respond to the Democratic ads, while the Democrats increased their spending to more than one million dollars per week on thirty-second TV ads throughout the fall. "The Republicans have given us great gifts," said White House political director Douglas Sosnik.[51]

POLITICAL CONFLICT AND
INSTITUTIONAL COMBAT

Political conflict in the United States has increasingly come to involve institutional struggle rather than electoral mobilization. As we have seen, fiscal policy, national security policy, the judiciary, and social policy have been both weapons and arenas in this struggle. These are not the only weapons or arenas of contemporary institutional combat. Others have included the federal bureaucracy, the complex of nonprofit organizations and public interest groups that has developed around federal domestic programs, and the national news media.

The Reagan administration, for example, made a determined effort to increase presidential control over cabinet departments and independent government agencies by centralizing authority over the appointment of personnel in the White House and over the issuance of regulations in the OMB. By centralizing control over appointments, the administration sought to ensure that officials would adhere to the administration's priorities rather than those of the agencies for which they worked. By requiring agencies to obtain OMB approval for all regulations they issued, the administration sought to diminish both the influence that congressional oversight committees exercised over administrative agencies and, more generally, the role that the federal bureaucracy plays in American life.[52] The number of pages of proposed new federal regulations published annually in the *Federal Register* did decline during the Reagan era.

These attempts to subject the federal bureaucracy to greater White House control did not go unchallenged.[53] Defenders of existing practices and programs asserted that the administration was trying to stack the bureaucracy with right-wing ideologues and to interfere with the lawful exercise by Congress of its oversight responsibilities. One way that federal employees responded to what they perceived as a threat to their agencies' integrity was to leak derogatory information about Republican appointees to Congress and the press. Investigations of Housing and Urban Development Secretary Samuel Pierce and Economic Development administrator Carlos Campbell, among others, were fueled by such leaks.

The national news media—which conservatives regard as liberal bastions—were also the target of a conservative political offensive in recent years. Libel suits were one weapon in the conservatives' campaign against the media. (The best known of these was General William Westmoreland's suit against CBS in the early 1980s.) These suits were encouraged and often financed by such conservative organizations as the Capitol Legal Foundation, the American Legal Foundation, and Accuracy in Media, Inc. When accused of chilling critical journalistic investigations of public officials, conservatives forthrightly stated that this was precisely their intent. For example, Reed Irvine, head of Accuracy in Media, asserted that Westmoreland's legal bills were "footed by contributions from individuals and foundations who believe that CBS deserves to be chilled for the way it treated the general. . . . What is wrong with chilling any propensity of journalists to defame with reckless disregard of the truth?"[54] For their part, Clinton administration officials see nothing wrong with hiring detectives to seek damaging information about their political opponents.

As the newly elected president, George W. Bush, organized his administration in 2001, Washington prepared for a new round of political struggle. Democrats vowed to resist Bush's tax cut, school voucher, and privatization plans, all of which threatened key Democratic bastions. Republicans sought to strengthen their own institutional base by seeking to expand defense spending. The GOP argued that the nation's level of military preparedness was inadequate. Both sides geared up for what promised to be bruising battle over court appointments.

American politics will continue to center on these and other forms of institutional combat as long as contending forces are unwilling to look to electoral mobilization as the key weapon through which to confront their foes. The continuation of this political pattern has profound implications for the conduct of government in the United States.

6

Bush v. Gore:
The Fracas Over Florida

IN LIGHT OF THE political trends that developed during the final quarter of the twentieth century, it should, perhaps, be no surprise that the first presidential election of the twenty-first century was ultimately decided in the courts rather than at the polls. After the nation's electoral machinery failed to produce a clear-cut winner, the Republican candidate, Governor George W. Bush of Texas, bested his Democratic rival, Vice President Al Gore, in a thirty-six-day-long institutional struggle over the twenty-five electoral votes from the state of Florida that would decide the race. Before it ended in mid-December, when Bush was declared to have won by a margin of a few hundred out of the more than six million votes cast in Florida, this battle embroiled legions of lawyers, many national political notables including two former U.S. secretaries of state, numerous county officials and election canvassing boards, most of Florida's executive institutions, the Florida state legislature, the national news media, many of Florida's courts, the Eleventh Circuit U.S. Court of Appeals, and, eventually, the U.S. Supreme Court.

Had the outcome of the 2000 race been determined solely on the basis of votes cast nationally, Gore and his running mate, Senator Joseph Lieberman of Connecticut, would have been elected president and vice president, perhaps by as many as five hundred thirty thousand of the more than one hundred million votes officially recorded throughout the nation. Bush, however, along with his vice-presidential partner, former defense secretary Dick Cheney, eked out the slimmest of victories in the electoral college, receiving 271 votes—one more than the constitutionally mandated majority. Because of the United States's electoral college system, established by Article II of the Constitution, every presidential election entails some risk that the electoral results will fail to mirror the popular outcome, especially in a close race. The 2000 election was the fifth such instance in U.S. history and, under other circumstances, might have become merely one more occasion for debate over the revision of this constitutional relic.

The matter of the electoral college, however, was eclipsed by the bitter controversy that erupted over the Florida results. The popular vote in Florida was so close and the vote count so fraught with ambiguity as to leave the actual outcome of the presidential balloting in the state open to question. This opened the way for a series of postelection challenges in several Florida counties and for a number of legal confrontations between the two presidential campaigns. During the course of this political battle, both Democrats and Republicans insisted they were committed to discovering and effectuating the popular will. But, while loudly professing their support for democratic principles, both campaigns endeavored to use every available means to invalidate votes that might help the other side.

During the actual 2000 presidential race, Bush and the Republicans had failed to outmobilize their Democratic foes. In the postelection battle, however, the GOP was able to assemble the more powerful constellation of institutional forces and, thereby, to capture the presidency. Over the past several decades, as we have seen, the vitality and centrality of U.S. electoral politics have been steadily eroded. On several occasions, forces defeated at the polls have used nonelectoral forms of political combat to circumvent election outcomes. In 2000 this decay of the nation's electoral institutions became even more manifest as the outcome of a national presidential contest was actually decided outside the electoral arena.

THE CAMPAIGN

During periods of economic prosperity, Americans generally return the party in power to office. The 2000 national elections were held during a period of peace and of greater economic prosperity than the United States has ever known. To further enhance the Democrats' prospects, Democratic partisans continue to outnumber Republican identifiers in the national electorate. Thus, all things considered, it seemed more than likely that Al Gore and Joe Lieberman would lead the Democratic party to victory against an inexperienced and little-known Republican presidential nominee. Indeed, most statistical models of election outcomes predicted an easy Democratic victory, with some forecasting a Gore landslide.[1]

Nevertheless, when the election finally ended, not only had Gore been defeated but Democrats failed to make much headway in House or Senate races either. The Democrats did gain some ground in both chambers but not enough to deprive the GOP of control of either the House or the Senate. Republicans would control the newly elected House by a margin of seven votes. The Senate would now be evenly divided, but with Vice President Dick Cheney casting tie-breaking votes, the GOP would continue to lead the upper chamber. In one note of Democratic triumph, former first lady Hillary Rodham Clinton was elected to the Senate from New York. Yet, against all odds, Republicans appeared to have eked out control of the elected branches of the U.S. government for the first time in almost fifty years. Given an extremely buoyant economy, a nation at peace, and an edge in partisan attachments, how could the Democrats have lost: How could the race even have been close?

The key reason Al Gore and the Democrats were unable to capitalize on a set of ideal conditions was the tenor of Gore's national campaign. Early in the 2000 campaign, Gore made the fateful decision to distance himself from the person and political strategy of his boss, President Bill Clinton. Gore said repeatedly, "I am my own man." In this way Gore sought to distance himself from the scandals of the Clinton administration and to present a picture of moral rectitude and respect for family that would prevent Republicans from linking him to the moral laxity associated with Bill Clinton. Gore made much of the strength of his marriage, and he refused to allow Clinton to participate in the campaign. Gore selected as his running mate Senator Joseph Lieberman, a man known for his strong religious beliefs and one of the first Democrats to have criticized Bill Clinton's conduct in the Monica Lewinsky scandal. Lieberman also had a long record of cooperation with Christian conservatives on such matters as legislation designed to limit religious persecution in third-world countries. Thus, Gore used the Lieberman nomination to distinguish himself from Clinton, the man.

Gore's assertion that he wanted to be his own man, however, had another component. He sought to distance himself not only from Clinton's morals but also from his politics. In his election campaigns, Clinton had adopted centrist positions on most domestic and foreign policy issues. In 1992 he presented himself as a "new Democrat," whose philosophy differed sharply from the liberalism of George McGovern and Walter Mondale that had carried the party to defeat. Clinton adopted moderate positions on economic policy and on civil rights. He talked about middle-class concerns like crime, welfare reform, and fiscal restraint. Clinton's moderation helped bring victory in 1992 and in 1996. In the 1996 race, Clinton pursued a strategy of "triangulation," in the words of his adviser, Dick Morris, which involved positioning himself midway between the liberalism of congressional Democrats and the conservatism of congressional Republicans. Holding the center was the key to victory in national elections, according to Morris, and the strategy succeeded.

A major way in which Gore chose to be his own man was by abandoning this Clintonite strategy. From Gore's perspective, the problem with moderation and triangulation was that they failed to energize core Democratic constituencies including organized labor, liberal public interest groups, and African Americans. Liberal groups had been furious with Clinton for his positions on welfare reform and education. Labor viewed Clinton as insufficiently committed to its cause. Indeed, some unions considered backing Ralph Nader's message of opposition to global capitalism. African Americans felt considerable rapport with Clinton and strongly supported him as an individual, but would expect more vigorous efforts on behalf of civil rights causes from his successor.

Confronting a restive Democratic base, Gore chose to depart from Clintonism and to move to the left. He attacked drug companies for charging too much. He promised African Americans stronger support for affirmative action. He promised expanded Social Security and Medicare coverage for the elderly. He courted organized labor by promising to raise the minimum wage and appealed to the teachers' unions by opposing school choice and voucher programs. Most importantly, Gore rejected the notion of using the projected government revenue surplus to cut federal income taxes. Gore promised tax cuts to selected Democratic constituencies but argued that an across-the-board cut would benefit the wealthiest 1 percent of Americans at the expense of everyone else. In short, Gore became his own man by abandoning triangulation in favor of a more traditional Democratic populism.

Gore's repositioning became clearly manifest to the public during the first presidential debate. Prior to the debates, most Americans had paid little attention to the presidential campaign. The conventions, for example, are only watched by small numbers of loyal partisans. This is why the television networks dropped their gavel-to-gavel coverage in favor of short excerpts. The debates, however, draw a huge audience of Americans hoping to see something that will help them make up their minds about the candidates. In the debates, especially the first, the candidates presented a study in contrasts. Gore was dynamic, sure of himself, even over-bearing. Bush seemed more nervous, less certain of facts, clumsy with language.

Yet the critical difference between the two candidates was less in their demeanor than in their political positioning. Bush pre-sented himself as a centrist who would "bring the country to-gether." He eschewed appeals based on race, class, or gender. He promised a tax cut for all Americans and espoused such middle-class issues as education reform. Gore, on the other hand, pursued the rhetoric of Democratic populism. He repeatedly said that Bush would give a tax cut only to the wealthiest 1 percent while ig-noring poorer Americans. Rather than wrap himself in Clinton's mantle of moderation—and years of unprecedented prosperity—Gore chose to appeal to the Democratic base with a message of populism and a hint of class warfare. Soon after the first debate, Gore's standing in the polls dropped while Bush's rose. By insist-ing that he was his own man and distancing himself from Clinton, Gore made it difficult to claim credit for the prosperity of the Clinton era.

Gore's strategy of shifting to the left might have been more ef-fective if it had been accompanied by a systematic effort to regis-ter and mobilize minority and working-class voters. During the campaign, the Democratic party announced plans for a $100 mil-lion, nationwide effort to attract new voters to the polls. For the most part, however, the Democrats and Republicans both focused on what Steven Schier has aptly called voter "activation" rather than mobilization.[2] A strategy of activation entails an attempt to energize existing supporters rather than the more difficult and challenging effort to bring new participants into the electoral arena. The Democrats, to be sure, did make some attempt to aug-ment their electoral strength in three key battleground states by launching voter registration drives among unionized workers in Michigan and Pennsylvania and among African Americans in Florida. After an extensive effort by the National Association for the Advancement of Colored People, African American voter turnout in Florida increased more than 70 percent over 1996 and 93 percent of these African American voters cast their votes for Al Gore. Without this marked increase in African American turnout in Florida, Gore would not even have come close to carrying the state and the postelection battle would not have been fought. Perhaps if the Democrats had extended their campaign to mobilize new voters throughout the nation, the outcome of the election would have been different. But for the reasons discussed earlier, neither party was willing to undertake such an effort, and voter turnout in 2000 remained near the 50 percent mark that has become the norm for U.S. presidential races.

In the closing days of the campaign, Gore abandoned his populist theme and focused instead on his opponent's qualifications for the presidency. Bush was said to be inexperienced and lacking the intelligence needed for the office. An old drunken driving conviction was revealed to cast doubt on Bush's veracity. This change of campaign tactics helped Gore close the gap in the final week of the campaign. On election day, Gore out-polled Bush by some five hundred thousand votes—leading to the first instance since 1888 that the winner of the popular vote lost in the electoral college. Yet, against the backdrop of peace and unprecedented prosperity, the election should not even have been close. Precisely this point was made by outgoing president Bill Clinton in a heated exchange with Gore after the election. Clinton told Gore that he lost the election because of his failure to run on the administration's record. Gore replied that Clinton's sex scandals had been a major impediment to his campaign.[3]

THE POSTELECTION STRUGGLE IN FLORIDA

Early on the election night it became clear that the outcome would hinge on the results in Florida, a state with twenty-five electoral votes. Initially, the television networks declared Gore the winner in Florida on the basis of exit poll results. Carrying

Florida meant that Gore was very likely to win the presidency. But after all of the votes were tallied, Bush seemed to have won by fewer than two thousand votes out of nearly six million votes cast across the state. Vice President Gore called Governor Bush and conceded defeat.

Within an hour, however, Gore was on the phone to Bush again—this time to withdraw his concession. Under Florida law, the narrowness of Bush's victory, less than one-tenth of 1 percent, triggered an automatic recount. Moreover, reports had begun to surface of election irregularities. For example, nearly twenty thousand votes in Palm Beach County had been invalidated because voters, apparently confused by a so-called butterfly ballot, had indicated more than one presidential choice. Many of these votes were cast in predominantly African American precincts and more likely than not were intended for Gore.[4]

Some civil rights groups, moreover, claimed that African American voters had faced long lines and harassment by election officials. Given the closeness of the race and the various uncertainties, Democrats decided to await the results of a statewide machine recount of the vote and quickly dispatched hundreds of Gore campaign workers to monitor the process. The recount narrowed Bush's margin to a mere 327 votes but still appeared to confirm his victory. Republican secretary of state Katherine Harris declared that she was prepared to certify this result on November 14, the date prescribed under state law, and to declare Bush the winner of the popular voting for president in the state of Florida.

At this point, the Gore campaign demanded a hand recount of the votes cast in four heavily Democratic counties—Miami-Dade, Palm Beach, Volusia, and Broward. Gore campaign workers argued that in these counties, all of which relied on punch card ballots, machine counts tended to miss large numbers of legitimate votes whose "chads" had not been fully perforated. The chad is the paper tab normally penetrated and dislodged from the ballot by the key-punch device manipulated by the voter.

Under Florida law, a defeated candidate has seventy-two hours to request a hand recount of the vote. In turn, county election boards are required to ascertain whether a recount might be warranted by the closeness of the vote of by possible problems surrounding the casting and counting of ballots. In preparation for recounts, Gore sent his top legal adviser, Ron Klain, to Tallahassee, the Florida state capital. Klain began to assemble what would eventually become a team of hundreds of attorneys, aides, and staffers for the battle.

The Gore campaign's demand for a hand recount was immediately denounced by Republicans as unnecessary and illegitimate. Gore forces knew, however, that the tabulation of ballots was less than an exact science and, before the November election, had actually prepared manuals of recount tactics and collected summaries of recount laws and procedures for twenty key states in preparation for possible recount battles. The balloting methods used in the United States are notoriously fraught with error. During a typical national election, more than a million ballots are discarded by local officials as uncountable for one reason or another, such as being marked for more than one candidate for the same office. In state and local races across the nation, balloting controversies have generated thousands of recounts and hundreds of lawsuits in recent years, including, as it happens, several major cases in Florida. Election law has become a lucrative legal specialty.

The ballots used in the United States are a mix of forms developed as long ago as the 1890s when the states took over the printing of ballots from the political parties. These were modified during the 1940s and 1950s, when voting machines and punch card ballots were introduced, and updated in some jurisdictions during the 1990s, when more modern and accurate computerized voting methods were introduced. The choice of ballot format is a county matter and, within any state, various counties may use different formats depending on local resources and preferences. For example, the Palm Beach County butterfly ballot, which seemed to confuse many voters, was selected by Democratic election officials who thought its larger print would help elderly, predominantly Democratic voters read the names of the candidates. Not infrequently, as turned out to be the case in Florida, neighboring counties use completely different ballot systems. For example, Baltimore City, Maryland, introduced voting machines many years ago and continues to use them. Baltimore County, Maryland, uses more modern ballots that are optically scanned by computers. Neighboring Montgomery County, Maryland, employs a cumbersome punch card system that requires voters to punch several different cards on both sides—a bewildering process that usually results in large numbers of spoiled ballots. In some states, including Florida, different precincts within the same county may use different voting methods, causing still more confusion.

As became only too evident during the struggle over Florida's votes, the United States's overall balloting process is awkward, confusing, riddled with likely sources of error and bias, and in cases of close races, incapable of producing a result that will stand up to close scrutiny. Results can take several days to process, and every recount appears to produce a slightly different result. Often, too, the process of counting and recounting is directed by state and county officials with political axes to grind. The "Votomatic" punch card machines used in a number of Florida counties are notoriously unreliable. The Votomatics are popular with many county governments because they are inexpensive. About 37 percent of the precincts in the United States's 3,140 counties use Votomatics or similar machines.[5] However, voters often find it difficult to properly insert the punch cards, frequently punch the wrong hole, or do not sufficiently perforate one or more chads to allow the punch cards to be read by the counting machine. Votomatics and other punch card voting devices generally yield a much higher rate of spoiled votes than other voting methods. Indeed, a 1988 Florida Senate race was won by Republican Connie Mack in part because of thousands of spoiled Votomatic ballots. To make matters worse, precinct-level election officials—frequently elderly volunteers—often do not understand the rules themselves and are unable to help voters with questions. These difficulties were not subject to public and media scrutiny so long as they affected only local races. In 2000, however, the United States's antiquated electoral machinery collapsed under the weight of a presidential election, revealing its flaws for all to see.

Thus, the Gore campaign's request for a hand recount of Florida votes was perfectly reasonable. Bush's apparent winning margin in the state was well within the potential margin of error. Another count might well have yielded a different result. The Gore campaign, however, was not simply interested in a more accurate tally. It wanted a vote count that would give Al Gore the presidency. Accordingly, rather than ask for a hand recount in all the state's counties, Gore campaign workers targeted four large South Florida counties—Miami-Dade, Palm Beach, Volusia, and Broward— where unreliable punch card ballots were used, where the electorate was heavily Democratic, and, perhaps most important, where Democrats controlled the local canvassing boards that would perform the had recounts.

Under Florida law, local canvassing boards have considerable discretion when conducting hand recounts. They are required, if possible, to ascertain the intent of the voter from the ballot. Depending on a particular board's outlook, voter intent might be divined from a partially perforated chad, a buckled but unperforated chad (sometimes called a dimpled or pregnant chad), or even a perforation in the vicinity of the chad. Gore strategists reasoned that friendly canvassing boards, sifting through thousands of so-called undervotes, ballots whose chads in the presidential column had not been sufficiently perforated to register in the machine counts, would have ample opportunity to identify enough Gore votes to overcome Bush's narrow lead. All four counties targeted by the Democrats agreed to begin the laborious process of recounting hundreds of thousands of votes by hand. The first recounts started in Palm Beach County on Saturday, November 11; the others got under way on Monday, November 13.

For their part, Republicans were bitterly opposed to any effort to recount votes. From the GOP's perspective, Bush had already won the election and had nothing to gain from any further tabulation of the votes. Like their Democratic counterparts, Republican campaign workers were not interested in obtaining the most accurate tally. They were interested in winning the election. Accordingly, Republicans launched the first salvo in what turned out to be a protracted judicial battle. Over the weekend following the election, GOP attorneys appealed to the federal district court and, subsequently, to the Eleventh Circuit Court of Appeals in Atlanta, arguing that the absence of a clear and consistent standard for hand recounts would lead to disparate standards across counties. Republican attorneys argued that this would constitute a violation of equal protection under the Fourteenth Amendment. But both the U.S. district judge and the Eleventh Circuit Court turned down the GOP suit. The court of appeals said state courts "have the primary authority" to handle election law disputes. The appellate court, however, left open the possibility of a rehearing at a later stage in the dispute. Though the Eleventh Circuit Court was asked at several subsequent points to intervene in the vote counting, it steadfastly refused to do so. Eventually, however, the GOP's equal protection argument proved to be critical in the U.S. Supreme Court's decision that ended the election.[6]

MOBILIZATION FOR POLITICAL COMBAT

While Democrats pursued and Republicans sought to block hand recounts, both sides assembled substantial legal and political teams in Florida. Interestingly, each camp chose as its chief spokesperson a former U.S. secretary of state. Democrats were represented by Bill Clinton's secretary of state, Warren Christopher, while George H. W. Bush's secretary of state, James Baker, spoke for the Republicans. These individuals were seen by their respective camps as giving weight and credence to their claims. The choice of secretaries of state as spokespeople, however, also represented interesting political symbolism. The secretary of state is the United State's chief diplomat, representing the national interest in a sometimes hostile world. Appropriately enough, the Bush and Gore campaigns viewed one another as the near equivalents of hostile foreign foes. Said one GOP chairperson in Florida, "We were fighting for our lives and we were fighting for a righteous cause."[7] Indeed, the rhetoric employed by both Baker and Christopher against the other's political party was as tough as any either had ever directed against the United States's foreign foes.

Beginning November 8 Democrats assembled what became a staff of more than three hundred attorneys and party workers in Florida, augmented by hundreds of locally recruited volunteers.[8] The Democratic political operation was led by Gore's campaign chair, William Daley, son of the famed boss of Chicago's political machine. The Democratic legal effort was led by Klain, a former top aide to Attorney General Janet Reno, and by David M. Boies, the New York attorney who led the Justice Department's successful case against Microsoft and who is regarded as one of the nation's top litigators. Additional legal firepower was provided the Democratic team by Harvard law professor Lawrence Tribe. Democrats also flew the Reverend Jesse Jackson to Florida to bolster African American support for Gore. Jackson also denounced Florida ballot procedures as racist.

Democratic workers, along with locally recruited volunteers, collected depositions from voters who claimed polling irregularities. Democratic attorneys answered Republican court challenges while preparing a legal offensive of their own. In Washington and New York, in the meantime, Democratic party activists and elected officials launched a barrage of claims on the various national news and talk programs, lambasting the GOP for attempting to block a full and accurate recount of the Florida vote. Also, prominent intellectuals in the Democratic camp wrote numerous magazine articles and newspaper columns and op-eds supporting Gore. A number of academics allowed their names to be used in full-page ads supporting Gore's cause in major newspapers such as the *New York Times* and the *Washington Post*. Several renowned law professors, including Harvard law professor and ex–O. J. Simpson "Dream Team" member Alan Dershowitz, volunteered their services to the Gore campaign. Dershowitz made numerous talk show appearances promoting the Gore cause.

Republicans lost no time in responding to the Gore campaign's mobilization for the Florida battle. Employing the party's nationwide fund-raising machinery, the Bush campaign quickly built a campaign chest of more than $5 million to fund its efforts. The GOP's legal strategy was developed under the supervision of Washington attorney Benjamin L. Ginsberg, the Republican party's leading election law expert. Former secretary of state Baker led the Bush campaign's political efforts. Ginsberg and Banker recruited attorneys Barry Richard and Philip Beck to argue on Bush's behalf in the Florida courts, while the GOP's foremost appellate litigator, Washington attorney Ted Olson, was retained to present Bush's case in two appearances before the U.S. Supreme Court. During the course of the battle, the Bush campaign retained the services of a number of major national firms.[9] A small army of Republican lawyers was also recruited in Florida to prepare briefs and depositions at a moment's notice, matching and eventually surpassing the democratic effort.

In addition to the lawyers, Republicans mobilized a force of campaign workers, party officials, and volunteers to press their cause. In Washington, Republican House whip Tom DeLay recruited more than five hundred volunteers, including large numbers of young GOP congressional staffers, to go to Florida to observe and, if possible, thwart recount efforts. In New York, Republican state committeeperson J. Brandon Quinn and GOP activist Brad Blakeman recruited another group of volunteers, who were provided housing and meals and sent to demonstrate in

Miami, Palm Beach, and Fort Lauderdale. Other Republican workers were recruited in Florida itself. Many of Florida's Republican party county chairpeople mobilized Republican workers in their jurisdictions and deployed them in South Florida to help the Bush effort. These various Republican volunteers were dispatched in teams to the disputed counties with orders to monitor recount efforts and to direct the news media to stories involving dubious counting practices. They were asked to create generally an atmosphere of chaos and disorder, which presented on national television, would cast doubt on the legitimacy of Gore's efforts to continue the battle in Florida. Round-the-clock shifts of Republican party workers also watched every Florida circuit court clerk's office to detect surprise Democratic motions or court orders.[10] Republican party officials closely directed the activities of the GOP activists and held two daily conference calls to coordinate their activities.[11] Republican officials also held Florida election law seminars for volunteers to acquaint them with the intricacies of state law and the techniques that could be used to challenge a ballot. Volunteers were issued cameras to record questionable vote-counting practices for possible later legal or public relations use.

At the same time, prominent national Republican party officials such as Michigan governor John Engler and Montana governor Marc Racicot went to Florida and did battle with their Democratic counterparts on television and radio talk shows, as each campaign sought to secure the support of political activists and financial contributors for its efforts. Republican luminaries also journeyed to Florida to serve as observers during hand recounts. Along with Engler and Racicot, former senator and presidential candidate Bob Dole, New Jersey governor Christie Whitman, New York governor George Pataki, and a score of other GOP officials took turns monitoring the activities of county canvassing boards. Republicans hoped that in the presence of nationally prominent witnesses, the boards would be less likely to interpret every dimpled chad as a Gore vote.

As they mobilized lawyers and political operatives, Republicans also secured the support of several of the executive institutions of the Florida state government. The Democrats, to be sure, controlled several South Florida canvassing boards. Republicans, however, controlled most of the executive offices of the state, including the governor's mansion. Indeed, Florida's governor was Jeb Bush, younger brother of Republican presidential candidate George W. Bush. Jeb Bush adopted a public posture of neutrality but worked tirelessly behind the scenes to advance his brother's cause. Certainly, too, it required little imagination on the part of state and local officials—many of them dependent on the governor's good will—to perceive that support for George W. Bush would help their standing with Governor Jeb Bush.

In the context of the battle over Florida's votes, another state executive official was even more important than the governor. This was the secretary of state who, as head of Florida's Election Canvassing Commission, also serves as the state's chief election officer. The sitting secretary of state, Katherine Harris, was an ambitious Republican, politically tied to Jeb Bush, and one of the co-chairs of the George W. Bush presidential campaign committee in Florida. Democrats viewed Harris as a determined adversary and had previously charged her with purging the state's electoral rolls of thousands of minority voters who were inaccurately classified as felons.[12]

Harris proved to be critically important to Bush's success in the postelection battle. As Democrats were demanding hand recounts in South Florida, Harris announced that she would not accept the results of hand tallies concluded after November 14. She unequivocally said she planned to certify the results from the machine recounts on November 14, the date stipulated under state law. Democrats filed suit in Leon County circuit court asking that Harris be compelled to allow hand recounts. The presiding judge, Terry P. Lewis, ruled that Harris had discretion in the matter but could not arbitrarily refuse to consider recounted votes. To avoid the appearance of arbitrary conduct, Harris deliberated for a time and then announced once again that she would strictly enforce the November 14 statutory deadline for the submission of revised vote tallies. This decision effectively negated hand recounts in all but one county, Volusia, which had completed its recount with a gain of only twenty-seven votes for Gore. Judge Lewis subsequently ruled that Harris had properly exercised her discretion. At this point, taking account of machine recounts across the state, the hand recount in Velusia County and several hundred overseas ballots, Bush's lead had actually grown to more than nine hundred votes.

Democrats immediately launched a media campaign of personal vilification against Harris. Chris Lehane, Gore's campaign press secretary, called Harris a "hack" and referred to her as "Commissar Harris." Other Democratic media personalities criticized Harris's makeup, wardrobe, and personal mannerisms. One compared Harris's appearance to that of Cruella De Vil, the villainess in a popular animated feature film. Some members of the Gore campaign evidently forgot their party's strong commitment to feminism and ardent opposition to comments directed at the personal appearance or wardrobe of a woman in public life. Al Gore rebuked at least one aide for the tenor of his attacks on Harris.

More important than their attacks on Harris, Democrats filed an appeal of Judge Lewis's decision with the Florida Supreme Court. While Florida's executive branch was in the hands of the Republicans, one important branch of the Florida government, the judiciary, was controlled by the Democrats. In particular, all seven justices of the Florida Supreme Court were Democratic appointees, most had been trial lawyers, and at least three had been liberal activists before being appointed to the bench. Over the previous year, the court had been embroiled in several conflicts with the state's Republican legislature and with Governor Jeb Bush. Bush and the legislature had recently threatened to cut the court's budget and staffing. Given this background, attorneys for the Gore campaign had reason to believe the Florida Supreme Court would look favorably on their appeal. To help with their case, the Gore legal team retained the services of semi-retired Florida attorney Dexter Douglass. As counsel to Florida's former Democratic governor Lawton Chiles, Douglass had played a major hand in selecting the six justices who were Chiles's appointees.[13]

THE LEGAL BATTLE

Thus prepared, Gore attorneys appealed Harris's decision to the state supreme court. The court immediately ordered Harris to delay certifying the vote totals until it could hear oral arguments. In its brief, the Gore legal team asked the Court to allow more time for recounts. "There is an overwhelming interest to ensure that every vote is counted," said Gore's lawyers. Their brief went on to argue that "it is critical that the Election Canvassing Commission's decision [to certify the election] be made on the basis of the most accurate vote count possible."[14]

Bush campaign lawyers argued vigorously that the state legislature had created a process for counting and certifying votes that gave the secretary of state and the state's election canvassing board discretion in overseeing the counting and certification of votes. They asserted, also, that the certification deadline of November 14 had been established by the legislature to ensure that Florida's slate of electors would be selected and presented to Congress by December 12, as required under federal law. December 12 was a so-called safe-harbor date. According to federal law, a slate of electors designated on or before that date was not subject to legal challenge. The vote of the electoral college was not to take place until December 18. Under federal law, this would be followed by the official counting of electoral votes in Congress on January 6 and the inauguration of a new president on January 20. Hypothetically, if Florida failed to properly identify a slate of electors by December 12, it was possible that Florida's electoral votes might not count toward the selection of the next president.

Some constitutional authorities believed that a failure to select Florida electors would automatically give the presidency to Al

Gore, who, absent Florida, would have a majority of the remaining electoral votes. Other experts argued that the Constitution required the winner to receive a majority of the possible electoral votes even if one or more states failed to choose electors. These experts believed that in the absence of Florida's electoral votes, neither candidate would have the majority of 271 electoral votes required under the Constitution. In this case the president would be chosen by the U.S. House of Representatives with each state casting one vote. Since in the new House, Republicans would control a majority of the state delegations, the House would almost certainly select George W. Bush.[15] The entire matter, if it came about, was sure to generate fierce litigation and would probably wind up being decided by the U.S. Supreme Court.

In the case before the Florida Supreme Court, the Bush attorneys argued that the state legislature had established a set of procedures for counting and reporting votes and it was not up to the court to substitute its own rules and timetables for those of the legislature. Any extension of the legislative timetable for counting votes or interference with the discretionary authority of the secretary of state would constitute a "judicial fiat" and would usurp the power of state officials. Another Bush attorney argued that Democrats were asking the court to violate the principle of separation of powers by ruling that the secretary of state did not have the discretion over recount procedures that had been assigned to her by the state legislature.[16] Gore's lead attorney responded that the court certainly possessed the authority to extend the legislature's timetable and could do so without jeopardizing the December 12 deadline.

On November 21, the Florida Supreme Court handed Gore what seemed to be a major victory. In a unanimous decision, the state's high court extended the deadline for the submission of revised tallies. The court ruled that Ms. Harris must accept manual recount tallies until 5 P.M. on November 26. This new date seemed to provide enough time for full hand recounts in the three disputed counties. Recounts resumed in Broward and Palm Beach Counties, while Democrats renewed their pressure on Miami-Dade, which had suspended its earlier recount, to begin counting ballots again.

The Gore campaign was elated by its victory. Republicans, however, denounced the Florida Supreme Court and rushed to appeal its decision to the U.S. Supreme Court, where they hoped a Republican majority would give Bush a favorable hearing. In its emergency filing, the Bush campaign argued that the hand counts authorized by the Florida Supreme Court opened the door to an "electoral catastrophe" and to "the ascension of a president of questionable legitimacy, or a constitutional crisis."[17]

In its legal briefs, the Bush campaign made two major points designed to demonstrate that the Florida case raised significant federal issues and, hence, should be decided by the federal courts. Bush attorneys argued, first, that Florida's Supreme Court violated the principle of separation of powers by intruding into an area reserved, under Article II of the U.S. Constitution, to the legislature. Article II specifies that "Each state shall appoint, in such a manner as the legislature thereof may direct," the appropriate number of presidential electors. The Bush attorneys argued that this language gave the state legislature, not the judiciary, the ultimate authority to establish the rules governing the selection of electors. The second point made by the Bush legal team was that a recount in selected counties denied Bush and those who voted for him equal protection of the laws in violation of the Fourteenth Amendment of the U.S. Constitution. In particular, the Bush attorneys charged, the hand-count procedure authorized by the Florida court disenfranchised Republican votes by giving officials in heavily Democratic counties too much discretion in deciding whether a challenged ballot indicated that a voter had intended to vote for Vice President Gore.[18] Similar arguments had been rejected by federal district and appellate judges and many observers predicted that the U.S. Supreme Court would decline to hear the case.

THE RECOUNT

While the U.S. Supreme Court weighed the merits of accepting the Bush appeal, the fund recounts continued. Democratic hopes of achieving a quick victory through South Florida recounts were, however, soon dashed. The Miami-Dade canvassing board refused to initiate a new hand count. In the aftermath of the election, Miami-Dade had begun a recount by sampling several precincts for tabulation errors. Though the sampling procedure suggested that hundreds of presidential votes in the county might not have been tabulated, the canvassing board announced on the evening of November 16 that it had decided not to undertake a full hand recount. The supervisor of elections for Miami-Dade County asserted that, despite their problems, machine counts were more reliable than hand counts and, in the absence of information suggesting the machines suffered from actual mechanical problems, the board would not proceed with a recount.[19]

The Gore campaign blamed the board's decision on intimidation by Republican "thugs." A group of noisy Republican demonstrators had been active outside the board's offices, waving placards and chanting, but the so-called thugs consisted mainly of Republican Capitol Hill staffers, many with children in tow. Members of the canvassing board denied they had been influenced by the demonstrators. The Miami-Dade canvassing board's closing its operations dashed Gore's hopes of finding hundreds of new votes in heavily Democratic precincts. Even after the Florida Supreme Court extended the time limit available for recounts, Miami-Dade declined to resume counting votes.

In Broward County, on the other hand, a manual recount continued during the period mandated by the Supreme Court, yielding significant new support for Gore's presidential bid. Despite Republican efforts to slow the process through legal challenges and objections, the Broward County canvassing board proceeded with its recount effort. The board, which consisted of two

Democrats and one rather acquiescent Republican, decided on a very liberal standard for ascertaining the voter's intent with regard to ballots that had not been read by the electronic counting machines. Initially, the board held that only ballots that showed two or more corners of the chad punched through would be counted as votes. However, when this standard failed to produce many new Gore votes, midway through the recount, the board voted 2–1 to relax the standard and accept ballots with only one corner of a chad dislodged as indicating that the voter intended to cast a ballot—usually for Al Gore.

It appeared to angry Republicans that Broward's Democratic officials were willing to accept almost an partial perforation of a chad however slight, or even an indentation of a chad as indicative of an effort to cast a ballot. Republican governor Marc Racicot of Montana said, "They changed the rules so they could manufacture additional votes for Gore."[20] Republican observers challenged virtually every action undertaken by the board. At one point, Republicans even charged that a Democratic counter had removed a chad from a ballot and eaten it.[21] Since the canvassing board often concluded that so-called undervotes had actually been votes for Al Gore, Gore added a net of more than four hundred votes to his total, brining him to within roughly five hundred votes of George W. Bush. Victory seemed to be within Gore's grasp despite what had happened in Miami-Dade.

The Gore campaign hoped that Palm Beach County, whose canvassing board consisted entirely of Democrats, would provide the winning margin. Unfortunately for Gore, however, the Palm Beach canvassing board, chaired by county judge Charles Burton, adopted a more stringent standard for counting votes than the one used in Broward. Pregnant and dimpled chads were not counted as votes. The board would only consider ballots whose chads had been clearly dislodged, even if not fully removed, by the punching device. Moreover, while Broward County had only examined so-called undervotes, the Palm Beach County canvassing board looked at all the votes. In some instances, this meant that votes that had been counted by a machine were now rejected afterhand examination revealed that more than one hole had been punched. As it happened, Gore lost almost as many votes that had been double punched as he gained from the undervotes. Palm Beach County's strict standards meant that the vote bonanza expected by the Gore campaign would probably not be realized.

Republican observers, meanwhile, sought to slow the process and prevent completion of the recount by the court-mandated deadline. Their strategy consisted of raising numerous objections at every stage of the process. Republicans claimed that they saw ballots intended for Bush with their chads taped back into place as well as Bush ballots in the Gore pile. Each objection took time to resolve. As the count slowly progressed, Gore added dozens, rather than hundreds, of votes. It began to appear that Gore would fall short. To make matters worse, the Palm Beach board voted to suspend operations for the November 24 Thanksgiving holiday. When it resumed counting on November 25, observers calculated that Palm Beach county would not complete its work by the 5 P.M. deadline the next day.

As the deadline approached, news agencies reported that Gore had netted only 215 new votes in Palm Beach County. But, with several thousand undervotes left to count, there was still some slight chance of success. The board asked Secretary Harris for an extension of several hours past the 5 P.M. deadline to complete its count. Harris refused to grant the extension, pointing to the fact that the deadline had been set by the Florida Supreme Court. In the absence of a complete tally, Harris also refused to accept the board's partial recount and 215 vote gain for Gore. She declared that she would certify the results produced by Palm Beach County's earlier machine recount. Thus, Gore was stripped of even his modest success.

On November 27, in a nationally televised ceremony attended by Florida notables and the news media, Katherine Harris officially certified the Florida totals and proclaimed George W. Bush the winner of the popular vote in the state. It was a moment of triumph for Bush and for Harris, who had survived a fierce personal attack. For the Gore campaign, Bush's certification represented both a public relations and a legal challenge. From the public relations perspective, the danger was the Americans would begin to regard Bush as the legitimate winner and view Gore as little more than a sore loser—a sentiment captured in the "Sore Loserman" placards waved by Republicans to mock the official Gore-Lieberman campaign signs. Indeed, public opinion polls taken after the certification ceremony indicated growing public skepticism about Gore's effort.

Gore's political standing had also been damaged by a flap over military votes. Democrats quietly sought to disqualify several thousand absentee military ballots cast by members of the armed forces registered in Florida but serving on active duty abroad. On the basis of past experience, both parties expected military personnel to give Republican candidate Bush the bulk of their votes. Eventually, absentee military votes in 2000 did support Bush by roughly a two to one margin. Under Florida law, military voters had ten days from the November 7 election to return their ballots. As military ballots were received, a team of Democratic lawyers in each Florida county stood ready to challenge their validity. These lawyers were armed with a five-page memorandum from Gore campaign headquarters detailing the possible grounds for such challenges including the lack of a proper postmark, witness signature, or date. Democratic challenges initially resulted in about 40 percent of the overseas military ballots being declared invalid.[22]

This initial legal success, however, turned into a political debacle for the Gore campaign. Republicans were quick to charge Gore with political duplicity—on the one hand, claiming to want more votes counted on the basis of guesses about voters' intent while, on the other hand, working to invalidate votes where intent was quite clear. Even worse, Republicans charged that Gore was insensitive to the heroism and sacrifice of U.S. service personnel and was working to disfranchise them even as they served their nation abroad. Montana governor Marc Racicot said, "We learned how far the vice president's campaign will go to win this election. And I am very sorry to say but the vice president's lawyers have gone to war in my judgement against the men and women who serve in our armed forces."[23] Retired General Norman Schwartzkopf, hero of the Persian Gulf War, was also enlisted by the GOP to castigate Gore's efforts and question his fitness to serve as commander in chief.

Democrats moved quickly to attempt to limit the political damage. Vice-presidential candidate Joe Lieberman made a number of television appearances to deny that the Gore campaign had targeted military voters. Lieberman asserted that he and Gore wanted every military absentee vote to count. "Al Gore and I don't want to ever be part of anything that would put an extra burden on the military personnel abroad," Lieberman said.[24] Despite Lieberman's protestations, however, Democratic attorneys continued to work to disqualify overseas military ballots. Republicans subsequently brought suit in a number of counties and were eventually able to count some but not all of the previously disqualified military votes.

The "Contest" Phase

From a legal perspective, the certification of Bush as the official Florida winner presented an enormous challenge to the Gore camp. Florida law provided the loser in a state race with the opportunity to contest the result after the winner was certified. The burden of proof in such a contest, however, was on the plaintiff. Absent actual election fraud, it was difficult to overturn the certified results of an election. In addition, the clock was also running against Gore as the December 12 deadline was approaching quickly. The Gore campaign had spent nearly two weeks in an unsuccessful effort to secure recounts and block Bush's certification as the winner. Now there were fewer than two weeks left to mount a legal contest asking the courts to undo Bush's certification and order new ballot tallies. Gore attorneys began their legal maneuvers but knew they faced an uphill struggle. Previous election contests in Florida had taken years to resolve, and the Gore attorneys had only days.[25] Some pundits suggested that Gore had made a major tactical blunder devoting so much time to fruitless recounts. Critics said Gore's attorneys should have allowed Harris to certify the results on November 14 as she initially sought to do, thus allowing more time for the postcertification "contest" phase of the process.

While Gore's attorneys prepared to contest the certified election results, two additional legal struggles were taking place that could potentially affect the outcome of the election, even if Gore's formal contest was unsuccessful. In Seminole and Martin Counties, local Democratic activists charged that Republican election officials had violated Florida law by allowing Republican party workers to correct errors in absentee ballot requests submitted by Republican voters. Apparently some ballot request forms had been incorrectly prepared by the printing companies hired by the GOP.[26] These forms omitted voter identification information required under Florida law for a valid absentee ballot request. In the two counties, Republican party officials had been allowed to correct more than four thousand request forms, in possible violation of state law. In the case of Seminole County, the county's Republican election supervisor had even allowed Republican party workers to correct the request forms.

Though some of the ballot requests were problematic, the more than twenty-five thousand absentee ballots eventually cast in the two counties were, in and of themselves, not tainted in any way. Moreover, it was impossible, after the fact, to ascertain which ballots had been cast by individuals who had filed the suspect request forms. Democrats, however, calculated that Bush led Gore among absentee voters in the two counties by several thousand votes. If all twenty-five thousand absentee ballots could be disqualified, Gore would suddenly take a substantial lead in the Florida voting. Accordingly Democratic party activists filed suit demanding that all the absentee ballots be discarded. Thus Democrats, who were demanding a full count of the vote in South Florida, were simultaneously asking for the disfranchisement of thousands of voters in Seminole and Martin Counties. Vice President Gore, himself, did not wish to be associated with efforts to invalidate legitimately cast ballots. Thus, the suits were nominally not associated with the Gore campaign. The Seminole County suit, for example, was filed by a flamboyant trial lawyer who was a member of the Democratic county executive board and was in frequent contact with Democratic party lawyers involved in the overall recount case.[27] For his part, Vice President Gore publicly indicated only that he thought the Seminole and Martin County suits were legitimate responses to what he characterized as unfair practices in the two counties.

THE FORMAL CONTEST IN THE COURTS: FROM LEON COUNTY TO WASHINGTON, D.C.

As the Seminole and Martin cases proceeded without Gore's ostensible involvement, the vice president's formal effort to contest the election began November 27 in the Leon County Circuit Court. Unfortunately for Gore, on the basis of random selection, the matter was assigned to Judge L. Sanders Sauls, the only one of the four jurists potentially eligible to hear the case who had been appointed by a Republican governor. Nevertheless, Gore's lead attorney, David Boies, argued that the judge should set aside the certification of the election and order full recounts of thousands of disputed votes in Miami-Dade and Palm Beach Counties. Boies demanded that the 215 votes netted by Gore in Palm Beach County's partial recount but rejected by Secretary Harris be added to Gore's tally. He asked also that all of other disputed votes in Palm Beach be recounted again, and this time according to the same liberal standard for counting votes that had been employed in Broward County. Democrats believed that Gore stood to gain more than 3,000 votes if Palm Beach County used the same standard as Broward. Boies also raised the issue of Nassau County.

There, the canvassing board had conducted two machine counts that resulted in slightly different tallies. The second count had given Gore fifty-one more votes than he received in the first count. The predominantly Republican board, however, decided to use the results of the first count. Boies demanded that Judge Sauls order the certification of the second count instead. Finally, Boies asked the judge to appoint a "special master" to oversee the recounts on an expedited basis. Were the court to accede to these requests, Gore would almost certainly be able to garner enough votes to win the election.

Republicans responded that these Democratic demands were preposterous. Attorneys for the GOP repeated their claim that Harris had properly certified the election results, using the discretionary authority given to her by Florida law. Bush attorneys argued further that Palm Beach County had failed to meet even the extended deadline for hand counts clearly established by the Florida Supreme Court. The central Bush position, however, was that in a contest procedure the burden of proof was on Gore to prove that one or more aspects of the election had been improperly conducted and that this improper or unlawful conduct had materially affected the outcome of the election. This, Bush attorneys argued, the Gore campaign had failed to prove.

While the case proceeded, a surprising turn of events took place in Washington, D.C. The U.S. Supreme Court decided that it would hear Bush's appeal from the earlier Florida Supreme Court decision ordering hand recounts. The High Court heard oral argument from the Bush and Gore attorneys—Ted Olson for Bush and Lawrence Tribe for Gore. Olson argued that the Florida Supreme Court had gone beyond the scope of its authority when it "overturned and materially rewrote" the section of Florida law dealing with the conduct of presidential elections, including changing the legislatively specified date for the certification of the vote. The federal courts, said Olson, had a compelling reason to deal with this issue because the U.S. Constitution and federal statute specifically assigned state legislatures authority over presidential elections.

Tribe countered that the entire issue was a matter of Florida law, which was a matter for the Florida courts to interpret, and the federal judiciary had given state courts wide latitude in interpreting the laws and constitution of their own state.

Significantly, during oral argument, the justices seemed to take positions that ran counter to their normal stances on matters of state versus federal power. For example, Justice Sandra Day O'Connor, normally one of the Court's most ardent proponents of the notion that the states retain important governmental powers under the U.S. Constitution, was concerned that the Florida Supreme Court had intruded on federal prerogatives. At the same time, Justice Ruth Bader Ginsburg, normally skeptical of doctrines of states' rights, accused Olson of "impugning" the Florida Supreme Court. It appeared from the questioning that the court's liberal-conservative division would carry more weight than other doctrinal considerations. The five more conservative justices—Scalia, Rehnquist, O'Connor, Thomas, and Kennedy—appeared to be siding with Bush while the four more liberal justices—Breyer, Souter, Ginsberg, and Stevens—saw more merit in Gore's position.

Since Bush had already been certified the winner in Florida, it was not certain what role the Supreme Court could now play. If the High Court ruled that the Florida Supreme Court had acted properly, the contest phase of the election, currently under way, would simply continue. If, on the other hand, the U.S. Supreme Court declared that the Florida Supreme Court had acted improperly in extending the state's certification deadline and ordering hand recounts, possibly this would mean that Gore would lose the four hundred or so votes he gained in Broward County's recount. Gore's ongoing challenge to the certified outcome of the election, however, would continue. Alternatively, the High Court might be able to extend its reach beyond these narrow possibilities and craft a decision that would have a larger impact on the election's outcome.

On December 4, the U.S. Supreme Court issued its opinion. In a unanimous decision, which appeared to reflect a compromise between the Court's liberal and conservative wings, the High Court vacated the Florida Supreme Court's extension of the deadline for hand counts and remanded the case to the Florida court asking it to clarify its authority for extending the original recount deadline. The U.S. Supreme Court said in its opinion that it was uncertain of the grounds on which the Florida court had based its decision. The state court was told to explain whether its decision was merely an interpretation and clarification of existing state law or an attempt to create new electoral law in Florida.

The Bush and Gore camps each characterized the decision as a triumph for its side.[28] In point of fact, the decision had little immediate significance. The Court had not validated the original November 14 deadline, which would have added about four hundred votes to Bush's margin, nor had it done anything to improve Gore's position. At most, the High Court had served notice that it was willing to hear cases stemming from the Florida election dispute and was willing to overrule the state's supreme court if it found reason to do so. This turned out to be a significant portent.

THE FLORIDA LEGISLATURE

As litigation in the federal and state courts continued, another institution was preparing to step into the fray. This was the Republican-controlled Florida state legislature. In the new legislature that was preparing to convene in November, Republicans would hold a 77–43 advantage in the House and a 25–15 edge in the Senate. With these lopsided margins in both houses, the GOP would possess total control of the legislature's leadership structure, agenda, and deliberative processes. As noted above, Article II of the U.S. Constitution seems to specify that state legislatures should play the predominant role in deciding how presidential electors are chosen. Normally, this means merely that each state's legislature crafts statutory language governing the selection process. But, now that the Florida Supreme Court had revised the statutory formula by extending the timetable for the certification of votes, some Republicans in the legislature asserted that the U.S. Constitution gave state legislatures the authority to name the state's presidential electors. Indeed, this had been the common practice through the first third of the nineteenth century

Title 3, Section 2, of the U.S. Code, moreover, appears to confirm legislative authority in this realm. The federal statute states, "Whenever any state has held an election for the purpose of choosing electors and has failed to make a choice on the day prescribed by law, the electors may be appointed on a subsequent day in such a manner as the Legislature of such state may direct." This law had never been invoked, and any effort to make use of it would certainly have led to bruising legal and political battles. The Florida legislature, however, gave ample notice that it was prepared to attempt to exercise what it saw as its constitutional and statutory authority.

During the earlier, court-mandated recounts in Broward and Palm Beach Counties, the Speaker-elect of the Florida House, Thomas Feeney, had castigated the Florida Supreme court for extending the certification deadline and usurping authority from Secretary of State Harris. The Speaker-elect averred that the law gave the legislature "the power, authority and responsibility to intervene" if the results of the election were not clear by December 12. Feeney said that after the new legislature convened on Tuesday, November 21, it would begin preparing to "play a role should it become necessary."[29] Indeed, soon after the legislature began its regularly scheduled session, its attorneys began to formally examine the body's options and powers and, possibly, to prepare for a special legislative session to name Florida's electors.

As the legislature weighed its options, Florida governor Jeb Bush dropped all pretense of neutrality, saying it would be an "act of courage" for the legislature to hold a special session if Gore persisted in contesting the election.[30] He added that "The Constitution provides that the legislature be delegated this authority, not the court, not anybody else but the legislature." In response to Bush's remarks, Florida House Speaker-elect Feeney and Senate president John McKay established a joint select committee to discuss and plan for a special session to be held possibly as early as the first week in December. It seemed clear that the legislature's Republican leadership was prepared to appoint a slate of Bush electors if it appeared either that the election would not be decided by December 12 or that actions by the Florida courts threatened to make Gore the winner. Thus, another major governmental institution controlled by the GOP appeared ready to intervene on Bush's behalf. Jeb Bush and the Republican legislature saw their preparations as a kind of insurance policy designed to guard against the possibility that the Florida courts might order recounts that would give Gore the presidency. The implications of such a move by the Florida legislature were potentially far-reaching.

In one possible scenario, a Bush slate of electors chosen by the legislature would vie for formal recognition with a slate of Gore electors chosen through a judicially mandated recount provision. This would bring the Florida controversy to the steps of the U.S. Capitol. Under an 1887 federal statute, the U.S. Congress has the ultimate authority to decide the validity of a slate of electors on the basis of a majority vote in each house. In the next Congress, Republicans would control the House while the Senate would be evenly divided between the two parties, leaving the lame-duck vice president—Albert Gore—potentially to cast a tie-breaking vote for his own electors. Under these circumstances, a Bush slate of electors would certainly be accepted by the House and a Gore slate adopted by the Senate. Federal law provides that if the House and Senate split, the nod goes to the slate of electors approved by the state's governor. Undoubtedly, Governor Jeb Bush would approve the George W. Bush electors. The entire matter, however, would likely cause an enormous political upheaval and would em-

broil Congress and, possibly, the federal courts in a great constitutional crisis. Many members of Congress hoped that the struggle would somehow be resolved without involving them in this
way.[31]

THE DECISION AND THE APPEAL

Before the Florida legislature could act and in the wake of the
U.S Supreme Court's inconclusive verdict, Leon County Circuit
Court judge L. Sanders Sauls rendered his verdict in what turned
out to be the opening phase of Gore's effort to contest the certification of the election. On December 4, Judge Sauls ruled
against each and every point of Gore's legal case. Judge Sauls
held that Gore had failed to prove that the election had been
conducted improperly or that further hand counts would change
the results. Sauls declined to order further counts; refused to
award Gore any of the disputed or partially recounted votes in
Nassau, Miami-Dade, or Palm Beach Counties; refused to order
Palm Beach County to use the Broward County recount standard; and refused to appoint a special master as requested by
Gore. In short, Judge Sauls's decision was a total victory for
Bush.

Gore attorney David Boies immediately appealed Sauls's decision to the Florida Supreme Court, essentially raising the same issues that had been presented to Sauls. While the state supreme
court continued to deliberate, Gore was handed a setback by the
Seminole and Martin County Circuit Courts. The two courts ruled
that Republican election workers had engaged in improper activities, but these actions did not justify negating more than twenty
thousand ballots cast by innocent persons. Bush had won again
and seemed close to finally capturing Florida's vote and the presidency.

Later that same day, however, Bush's chances again appeared to
be in jeopardy. The Florida Supreme Court announced its verdict
in Gore's appeal of Judge Sauls's decision. While Sauls had given

Bush a total victory, Florida's highest court, in a 4–3 decision, reversed Sauls and ruled in favor of Gore. First, the court ordered the Leon County Circuit Court to begin an immediate review of approximately nine thousand ballots from Miami-Dade County, looking for lawful votes that might have been missed by the automatic tabulating machines. Second, the court ordered Gore credited with approximately 215 votes form Palm Beach County that had been counted after its own previous deadline and subsequently disallowed by Katherine Harris. Third, the court gave Gore a net of 168 votes from Miami-Dade that had been counted before that county decided to abort its hand recount. All in all, the Florida Supreme Court's ruling left Gore, in the immediate run, only about 150 votes behind Bush. This small difference could easily be made up from the nine thousand Miami-Dade votes, especially since the court provided no standard for counting beyond the vague "intent of the voter" criterion, which essentially left the determination of what constituted a vote to the total discretion of the canvassing board. With a single stroke, the Florida Supreme Court had given Gore's candidacy, earlier on the brink of death, new life.

The Florida court's decision sparked enormous controversy. The court's own chief justice, Charles T. Wells, dissented, saying that the decision would lead to a constitutional crisis that would do "substantial damage to our country, our state, and to this Court as an institution." Wells asserted that the trial court's decision should have been affirmed. The Florida state legislature immediately denounced the court and prepared to go into special session for the purpose of selecting a slate of presidential electors pledged to George W. Bush. "We will act at the right time," said Florida Senate president McKay. "It would be irresponsible of us if we failed to put a safety net in place under the current court conditions," he added.[32] Bush campaign spokesperson James Baker acknowledged that the legislature's efforts were being coordinated with those of the campaign. Baker said that Republicans were not prepared to accept a Gore victory stemming from court-ordered recounts. Should Gore emerge the winner as a result of such a re-count, Baker indicated that Republicans would have to make use of the "constitutional remedy" of having the state legislature choose a slate of pro-Bush electors and allowing Congress to choose between them.[33] For their part, Republicans in the U.S. Congress indicated they were now ready to do battle, castigating Florida's high tribunal as a "runaway court." As both sides prepared for an escalation in the political struggle, the stage seemed to be set for the naming of contending slates of electors and a ferocious battle on Capitol Hill.

THE SUPREME COURT REENTERS THE FRAY

Against this backdrop, attorneys for George W. Bush appealed the Florida court's new decision to the U.S. Supreme Court. Their brief declared that the vote recount mandated by Florida's Supreme Court was, "virtually guaranteed to incite controversy, suspicion and lack of confidence not only in the process but in the result that such a process would produce." "The U.S. Constitution," said Bush's attorneys, "leaves it to the legislature exclusively to define the method of effecting the object of appointing electors. . . . The Florida legislature effected a carefully crafted scheme to govern the appointment of presidential electors. . . . By rewriting that statutory scheme—thus arrogating to itself the power to decide the manner in which Florida's electors are chosen—the Florida Supreme Court substituted its judgement for that of the legislature in violation of Article II."

Bush's attorneys asked the U.S. Supreme Court to take the rather drastic step of halting the recounts ordered by the Florida court pending oral argument. Such a move would generally only be undertaken in extreme cases where a majority on the Court felt that the plaintiff was likely to prevail in the end while in the meantime, "irreparable harm" to the plaintiff's interests would occur if the offensive activity were allowed to continue.

In their own filing with the High Court, Gore's attorneys as-

serted that Florida votes needed to be recounted, as ordered by
the Florida Supreme Court, in order to make certain that the
choice of Florida's presidential electors comported with the actual outcome of the popular vote in the state. The Florida
Supreme Court, argued Gore's attorneys, held that "in order to
determine whether lawfully cast ballots have been wrongfully
excluded from the certified vote tally in this election, they must
be examined." The brief declared that U.S. Supreme Court intervention in the case "would run an impermissible risk of taint-
ing the result of the election in Florida—and thereby the
nation." The brief went on to warn that even if ballots were not
officially counted, Florida's "sunshine law," which opens access
to public documents, would guarantee that journalists and
scholars would eventually see the tallies and, perhaps, discover
that a sitting president had actually lost the election.[34] Gore
lawyers also contended that the December 12 deadline for the
naming of electors was not sacrosanct but could be extended to
allow time for additional recounts.

By a 5–4 vote, the High Court stunned most legal observers by
order the counting to stop. It appeared that the Court's conservative majority was determined to rule in favor of Bush's appeal and
feared that allowing the hand recount to continue might produce
evidence that Gore had really won the election. This, in turn,
might undermine the legitimacy of Bush's victory. As Justice Antonin Scalia put it in a separate opinion concurring with the stay
order, "Irreparable harm" might occur if "the counting of votes
that are of questionable legality" would impair the legitimacy of
the election. Democrats sought to put the best face on this turn of
events, but the outcome appeared foreordained. The fact that the
Court had ordered a stay of the tabulations virtually guaranteed
that a majority of the justices were prepared to rule in Bush's
favor.

The Supreme Court heard oral arguments on December 11.
Theodore Olson once again presented the Bush case, David Boies
presented Gore's case, and another attorney represented the

Florida secretary of state. Olson reasserted the points made many times by Bush's attorneys. The U.S. Constitution and federal statute, he said, gave the state legislature the preeminent position when it came to the selection of presidential electors. While courts might interpret the legislature's intent, the Florida court, he said "passed far beyond the normal limits of statutory construction" when it ordered recounts. Moreover, said Olson, to allow hand recounts of selected ballots, as mandated by the Florida Supreme Court, violated the basic constitutional principles of due process and equal protection of the law by not treating all ballots in the same way. David Boies presented Gore's case. Boies contended that the Florida court was simply interpreting Florida law when it ordered a hand recount. He argued that under longstanding Florida law, hand recounts were appropriate to discern voters' intentions where these could not be ascertained by machine tabulation.

As the justices questioned the attorneys, it became clear that members of the Court's liberal and conservative blocs had very different positions on the recount case. Conservative justices Kennedy, Rehnquist, Scalia, and O'Connor were sharply critical of the Florida Supreme Court and of Boies's contention that it was not superseding the intent of the legislature when it ordered recounts. O'Connor, for example, took sharp issue when Boies argued that the Florida Supreme Court was entitled to the deference the justices usually show to state courts. "You are responding as though there were no special burden [on the part of the Florida court] to show some deference to legislative choices," she said.[35] Justice Kennedy attacked Boies's contention that the so-called intent of the voter standard offered any real guidance for the uniform hand counting of ballots and suggested that this so-called standard was so general as to threaten equal protection.

Justice Scalia went so far as to intervene when Bush attorney Theodore Olson responded to a question from Justices Souter and Ginsburg. Scalia evidently sought to assure that Olson did not concede too much to the Gore argument. "It's part of your submission, I think," Scalia said, "that there is no wrong when a machine does not count those ballots that it's not supposed to count?" Scalia was seeking to remind Olson that when voter error rendered a ballot unreadable by a tabulating machine, it was not appropriate for a court to order them counted by hand. "The voters are instructed to detach the chads entirely," Scalia said, "and if the machine does not count those chads where those instructions are not followed, there isn't any wrong." Olson was happy to accept Scalia's reminder.[36]

For their parts, liberal justices Breyer, Souter, Stevens, and Ginsburg were quite critical of Olson's case. If the problem was uniformity, asked Souter and Breyer, why not send the case back to Florida for the imposition of a uniform recount standard? Justice Souter angrily attacked Olson's contention that the Florida court had acted improperly in ordering a recount making it "virtually impossible" resolve the election by the December 12 deadline. "If your concern was with impossibility, asked Souter, why didn't you let the process run instead of asking for a stay?" Liberal justices appeared to be experimenting with the idea of sending the case back to Florida with instructions to the state court to develop a uniform statewide standard for manually counting ballots. Olson, of course, resisted this idea as did Chief Justice William Rehnquist who said that sending the case back would only pave the way for more appeals and very likely another U.S. Supreme Court hearing.[37]

The Court deliberated for two days. During this period, a special session of the Florida House got under way and voted to approve a slate of Bush electors. The state Senate was poised to follow suit if necessary. The Supreme Court, however, made the issue moot when it handed down its verdict on December 13. In the appeal from the Florida Supreme Court's earlier recount decision, the High Court had been unanimous but equivocal. This time the Court was definitive but sharply divided. The Court ruled decisively in favor of Bush's position, effectively ending Al Gore's election contest and presidential hopes. Seven of the nine justices agreed that the recount ordered by the Florida Supreme Court violated the U.S. Constitution's equal protection provision because it failed to establish a consistent standard for counting the disputed ballots. The Court split 5–4 however, on the question of what to do. The Court's five conservatives said the deadline for states to choose their electors had been December 12, leaving no time for further recounts. Chief Justice Rehnquist, writing for the majority, also said that the Constitution provided that the state legislators, not the courts, should decide how presidential electors are appointed. Anticipating criticism of the Supreme Court's intervention, Justice Rehnquist wrote, "None are more conscious of the vital limits on judicial authority than are the members of this court. . . . When contending parties invoke the process of the courts, however, it becomes our unsought responsibility to resolve the federal and constitutional issues the judicial system has been forced to confront."

The four dissenting justices were divided among themselves. Justices Breyer and Souter agreed that the uneven standards existing for the counting of votes in Florida posed an equal-protection problem but thought there was still time for recounts with a more explicit standard. The remaining justices, Ginsburg and Stevens, found no constitutional problems with the Florida Supreme Court's ruling. In his dissent, Justice Stevens said the majority opinion smacked of partisan politics. The opinion, he said, "can only lend credence to the most cynical appraisal of the work of judges throughout the land." He concluded, "Although we may never know with complete certainty the identity of the winner of this year's presidential election, the identity of the loser is perfectly clear. It is the nation's confidence in the judge as an impartial guardian of the rule of law." Justice Stevens's dissent did not change the outcome. Throughout the nation, Democrats saw the Supreme Court majority's opinion as a blatantly partisan decision. Nevertheless, the contest was over. The next day Al Gore made a speech conceding the election and, on December 18, 271 presidential electors—the constitutionally prescribed majority—cast their votes for George W. Bush.[38]

POLITICAL CONFLICT AND INSTITUTIONAL STRUGGLE

George W. Bush won the 2000 national presidential election. The final battle, however, occurred outside the electoral arena and ordinary citizens were not the key participants. Rather it was fought in the courts, in the Florida state legislature, and in the executive institutions of the Florida state government by attorneys and a limited number of political activists. In this final battle, some forty lawsuits were filed in the Florida state courts and the U.S. federal courts.[39] Together, the two campaigns amassed nearly $10 million in legal fees during the month of litigation. This does not include the fees accrued by litigants who were not formally associated with either campaign, such as the plaintiffs in the Seminole and Martin County absentee ballot cases. In most of the courtroom battles, the Bush campaign prevailed. Despite two setbacks before the all-Democratic Florida Supreme Court, Bush attorneys won most Florida Circuit Court cases and the ultimate clash before the U.S. Supreme Court whose conservative majority seemed determined to prevent a Gore victory.

Bush defeated Gore not only because he prevailed in the courts but also because he and the Republicans were able to mobilize a powerful set of institutions that gradually wore down their Democratic foes. Democrats controlled the South Florida canvassing boards that endeavored to conduct manual recounts, but this advantage was trumped by GOP control of statewide Florida executive institutions, most notably the governorship and the secretary of state's office. The Republican-dominated Florida legislature, moreover, was prepared to select Bush electors even if the Texas governor lost the court battle, and so gave the GOP an insurance policy against judicial defeat. Republicans were also better able to mobilize political activists and party notables to exert pressure on the ground in Florida.

While they deployed their institutional resources, both sides sought to suppress large numbers of popular votes that had already been cast. Bush fought to block recounts that might have revealed additional votes, while forces supporting Gore worked to negate military ballots as well as thousands of absentee ballots in Seminole and Martin Counties. Although the national news media continually claimed that the so-called battle for public opinion was every bit as important as the legal and institutional struggle, this claim was patently false. Public opinion was not totally irrelevant, but the two candidates' occasional public appearances were not really designed to bolster popular enthusiasm. They were intended more to strengthen the resolve of important political allies and to induce contributors to continue financing a battle that cost at least $10 million. According to the Federal Election Commission, Bush raised $6 million for the Florida battle, mainly in small contributions, while Gore raised almost $4 million, primarily in large donations from Democratic party loyalists. These figures do not include the money spent for the battle by the two parties or Florida government agencies. While their public appearances were rare, the candidates spent hours on the telephone each day calling contributors. Al Gore, for one, fully understood the limited role of the mass public in the battle. In response to a reporter's question about the role of public opinion in the presidential struggle, Gore said, "I'm quite sure that the polls don't matter in this, because it's a legal question."[40] This was a rather significant observation from a candidate for the presidency of the United States.

During the course of the struggle, the media pointed with pride to the fact that an all-out battle between the nation's two major political parties was being resolved peacefully. There were no tanks or troops in the streets as there might have been in other countries. On a typical day, fewer than a score of protesters stood outside the vice president's residence on Massachusetts Avenue in Washington, D.C. The absence of political ferment was said by the national media to indicate the maturity of U.S. democracy and Americans' profound respect for the rule of law. To be sure, tanks in the streets are hardly to be desired. Yet the absence of expressions of popular political emotion, the paucity of demonstrators, and the near absence of any kind of popular political action or protest during the course of the battle for the presidency should not be seen as symptoms of the United States's political well-being. Quite the contrary. The final struggle over the presidency involved at most a few thousand political leaders and activists. As for citizens at-large, some watched the battle on television or followed newspaper accounts, but most paid limited attention to the Florida struggle. They were, as the polls suggested, prepared to accept either outcome. Little popular feeling was expressed and few demonstrators were in evidence, not because Americans are so mature but because most knew the political struggle they were witnessing did not involve them.

7

Electoral Mobilization, Institutional Combat, and Governmental Power

THE GROWING IMPORTANCE OF institutional forms of political combat has significant consequences for the coherence and vitality of American government. Contemporary American politics undermines governance in four ways.

WHO GOVERNS?

First, elections today fail to accomplish what must be the primary task of any leadership selection process: They fail to determine *who will govern*. An election should award the winners with the power to govern. Only in this way can popular consent be linked to effective governance. Today elections not only fail to determine who will govern but also do not definitively determine *who will not exercise power*. Given the political potency of nonelectoral modes of political struggle, electoral defeat does not deprive the losing party of the power to undermine the programs and policies of the winner. Indeed, as we have seen, electoral verdicts can now be reversed outside the electoral arena.

As a result, even as the "winners" in the American electoral process do not acquire firm control of the government, so the "losers" are not deprived of power. Instead "winners" and "losers" typically engage in a continuing struggle, which often distracts them from real national problems. Indeed, the failure of political leaders to organize and mobilize strong popular bases leaves them weak and vulnerable to the institutions and interests, including the mass media, upon which they are now so dependent. Party politicians once had stable, organized, popular followings that could be counted upon when their leaders came under fire. As Chicago's longtime machine mayor Richard J. Daley once said in response to media attacks, "When you've got the people behind you you don't need the media. . . . The media can kiss my ——!" Contemporary politicans seldom have well-organized followings. Lacking such a base of support, they seldom can afford Mayor Daley's indifference to his media image.

Today elected officials subjected to RIP attacks often find that their poll standings (today's substitute for an organized popular base) can evaporate overnight and their capacity to govern disappear with them. Thus, the Nixon administration was paralyzed for three years by the Watergate affair, the Reagan White House for two years by the Iran-contra affair, the Clinton White House was distracted by Whitewater, and Newt Gingrich's popularity and leadership were compromised by attacks on his character. This is hardly a recipe for a strong government able to deal with America's problems.

An extremely strong economy helped President Bill Clinton maintain high approval ratings despite the media frenzy surrounding the Monica Lewinsky scandal. For months in 1998, however, the president and his closest advisers were preoccupied with the investigations and the avalanche of subpoenas demanding testimony and records. Many top White House aides were able to do little but deal with daily media disclosures and hope they might avoid further subpoenas and legal bills.[1] During this period, the president's ability to promote his domestic agenda was sharply reduced, much as Newt Gingrich's ability to advance the GOP's agenda had been derailed by RIP attacks two years earlier. Thus, the postelectoral attack on Clinton brought about a collapse of Democratic leadership in the White House, something the 1996 elections had failed to accomplish. Even as America sought to cope with terrorism in 2001–02, some of President Bush's foes considered attempting to link the administration to the Enron scandal, a move that would surely place political considerations above the national interest.

DUAL SOVEREIGNTY

The second way in which contemporary political patterns undermine governance in the United States has to do with the separation of powers. Conflict between the political forces controlling Congress and those controlling the presidency is built into the American system of government. Today, however, the separation of powers mandated by the Constitution is becoming what amounts to a system of dual sovereignty. In a separation of powers system, the power to govern is shared by disparate institutions. If government is to function, each branch must secure a measure of cooperation from the others. For example, the framers of the Constitution provided roles for both the president and Congress in the enactment of legislation. However, the growing prominence of institutional combat in America means that such cooperation often cannot be secured.

By disrupting the traditional system of shared powers, the increasing prevalence of institutional combat has encouraged the major branches of government to develop various formal and informal means of governing autonomously. Thus, forces controlling the White House have often undertaken to strengthen the presidency and to enhance its ability to pursue both foreign and domestic objectives independently of Congress. As we have seen, the Reagan administration sought to place control of major foreign and defense policies in the hands of the president's National Security Council. Moreover, it sought to circumvent Congress and rely on the Treasury Department and the Federal Reserve to manage the nation's economy. In a similar vein, through Executive Order 12291, which centralized control over federal regulations in the OMB, President Reagan sought to disrupt ties between Congress and administrative agencies, a disruption that would greatly enhance the legislative powers of the presidency.

Similarly, political forces controlling Capitol Hill have often sought to strengthen Congress and to provide it with the capacity to develop and implement policies independently of the White House. Congress has greatly increased its autonomous control over policy formulation by establishing or bolstering such congressional agencies as the Congressional Budget Office (CBO) and the General Accounting Office (GAO), as well as by expanding the staffs of its committees and subcommittees. Over the past decades the size of committee staffs has nearly doubled in the Senate and more than tripled in the House. Congress has also enhanced its ability to act autonomously by drafting detailed statutes that reduce the discretion of executive agencies and by deploying its augmented staff to monitor agency compliance with the priorities of Congress, its committees, and its subcommittees.

Congress and the White House are thus able to pursue independent and even contradictory policies. The example that has most frequently been commented on involves policy toward Central America. At the same time that the Reagan administration was seeking to mobilize support in the Central American region for the contra forces in Nicaragua, House Speaker Jim Wright and other members of Congress were conducting their own negotiations with Central American heads of state premised upon American abandonment of the contras. Moreover, this was not the only time Congress and the president embarked upon contradictory courses of action. While the Reagan administration was pursuing policies of "constructive engagement" in South Africa, Congress enacted trade sanctions against the Afrikaner regime. Similarly, while the Reagan administration, concerned with the fate of American military bases, sought to buttress the power of Philippine dictator Ferdinand Marcos, Chairman Stephen Solarz of the House Subcommittee on Asian Affairs was conducting hearings on Marcos's business dealings with the intention of discrediting him. Ultimately, opposition to Marcos in the U.S. Congress and the American media played a central role in the chain of events that led to his ouster.

Despite their various efforts, neither presidents nor Congress have acquired sufficient formal authority to govern autonomously. As a result, they have frequently sought to work through other institutions, including nongovernmental entities. The problems confronting presidents and Congress are akin to those faced by rulers in early modern Europe. Seeking glory abroad and grandeur at home, but not commanding the apparatus of a modern state, those rulers were compelled to draw on the resources of nongovernmental institutions. Contemporary America possesses such a state apparatus, but neither the White House nor Congress acting on its own is able to control it fully. The institutional expedients executive and legislative officials have adopted to cope with this problem bear striking resemblances to those devised by Renaissance princes.

Lacking adequate revenue systems, monarchs in the sixteenth and seventeenth centuries made use of tax farmers and bankers for funds.[2] This, in effect, is what the Reagan and Bush administrations have done over the past decade. The United States of course created an enormously productive revenue system in the 1940s based upon the progressive income tax. This system permitted politicians to win the support of a host of disparate interests by regularly enacting new spending programs. The Reagan administration managed, through the rate reductions and indexing provisions of the 1981 tax act, to disrupt this regime of interest group liberalism by reducing the flow of tax receipts upon which it depended.

Unable to secure commensurate reductions in domestic spending, however, and committed to an enormously costly military buildup, the administration was compelled to tap new revenue sources. It did so by devising twentieth-century equivalents of the fiscal techniques of Renaissance monarchs, techniques that endured during the Bush years.

To make up the difference between tax receipts and governmental expenditures, the Reagan and Bush administrations were compelled to borrow two trillion dollars through banks and other financial institutions. Approximately one-third of this sum was supplied by foreign creditors, principally the Japanese. As noted previously, the Reagan and Bush administrations fought to keep American markets open to Japanese products. Japanese financial institutions in turn used profits earned in the American market (by such firms as Toyota and Sony) to purchase U.S. Treasury securities. The financial relationship between America and Japan was codified in the May 1984 report of the Japan-United States Yen-Dollar Committee.[3] Through this extraordinary relationship, the Japanese supply the U.S. Treasury with monies they collect from American consumers, while of course retaining a healthy share for themselves. This is a system of tax farming in all but name. Likewise, the Clinton administration proposed to use the tobacco companies and trial lawyers as its tax collectors. Clinton's 1998 budget proposals called for financing new social spending through the federal government's share of the proposed tobacco settlement between the major tobacco companies and the trial lawyers in 1997.

During the Reagan era the White House also resorted to fifteenth- and sixteenth-century practices in the realm of foreign and military policy. To bolster their military strength, Renaissance princes depended upon condottieri, mercenaries, and privateers.[4] Although the United States possesses an enormous military and intelligence apparatus, since the Vietnam War presidents have had to contend with congressional restrictions on its use. To circumvent limits on its freedom of action in such areas as Central America and Iran, the Reagan administration raised funds from foreign potentates and worked through private firms and freelance operators like Richard Secord and Albert Hakim to hire mercenaries, organize military operations, and conduct diplomatic negotiations. As in early modern Europe, the conduct of public affairs was placed in private hands. For its part, the Bush administration relied heavily on foreign governments to finance America's war effort in the Persian Gulf.

In modern Europe's formative period, rulers employed private parties not only to make war abroad but also to enforce the law at home. Lacking an extensive administrative apparatus, they relied upon such practices as bounty hunting and rewarding complainants and witnesses in order to assist the identification, apprehension, and prosecution of lawbreakers. For similar reasons, bounty hunting was common on the American frontier through the nineteenth century. Lately the Congress, lacking full control over an administrative apparatus, has revived these techniques. In such realms as environmental and consumer legislation as well as disability law and civil rights, Congress has sought to involve private parties in law enforcement by authorizing citizens to bring suit against alleged malefactors.[5] An incentive for such "private attorneys general" has been provided by requirements that convicted offenders pay attorneys' fees that generally far exceed costs to those who brought the suit.

This reversion to tax farming, privateering, and bounty hunting carried with it serious administrative costs. Modern states abandoned these practices precisely because they were inefficient, prone to abuse, and ultimately incompatible with popular sovereignty. Tax farming imposed heavy burdens on citizens while yielding inadequate revenues to the state. Over two decades, for example, the profits collected from American consumers by foreign manufacturers greatly exceeded the funds provided by foreign financial institutions to the U.S. Treasury—to say nothing of the interest that the Treasury obligated itself to pay to foreigners in order to secure these funds. Moreover, this method of raising revenue gave creditors inordinate leverage over the state. As John Brewer

says of tax farming in seventeenth-century England, "in surren-
dering the task of tax gathering to some of its major creditors, the
government ran the risk of financial subordination to . . . [a] con-
sortium controlling the two major sources of state income, namely
loans and taxes."[6] The United States faced precisely this problem
with regard to Japan, which is why the Reagan and Bush administrations were not in a position to insist that it open its markets
to American firms or purchase military aircraft directly from U.S.
manufacturers.

States abandoned the use of mercenaries and privateers because
lacking loyalty to the nation they ostensibly served, they typically
placed their own interests first. America relearned this lesson in its
dealings with arms merchants and private military contractors in
the Iran-contra affair. Moreover, just as bounty hunters were indifferent to larger public concerns such as the rights of the accused, so private litigants cannot be expected to consider the
ramifications for other public goals and policies of the suits they
choose to bring—for example, the economic burden of alternative
methods of pollution control. Thus, administrative expedients that
were already inadequate in the early modern era are even less well
suited to the governance of a twentieth-century state.

THE DESTRUCTION OF ADMINISTRATIVE CAPACITY

Third, contemporary patterns of institutional combat exacerbate
the administrative incoherence of the American state. Over the
past two decades Congress and the political forces with which it is
allied have sought to acquire administrative capacities independent
of the White House. Congress has restricted the discretion of presidentially appointed administrative officials, increased committee
and subcommittee involvement in agency decision making, opened
agencies to direct interest group participation in administrative
rule making, and expanded opportunities for judicial intervention
in administration. These efforts promote fragmentation in the

executive branch and can disrupt administrative processes. Attempts by the White House to reassert its authority over the executive branch have often done more to intensify than to remedy these problems.

One way in which Congress and its allies have sought to gain control over administrative processes is by drafting legislation that specifies in great detail the standards governing administrative conduct. The most familiar examples are the environmental statutes enacted during the 1970s, which set strict standards for air and water quality and the means through which they are to be met. The statutes have often precluded administrators from taking account of changes in technology, cost considerations, economic impact, and other public ends in supervising industry compliance with the legislation.[7]

Congress has also undertaken to subject administrative agencies to control by its committees and subcommittees.[8] Over the past twenty-five years the number of subcommittees in the House of Representatives has increased by more than 25 percent to 130, and the size of committee and subcommittee staffs has more than tripled. These increases have enabled Congress to scrutinize more closely than ever before the activities of administrative agencies, both through direct supervision by congressional staff and through frequent oversight hearings. In addition, by including legislative veto provisions in statutes and issuing detailed committee reports that the courts recognize as evidence of legislative intent, Congress gives its committees control over agency decisions.

Congress's ability to prevent the Reagan administration from imposing its own priorities on the Legal Services Corporation (LSC) provides some of the most striking examples of this phenomenon.[9] During the 1960s and 1970s Legal Services attorneys won numerous class action suits expanding the rights of welfare recipients, tenants in public housing projects, and the clients of other public programs serving the poor. In its first year in office the Reagan administration sought to abolish the corporation, but this move was blocked by Congress. The administration was able, however, to appoint a majority of the corporation's directors, and they urged that agency attorneys focus their efforts exclusively on routine domestic relations and personal credit problems rather than class action suits and political advocacy.

Congressional subcommittees with jurisdiction over the agency were able to frustrate completely the administration's efforts. When the new board sought to introduce accounting and reporting requirements that would enable it to monitor the activities of staff attorneys, Congress responded to appeals from agency staffers and killed the requirements. This effectively prevented the board from ascertaining how agency funds were spent and how employees spent their time. Congressional subcommittees also blocked the board's efforts to eliminate funding for programs it sought to abolish. In addition, the chairman of the Senate subcommittee with jurisdiction over the agency's appropriations prevented the board from implementing a regulation that would have prohibited Legal Services lawyers from engaging in lobbying and other political activities. In the case of the LSC, as in many others, congressional committees and subcommittees all but took charge of running the agency. Because there are more than 250 of these congressional units, their increasing role in administration is leading toward the emergence of a plural executive in the United States. During the mid-1990s the destruction of national administrative capacity as a result of partisan struggle took a new form. As we saw earlier, this was called devolution. Republicans proposed devolving administrative responsibilities for most, if not all, social services from the national government to the states. The welfare reform bill enacted in 1997 represented a step in this direction. GOP leaders regard the national government's social service and regulatory agencies as part of the Democratic party's bureaucratic empire and see devolution as a means of reducing the political power of their foes. In so doing, however, Republicans are also robbing the national government of significant portions of its administrative capacity.

During the past two decades the coherence of the American state has also been undermined by the growing involvement of interest groups in administrative decision making. Having no commitment to executive prerogatives, Congress increasingly has authorized interest groups to participate directly in administrative rule making. Groups that enjoy access to Congress can in effect write their own priorities into law.

For example, the 1972 act authorizing the Consumer Product Safety Commission (CPSC) established a process through which consumer groups could petition the agency to regulate new products and even develop specific rules for the agency to adopt. In 1981 probusiness forces were able to defeat consumer forces in Congress, amending the act so as to give business the same sort of influence over CPSC rule making that consumer groups had formerly enjoyed. The agency, for instance, was now required to invite product manufacturers to propose voluntary safety standards and to give these preference over its own mandatory rules.[10]

Finally, Congress has greatly increased the role of the courts in administrative processes. The courts' increased role provides another channel for interest groups to exert influence over executive agencies, and it often hinders agencies from carrying out any administrative task opposed by any group or individual with the resources to hire a lawyer. For example, the 1970 statute that established the EPA provided interest groups with opportunities to appeal virtually every agency decision in the courts. This has compelled the EPA to adopt such cumbersome decision-making procedures that it has difficulty accomplishing anything at all.[11]

The White House's response to efforts by Congress and its allies to assert control over administrative agencies has often sparked conflicts that further undermine the capacity and coherence of the executive branch. During the Nixon years, for example, the administration imposed personnel ceilings on agencies it deemed to be too closely tied to Congress, resulting in hampered agency performance. Congress responded by adopting legislation setting strict personnel floors for the agencies involved. Frozen by statute, these floors reduced managerial flexibility and agency efficiency.[12] In the Reagan and Bush years, conflicts between the White House and Congress disrupted the functioning of a number of departments and agencies, including the Justice Department, the EPA, the Civil Rights Commission, and the Economic Development Administration.

WHY WOULD ANYONE WANT THIS JOB?

Finally, in the current political climate, what possible reasons do able individuals have to seek careers in government and politics? In an era when policy disagreements lead to smear campaigns in the media, when independent counsels spend years and millions of dollars probing every last detail of a cabinet secretary's life, when White House staffers can expect continually to need the services of expensive lawyers, why would any reasonable individual seek a career in public life? "People who are thinking about running for office, they're asking themselves, 'Do I want to go down this road?'" said Colorado Democratic Party Chairman Philip Perington.[13] Anyone considering a career in public life would do well to recall the calamitous personal fates of so many of the individuals who came to Washington with Bill Clinton in 1992. Vincent Foster committed suicide. Webster Hubbell was sent to prison. Mike Espy and Henry Cisneros were indicted by federal grand juries. Nearly forty staff members, not charged with the commission of any crime, nevertheless faced enormous legal bills as a result of being called to testify before congressional committees and federal grand juries. Margaret Williams, the former chief of staff to Hillary Rodham Clinton, incurred $350,000 in personal legal expenses. Clinton aide Harold Ickes incurred more than $250,000 in legal fees. Even a minor state official caught up in a national political struggle might face the prospect of debilitating legal fees. For example, during the Florida recount struggle in 2000, Republican secretary of state, Katherine Harris, incurred more than quarter of a million dollars in personal legal expenses after she came under withering Democratic fire. "You

have to remember that we're all young people who came into public service with basically no assets and left with exorbitant legal
bills that none of us can afford to pay," said one former White
House staffer.[14] Why, indeed, would any reasonable individual
seek a career in government?

In these ways RIP has become not only a central tactic in the political process but also an epitaph for democratic politics in America.

Electoral Mobilization and Governmental Power

The relationship between political patterns and governmental
effectiveness is a complex one. Practices that severely undermine
governmental capacities in some settings may not in others; witness the ability of Japan to thrive for many decades despite wide-
spread political corruption. But in the United States and elsewhere
political patterns that have seriously inhibited governments from
pursuing collective purposes have at times emerged. For example,
in Israel during the late 1980s electoral stalemate between the
Labor and Likud parties paralyzed the government. The stalemate
prevented the government from responding effectively to uprisings
in the occupied territories and to diplomatic initiatives by the
Palestine Liberation Organization, thereby threatening the relationship with the United States, which is a necessary condition for
Israel's very survival.

Similar examples may be found in American history. In the
United States during the early 1930s prevailing political patterns
led the government to pursue policies that exacerbated rather than
ameliorated the Depression. A particularly notable example is the
Smoot-Hawley Tariff of 1930. The logrolling practices that at the
time characterized the formulation of trade policy in the U.S. Congress led to the adoption of the highest tariffs in American history.
This precipitated foreign retaliation and a virtual collapse of international trade, and it helped turn what could have been an or-

dinary cyclical downturn into the most severe economic crisis of the modern era. Even more striking than the events of the early 1930s were those preceding the Civil War. Political paralysis during the Buchanan administration prevented the government from responding to its own dismemberment as southern states seceded from the Union.

Historically efforts to overcome political patterns that undermine governmental effectiveness have taken one of two forms in the United States: political demobilization or mobilization. Demobilization involves attempts to free government from "political interference" by insulating decision-making processes, restricting political participation, or both. Mobilization consists of efforts by one or another contender for power to overcome political stalemate and governmental paralysis by bringing new voters into the electorate and winning over some of the opposition's supporters. In this way a party can overwhelm its opponents in the electoral arena and take full control of the institutions of government. Such a strategy also provides a party with a mass base of support that can enable it to confront and prevail over entrenched social and economic interests.

Demobilization and insulation were the paths followed by institutional reformers in the United States during the Progressive Era. The Progressives, who spoke for a predominantly middle-class constituency, sought to cope with the problems of turn-of-the-century America by strengthening the institutions of national, state, and local government. Progressives undertook to strengthen executive institutions by promoting civil service reform, creating regulatory commissions staffed by experts, and transferring fiscal and administrative responsibilities from elected to appointed officials.[15] In addition, asserting that the intrusion of partisan considerations undermined governmental efficiency, the Progressives attacked state and local party organizations. They sponsored legislative investigations of ties between party leaders and businessmen and the criminal prosecution of politicians they deemed to be corrupt.[16] They also supported the enactment of personal registration requirements for voting that served to reduce turnout among the poorly educated, immigrant, nonwhite, and working-class voters who had provided party organizations with their mass base.[17] Partly as a result of these measures, voter participation rates in the United States fell by nearly thirty percentage points during the first quarter of the twentieth century, a decline from which they never fully recovered.[18]

In the short run the Progressive strategy of administrative reform did help enhance governmental capacities in the United States. Government agencies penetrated by parties and rife with patronage are not well suited to performing the functions of a modern state. However, politicians are not in a position to prevail over entrenched social and economic forces when they lack the support of an extensive and well-organized mass constituency. In the long run the Progressive strategy of insulation and demobilization undermined the strength of American government relative to powerful interests in civil society and helped produce the low rates of voter turnout that contribute to an indecisive electoral politics in the United States today.

The second strategy—political mobilization—was used most effectively in the United States by the administrations of Abraham Lincoln and Franklin D. Roosevelt. To fight the Civil War and break the power of southern slaveholders, the Lincoln administration vastly expanded the scope of the American national state. It raised an enormous army and created a national system of taxation, a national currency, and a national debt. The extensive organizing and extraordinary popular mobilization that brought the Republicans to power in 1860 enabled them to raise more than two million troops, to sell more than two billion dollars in bonds to finance the military effort, and to rally popular support for the war. The higher levels of party organization and political mobilization in the North than in the South, as much as the superiority of northern industry, help explain the triumph of the Union cause in the Civil War.[19]

The Roosevelt administration permanently transformed the American institutional landscape, creating the modern welfare and regulatory state.[20] The support that the administration mobilized through party organizations and labor unions helped it contend with opposition to its programs both inside and outside the institutions of government. A marked increase in electoral turnout, a realignment of some existing blocs of voters, and a revitalized Democratic party apparatus provided Roosevelt with the enormous majorities in the electoral college and Congress that allowed him to secure the enactment of his programs.[21] Worker mobilization through unions and strikes forced businessmen to accept the new pattern of industrial relations the administration was seeking to establish.[22]

Demobilization versus Mobilization in Contemporary Politics

The problems facing the United States at the dawn of the twenty-first century are not as acute as those that the nation confronted on the eve of the Civil War or in the aftermath of the 1929 stock market crash. Nevertheless, America's political processes impede governmental responses adequate to the challenges that the nation faces, including the maintenance of prosperity and American security in the post–Cold War Era.

Of the political expedients adopted and the solutions proposed in recent years for the nation's problems, the majority follow the former of the aforementioned paths—that of political insulation and demobilization. Thus, the often-proposed constitutional amendment requiring a balanced budget would deprive elected officials of discretion over fiscal policy. The bipartisan commissions—increasingly used to overcome governmental stalemate—represent an attempt to insulate government decisions from political pressure. The line-item veto was a misguided attempt to remove "political" criteria from budgeting.

Whatever advantages might be derived from such expedients in the short run, they raise issues of democratic legitimacy, and as the experience of Progressivism suggests, in the long run they are likely to weaken government. The founders of the American

Republic recognized that a strong national government could not be built in the United States on a narrow popular base. As James Wilson observed at the Constitutional Convention of 1787, "raising the federal pyramid to a considerable altitude" required giving it "as broad a base as possible."[23]

It is precisely the narrow base of the "federal pyramid" that underlies governmental disarray in the United States today. As we have suggested in this book, the decay of American electoral democracy—particularly the destruction of party organizations and erosion of voter turnout—has contributed to the emergence of alternative forms of political struggle. This pattern of politics undermines governmental institutions and further discourages voter participation. In its origins, character, and consequences, America's postelectoral political order is linked to low levels of popular participation in politics.

Were one of the parties to mobilize and forge organizational links to new voters, it might put itself in a position to gain control of all the major institutions of government. At the same time mobilization could provide the party with a political base enabling it to prevail over entrenched interests and powerful social forces for the sake of achieving collective national purposes. Under such circumstances, the most debilitating features of the contemporary American policy-making process might be contained.

For the Democrats, a strategy of mobilization presumably would involve a serious effort to bring into the electorate the tens of millions of working-class and poor Americans who presently stand entirely outside the political process. There exists a large gap between the voting participation rates of Americans in upper-middle-, lower-middle-, and working-class occupations. Bringing citizens who currently do not vote into the Democratic party would probably require an organizational and programmatic focus on economic issues that unite poor, working-, and lower-middle-class voters rather than the racial and cultural issues that divide them.

Though it is generally assumed that only the Democrats could benefit from any substantial expansion of the electorate, it is important to note that mobilization is a strategy that could be employed by the Republicans as well.[24] Indeed, in the late 1970s and early 1980s it was the GOP, through its alliance with conservative evangelicals, that made the more concerted effort to bring new voters into the electorate. The extent of Republican organizational efforts was limited, however, and thus so was the party's ability to construct a base of support for conservatism large enough to pose a challenge to Democratic congressional hegemony.

By contrast, Europe's great conservative mobilizers of the nineteenth century, Otto von Bismarck and Benjamin Disraeli, brought millions of new working-class voters into the electorate and constructed extensive party organizations to link them securely to the conservative cause. By sponsoring factory and social legislation, moreover, they appealed to these voters on the basis of their long-term economic concerns, not simply their religious and nationalistic passions. Their counterpart in the United States, Abraham Lincoln, proceeded along similar lines. Nineteenth-century Republican electoral mobilization entailed the construction of party organizations throughout the North and relied on economic appeals as much as on the issues of slavery and union. The most important Republican slogan in 1860, after all, was "Vote yourself a farm, vote yourself a tariff." As these examples suggest, its position as the more conservative of the two major parties does not preclude the contemporary GOP from organizing a broad popular base for itself.

It is not likely, however, that either Democrats or Republicans will be willing to embark on the path of full-scale political mobilization. The electoral histories of both America and Europe demonstrate that strong party organizations are necessary to achieve high levels of electoral participation, particularly at the bottom half of the social scale. Massive organizational efforts would be required to reach the 50 percent of the potential electorate not drawn to the polls by present-day electoral techniques and appeals. These efforts would be difficult in the face of legal and institutional impediments—ranging from voter registration laws to communications technologies—that currently work against higher levels of mobilization. The enactment of legislation such as the 1993 Motor Voter Act might be a halting step in the direction of fuller electoral participation. But by continuing to leave the burden of registration on the individual voter, such legislation hardly seems likely to reach the millions of poor and poorly educated individuals who constitute the hard core of the nonvoting population.

The most important barriers to full-scale voter mobilization in the United States, however, are not legal or technological; they are political. The politicians who have risen to the top in contemporary America learned their skills and succeeded in a low-mobilization environment. And the weapons of institutional combat that have become central in American politics contribute to maintaining such an environment. When they rely mainly on these weapons to compete with one another, politicians provide voters with little opportunity or reason to participate in politics. Indeed, the pattern of smear and endless investigation that characterizes contemporary politics discourages citizens from voting. If all politicians are scoundrels, why bother voting?

Thus, contemporary weapons of institutional combat leave little room for popular participation. Indeed, when they use weapons of institutional combat to discredit one another, political leaders give voters new reasons to refrain from participating.

Conversely, politicians competing for the support of a highly mobilized electorate would have to deal with questions of concern to tens of millions of voters from the bottom of the social hierarchy and would not find it possible to focus on the issues of personal impropriety that loom so large in American politics today. Nor would they find themselves so vulnerable to such charges. In 1944, for example, when Republicans charged that Franklin Roosevelt had used government property for his personal benefit by sending a U.S. Navy destroyer to retrieve a pet he had left behind on the Aleutian Islands, the president ridiculed them for attacking "my little dog, Fala."[25] FDR's links to a mass constituency were too strong to be threatened by the GOP charges, and therefore he was in a position to dismiss them with a derisive quip. Lacking such support, elected officials today are much more vulnerable to personal attacks.

In contrast with the immediate gains that can be realized today by using revelations and investigations to drive opponents from office, the path of mobilization would entail major risks for both parties. For the Republicans, expansion of the electorate could threaten to bring millions of traditionally Democratic poor and minority voters to the polls. As for the Democrats, whatever the potential benefits to the party as a whole, an influx of millions of new voters would create serious uncertainties for current officeholders at the local, state, and congressional levels. Moreover, various interests allied with the Democrats—notably upper-middle-class environmentalists, public interest lawyers, antinuclear activists, and the like—could not be confident of retaining their influence in a more fully mobilized electoral environment. Finally, though it is seldom openly admitted, the truth is that many members of both the liberal and conservative camps are wary of fuller popular participation in American politics. Conservatives fear blacks, and liberals often have disdain for working- and lower-middle-class whites.

As long as these conditions persist, the path of electoral mobilization will not be taken. America's postelectoral political patterns, governmental incapacities, and economic difficulties will endure—and America will continue to pay the price of its undemocratic politics. It is worth noting that during the decade of the 1990s, while American politicians were transfixed by scandals, the nation's foes were gathering strength and plotting their own politics by other means.

Notes

CHAPTER 1

1 In the late nineteenth century, electoral turnout was lower in the states of the former Confederacy than in the rest of the country because blacks were excluded from voting and there was no party competition in the "Solid South."

2 E. E. Schattschneider, *The Semi-Sovereign People* (New York: Holt, Rinehart and Winston, 1960), p. 5; V. O. Key, Jr., *Politics, Parties and Pressure Groups,* 4th ed. (New York: Crowell, 1958), p. 201.

3 Richard Jensen, *The Winning of the Midwest* (Chicago: University of Chicago Press, 1971), chap. 6.

4 In 1868 President Andrew Johnson was impeached by the House of Representatives and avoided conviction and removal by only a single vote in the Senate. Presidents Abraham Lincoln, James Garfield, and William McKinley were assassinated in 1865, 1881, and 1901 respectively. Among the numerous public officials subject to criminal indictments and

prosecutions were the agents of the Treasury Department involved in the Whiskey Ring scandals of the 1870s. Southern politics was beset with extralegal violence by groups such as the Ku Klux Klan. See J. Morgan Kousser, *The Shaping of Southern Politics: Suffrage Restriction and the Establishment of the One-Party South, 1890–1910* (New Haven: Yale University Press, 1974).

5 On the magnitude of electoral fraud and its effect on voter turnout historically, see the debate between Philip Converse and Walter D. Burnham: Philip E. Converse, "Change in the American Electorate," in *The Human Meaning of Social Change,* ed. Angus Campbell and Philip Converse (New York: Russell Sage Foundation, 1972), pp. 263–337.

6 Benjamin Ginsberg, Walter R. Mebane, Jr., and Martin Shefter, "The Disjunction between Political Conflict and Electoral Mobilization in the Contemporary United States." Annual meeting of the American Political Science Association, Washington, D.C., September 1993.

7 Daniel Boorstin, *The Genius of American Politics* (Chicago: University of Chicago Press, 1953).

8 David von Drehle, "Feat of (Henry) Clay: A Defense of the Lost Art of Compromise," *Washington Post,* June 20, 1993, p. C1; Thomas L. Friedman, "Clinton's Gay Policy: Cave-In or Milestone," *New York Times,* July 25, 1993, p. I1.

9 Ginsberg, Mebane, and Shefter, op. cit.

10 Robert Shogan, "Politicians Embrace Status Quo as Nonvoter Numbers Grow," *Los Angeles Times,* May 4, 1998, p. A5.

11 Helen Dewar, "Motor Voter" Agreement Is Reached," *Washington Post,* April 28, 1993, p. A6.

12 Peter Baker, "Motor Voter Apparently Didn't Drive Up Turnout," *Washington Post,* November 6, 1996, p. B7.

13 Owen Ulmann, "What Clinton Has to Fear from a Landslide," *Business Week* (November 11, 1996), p. 51.

14 Paul Gigot, "Scandal's Price: GOP Chops Up Bills Agenda," *Wall Street Journal,* May 1, 1998, p. A14.

15 David R. Mayhew, "Does It Make a Difference Whether Party Control of American National Government Is Unified or Divided?" Paper presented at the annual meeting of the American Political Science Association, Atlanta, Georgia, 1989.

16 R. H. Melton, "Ethics Probe Reaching Critical Stage for Frustrated Gingrich," *Washington Post,* November 4, 1996, p. A17.

17 Jeremy Rabkin, *Judicial Compulsions* (New York: Basic Books, 1989).

18 Martin Shapiro, "The Supreme Court's 'Return' to Economic Regulation," *Studies in American Political Development* 1 (1986), pp. 91–142.

19 78 F. 3rd 1313 (8th Cir.) 1996.

20 Quoted in John Harwood and Edward Felsenthall, "Independent Counsels Range Far Afield," *Wall Street Journal,* January 29, 1998, p. 1.

21 Clarence Page, "Party, Media Get Their Chances," *Memphis Commercial Appeal,* August 20, 1996, p. 8A.

22 Mark Steyn, "The Big Turn-Off," *Sunday Telegraph,* October 13, 1996, p. 36.

23 Howard Kurtz, "The Media and the Fiske Report," *Washington Post,* July 3, 1994, p. A4.

24 David Streitfeld and Howard Kurtz, "Literary Agent Was behind Secret Tapes," *Washington Post,* January 24, 1998, p. 1.

25 Jill Abramson, "Washington's Culture of Scandal Is Turning Inquiry into an Industry," *New York Times* April 26, 1998, p. 1.

CHAPTER 2

1 For a discussion, see Thomas Edsall, "The Democrats Pick a New Centerpiece," *Washington Post National Weekly Edition,* August 24, 1992, p. 14.

2 Thomas B. Edsall and E. J. Dionne, Jr., "Younger, Lower-Income Voters Spurn GOP," *Washington Post,* November 4, 1992, p. 1.

3 Robin Toner, "Pollsters See a Silent Storm That Swept Away Democrats," *New York Times,* November 16, 1994, p. A14.

4 John Judis, "The Contract with K Street," *New Republic* (December 4, 1995), pp. 18–25.

5 Richard L. Burke, "Religious Right Coalition Gains as GOP Turnout Rises," *New York Times,* November 12, 1994, p. 10.

6 Rich Lowry, "How the Right Rose," *National Review* (December 11, 1995), pp. 64–76.

7 Ibid.

8 Ibid.

9 Theda Skocpol, *Boomerang: Clinton's Health Care Effort and the Turn against Government in U.S. Politics* (New York: W. W. Norton, 1996).

10 Neil Peirce, "Second Thoughts about Takings Measure," *Baltimore Sun,* December 18, 1995, p. 13A.

11 Chris Warden, "A GOP Revolution That Wasn't," *Investor's Daily,* January 2, 1996, p. A1.

12 Judis, op. cit.

13 Lorraine LaFemina, "LI Small Firms Petition DC," *LI Business News,* July 3, 1995, p. 1.

14 Edward Segal, "Elect an Entrepreneur," *Home Office Computing* (January 1996), pp. 9–11.

15 Rhodes Cook, "Race of Muted Differences Has the Nation Yawning," *Congressional Quarterly Weekly Report,* vol. 54, no. 42 (October 19, 1996), pp. 2950–53.

16 George Hager, "A Battered GOP Calls Workers Back to Job," *Congressional Quarterly Weekly Report,* vol. 54, no. 1 (January 6, 1996), pp. 53–57.

17 George Hager, "Republicans Throw in Towel on Seven-Year Deal," *Congressional Quarterly Weekly Report,* vol. 54, no. 4 (January 27, 1996), pp. 213–16.

18 Ibid., p. 213.

19 David Rogers, "Spending Pact Marks Major Retreat by GOP Leaders," *Wall Street Journal,* September 30, 1996, p. A20.

20 Elizabeth Drew, *Showdown: The Struggle between the Gingrich Congress and the Clinton White House* (New York: Simon & Schuster, 1996).

21 John E. Harris, "Clinton Had Ingredients for Victory a Year Ago," *Washington Post,* November 4, 1996, p. 1.

22 Rhodes Cook, "Dole's Gamble Gets Spotlight, but Questions Remain," *Congressional Quarterly Weekly Report,* vol. 54, no. 20 (May 18, 1996), p. 1401.

23 Thomas B. Edsall, "Dole Vows to Sign Partial-Birth Abortion Ban," *Washington Post,* September 15, 1996, p. A16.

24 John Harwood, "Dole Presses Hot-Button Issues to Try to Rouse GOP Activists Missing from Campaign So Far," *Wall Street Journal,* October 16, 1996, p. A22.

25 Ira Rifkin and David E. Anderson, "For the Religious Right This Was Certainly No '94," *Washington Post,* November 9, 1996, p. B6.

26 Alison Mitchell, "Stung by Defeats in '94, Clinton Regrouped and Coopted G.O.P. Strategies," *New York Times,* November 7, 1996, p. B1.

CHAPTER 3

1 On the role of nonprofit organizations in the delivery of public services, see Lester M. Salamon, "Rethinking Public Management: Third Party

Government and the Changing Forms of Government Action," *Public Policy,* vol. 29 (Summer 1981), pp. 255–75.

2 Joel Aberbach and Bert Rockman, "Clashing Beliefs within the Executive Branch," *American Political Science Review,* vol. 70 (June 1976), pp. 456–68.

3 Calculated from data on the votes of individuals in identifiably public sector occupations in the 1984 National Election Survey of the University of Michigan Center for Political Studies.

4 Theodore J. Lowi, *The End of Liberalism* (New York: W.W. Norton, 1979).

5 *New York Times*/CBS News 1988 presidential election exit poll, *New York Times,* November 10, 1988, p. B6.

6 Richard Polenberg, *Reorganizing Roosevelt's Government* (Cambridge, Mass.: Harvard University Press, 1966), p. 167; see also Peri Arnold, *Making the Managerial Presidency* (Princeton: Princeton University Press, 1986).

7 Civil Service Assembly, *Civil Service Agencies in the United States, A 1940 Census* (Washington, D.C.: Government Printing Office, 1940), pamphlet no. 16.

8 See Sidney Milkis, "The New Deal, Administrative Reform, and the Transcendence of Partisan Politics," *Administration and Society,* vol. 18 (January 1987), pp. 433–72.

9 Elizabeth Sanders, "Business, Bureaucracy, and the Bourgeoisie: The New Deal Legacy," in *The Political Economy of Public Policy,* ed. Alan Stone and Edward Harpham (New York: Russell Sage Foundation, 1982), pp. 115–42.

10 James Sundquist, *Dynamics of the Party System* (Washington, D.C.: Brookings Institution, 1983), chap. 11.

11 Stephen Erie, *Rainbow's End* (Berkeley and Los Angeles: University of California Press, 1988), chap. 4.

12 Martin Shefter, "Political Incorporation and the Extrusion of the Left: Party Politics and Social Forces in New York City," *Studies in American Political Development,* vol. 1 (1986), pp. 50–90.

13 John Fenton, *Midwest Politics* (New York: Holt, Rinehart and Winston, 1966), chaps. 2–3; see also Richard Valelly, *Radicalism in the States* (Chicago: University of Chicago Press, 1989).

14 David Mayhew, *Placing Parties in American Politics* (Princeton: Princeton University Press, 1986), chap. 2.

15 David Greenstone, *Labor in American Politics* (New York: Knopf,

1969). On the power of organized labor during the postwar period, see Karen Orren, "Union Politics and Postwar Liberalism in the United States, 1946–1979," *Studies in American Political Development,* vol. 1 (1986), pp. 215–54.

16 Peter Marris and Martin Rein, *Dilemmas of Social Reform* (Chicago: Aldine, 1973); Frances Fox Piven and Richard A. Cloward, *Regulating the Poor* (New York: Pantheon, 1971), chap. 9.

17 Daniel Patrick Moynihan, *Maximum Feasible Misunderstanding* (New York: Free Press, 1969), chap. 2; Samuel Beer, "The Modernization of American Federalism," *Publius,* vol. 3 (Fall 1973), p. 75.

18 Robert Salisbury, "Urban Politics: The New Convergence of Power," *Journal of Politics,* vol. 26 (November 1964), pp. 775–97.

19 On the political mobilization of blacks through federal urban programs, see Peter Eisinger, *The Politics of Displacement* (New York: Academic Press, 1980); Rufus Browning, Dale Rogers Marshall, and David Tabb, *Protest Is Not Enough* (Berkeley and Los Angeles: University of California Press, 1984).

20 Lewis Anthony Dexter, "Congressmen and the Making of Military Policy," in *New Perspectives on the House of Representatives,* ed. Robert Peabody and Nelson Polsby (Chicago: Rand McNally, 1963), pp. 305–24.

21 David Vogel, *Fluctuating Fortunes* (New York: Basic Books, 1989), chaps. 3–5; James Q. Wilson, "The Politics of Regulation," in *The Politics of Regulation,* ed. James Q. Wilson (New York: Basic Books, 1980), pp. 357–94.

22 See Charles O. Jones, *Clean Air* (Pittsburgh: University of Pittsburgh Press, 1975); Charles Noble, *Liberalism at Work* (Philadelphia: Temple University Press, 1986); Graham Wilson, *The Politics of Safety and Health* (Oxford, U.K.: Clarendon Press, 1985).

23 Byron Shafer, *The Quiet Revolution* (New York: Russell Sage Foundation, 1985).

24 Nelson Polsby, *Consequences of Party Reform* (New York: Oxford University Press, 1983), chap. 2.

25 Jeremy Rabkin, *Judicial Compulsions* (New York: Basic Books, 1989).

26 Lawrence Dodd and Bruce Oppenheimer, "Consolidating Power in the House: The Rise of a New Oligarchy," in *Congress Reconsidered,* 4th ed., ed. Lawrence Dodd and Bruce Oppenheimer (Washington, D.C.: Congressional Quarterly Press, 1989), pp. 39–64.

CHAPTER 4

1 William Schneider, "The Political Legacy of the Reagan Years," in *The Reagan Legacy,* ed. Sidney Blumenthal and Thomas Byrne Edsall (New York: Pantheon, 1988), pp. 51–98.

2 Aaron Wildavsky, *The Politics of the Budgetary Process* (Boston: Little, Brown, 1964).

3 John Ferejohn, "Congress and Redistribution," in *Making Economic Policy in Congress,* ed. Allen Schick (Washington, D.C.: American Enterprise Institute, 1983).

4 Martha Derthick and Paul Quirk, *The Politics of Deregulation* (Washington, D.C.: Brookings Institution, 1985).

5 Peter Gourevitch, *Politics in Hard Times* (Ithaca: Cornell University Press, 1986), chap. 4.

6 Thomas Byrne Edsall, *The New Politics of Inequality* (New York: W.W. Norton, 1985), chap. 3; see also Thomas Ferguson and Joel Rogers, *Right Turn* (New York: Hill and Wang, 1986).

7 For an account of this conflict by a committed supply-sider, see Paul Craig Roberts, *The Supply-Side Revolution* (Cambridge, Mass.: Harvard University Press, 1984), chaps. 6 and 7.

8 Theodore J. Lowi, *The End of Liberalism* (New York: W. W. Norton, 1979).

9 Mike Davis, *Prisoners of the American Dream* (London: Verso, 1986), chaps. 4 and 5.

10 William Greider, *Secrets of the Temple* (New York: Simon and Schuster, 1987).

11 The 1984 election data in this chapter are from the National Election Survey of the University of Michigan's Center for Political Studies. The 1988 data are from the *New York Times*/CBS News exit poll, *New York Times,* November 10, 1988, p. B6.

12 Steven Brint, "New Class and Cumulative Trend Explanations of the Liberal Political Attitudes of Professionals," *American Journal of Sociology,* vol. 90 (July 1984), pp. 30–71.

13 Ira Katznelson, *City Trenches* (Chicago: University of Chicago Press, 1982); John Mollenkopf, *The Contested City* (Princeton: Princeton University Press, 1983), chap. 3.

14 Michael Goldfield, *The Decline of Organized Labor in the United States* (Chicago: University of Chicago Press, 1987).

15 Arthur Maass, "U.S. Prosecution of State and Local Officials," *Publius,* vol. 17 (Summer 1987), pp. 195–230.

16 Connie Paige, *The Right to Lifers* (New York: Summit, 1983).

17 V. O. Key, Jr., *Southern Politics* (New York: Random House, 1949); see also J. Morgan Kousser, *The Shaping of Southern Politics* (New Haven: Yale University Press, 1974).

18 Benjamin Ginsberg, *The Captive Public* (New York: Basic Books, 1986), chap. 4.

19 Daniel Wirls, *Buildup: The Politics of Defense in the Reagan Era* (Ithaca, N.Y.: Cornell University Press, 1992).

20 Barton Gelman, "Breaches by Nominee," *Washington Post,* July 8, 1993, p. A15.

21 Cf. Paul Peterson, "The New Politics of Deficits," in *The New Direction in American Politics,* ed. John Chubb and Paul Peterson (Washington, D.C.: Brookings Institution, 1985), chap. 13. On the electoral uses of macroeconomic policy, see Edward Tufte, *Political Control of the Economy* (Princeton: Princeton University Press, 1978); Douglas Hibbs, *The American Political Economy* (Cambridge, Mass.: Harvard University Press, 1987), chaps. 7–9.

22 Robert Gilpin, *The Political Economy of International Relations* (Princeton: Princeton University Press, 1987), chap. 8.

23 For discussions of the reforms mandated by the Republican leadership of the 104th Congress, see Mary Jacoby, "New GOP Rules Lock in Power," *Roll Call,* December 8, 1994, p. 1; John B. Judis, "House Repairs," *Washington Post,* December 18, 1994, p. C1.

24 Benjamin Sheffner, "Freshmen Make It to Subcommittee Chairs," *Roll Call,* December 15, 1994, pp. 9–11.

25 Gabriel Kahn, "Everyone Gets Fired," *Roll Call,* December 5, 1994, p. 1.

26 Margaret Weir, "In the Shadows: Central Cities' Loss of Power in State Politics," *Brookings Review,* vol. 13, no. 2 (Spring 1995), pp. 16–19.

27 Laurie Kellman, "Uphill Road for Advocacy Bill," *Washington Times,* December 5, 1995, p. A8.

CHAPTER 5

1 Paul E. Peterson and Mark Rom, "Macroeconomic Policymaking:

Who Is in Control?," in *Can the Government Govern?* (Washington, D.C.: Brookings Institution, 1989), pp. 139–84.

2 I. M. Destler, *American Trade Politics: System under Stress* (Washington, D.C.: Twentieth Century Fund, 1986).

3 Robert Gilpin, *The Political Economy of International Relations* (Princeton: Princeton University Press, 1987), pp. 156–70.

4 I. M. Destler and C. Randall Henning, *Dollar Politics* (Washington, D.C.: Institute for International Economics, 1989), chap. 4.

5 Walter LaFeber, *The American Age: United States Foreign Policy at Home and Abroad since 1750* (New York: W. W. Norton, 1989).

6 Benjamin Ginsberg, *The Captive Public* (New York: Basic Books, 1986), chap. 4.

7 Daniel Wirls, "Defense as Domestic Politics: National Security Policy and Domestic Alignments in the 1980s," Ph.D. dissertation, Cornell University, 1988.

8 Pat Towell, "Scandal Highlights Dilemma of Defense Purchasing Process," *Congressional Quarterly Weekly Report,* vol. 46, no. 25 (June 25, 1988), pp. 1723–25.

9 For a discussion of the genesis of this condition, see William Saletan and Nancy Waltzman, "Marcus Welby, J.D.," *The New Republic* (April 17, 1988), pp. 19–24.

10 L. Gordon Crovitz and Jeremy Rabkin, eds., *The Fettered Presidency* (Washington, D.C.: American Enterprise Institute, 1989), pp. 15–116.

11 U.S. Congress, *Report of the Congressional Committees Investigating the Iran-Contra Affair* (New York: Random House, 1988), 37–329.

12 See, e.g., "Europe vs. Arms Control," *Wall Street Journal,* October 24, 1986, p. 28.

13 Steven Pressman, "Public Sympathy Proves Effective Shield for North against Committee," *Congressional Quarterly Weekly Report,* vol. 45, no. 29 (July 18, 1987), pp. 1564–65.

14 This would appear to be consistent with one of Theodore J. Lowi's major points. See Theodore J. Lowi, *The Personal Presidency* (Ithaca: Cornell University Press, 1985).

15 Martin Shapiro, "The Supreme Court: From Warren to Burger," in *The New American Political System,* ed. Anthony King (Washington, D.C.: American Enterprise Institute, 1978), pp. 179–212; see also Martin Shapiro, "Fathers and Sons: The Court, the Commentators and the Search for Values," in *The Burger Court: The Counter-Revolution That*

Wasn't, ed. Vincent Blasi (New Haven: Yale University Press, 1983), pp. 218–38.

16 Jeremy Rabkin, *Judicial Compulsions* (New York: Basic Books, 1989).

17 Mark Silverstein and Benjamin Ginsberg, "The Supreme Court and the New Politics of Judicial Power," *Political Science Quarterly,* vol. 102 (Fall 1987), pp. 371–88.

18 Wards Cove v. Atonio, 109 S.Ct. 2115 (1989).

19 Joan Biskupic, "The Marshall Files: How an Era Ended in Civil Rights Law," *Washington Post,* May 24, 1993, p. 1.

20 Benjamin Weiser and Bob Woodward, "Roe's Eleventh-Hour Reprieve: 89 Drafts Show Court Poised to Strike Abortion Ruling," *Washington Post,* May 23, 1993, p. 1. Webster v. Reproductive Health Services, 109 S.Ct. 3040 (1989); Hodgson v. Minnesota, 110 S.Ct. 2926 (1990); Ohio v. Akron Center for Reproductive Health, 110 S.Ct. 2972 (1990).

21 Penry v. Lynaugh, 109 S.Ct. 2934 (1989); Stanford v. Kentucky, 109 S.Ct. 2969 (1989).

22 Board of Education of Oklahoma City Public Schools v. Dowell, 111 S.Ct. 630 (1991).

23 Rust v. Sullivan, 111 S.Ct. 1759 (1991).

24 Arizona v. Fulminante, 111 S.Ct. 1246 (1991).

25 Lucas v. South Carolina Coastal Council, 112 S.Ct. 2886 (1992).

26 Shaw v. Reno, 113 S.Ct. 2816 (1993).

27 Planned Parenthood of Southeastern Pennsylvania v. Casey, 112 S.Ct. 2791 (1992).

28 Joan Biskupic, "New Term Poses Test for Alliance at Center of Conservative Court," *Wall Street Journal,* October 4, 1992, p. A12.

29 *Chicago Daily Law Bulletin,* October 5, 1994.

30 Joan Biskupic, "Justices Follow a Mostly Conservative Course," *Washington Post,* July 4, 1994, p. 1.

31 Johnson v. DeGrandy, 92-519 (1994); Holder v. Hall, 91-2012 (1994).

32 Adarand Constructors v. Pena, 94-329 (1995); Missouri v. Jenkins, 63 USLW 3889 (1995); Miller v. Johnson, 63 USLW 4726 (1995).

33 Bush v. Vera, 116 S.Ct. 1941 (1996); Shaw v. Hunt, 64 USLW 4437 (1996); Abrams v. Johnson, 95-1425 (1997).

34 Rosenberger v. University of Virginia, 94-329 (1995); Agostini v. Felton, 96-522 (1997).

35 U.S. v. Lopez, 115 S.Ct. 1624 (1995); Printz v. U.S., 95-1478 (1997); Mack v. U.S., 95-1503 (1997); City of Boerne v. Flores, 95-2074 (1997).

36 Employment Division v. Smith, 494 U.S. 872 (1990).

37 Raines v. Byrd, 96-1671 (1997); Clinton v. Jones, 95-1853 (1997).

38 Reno v. A.C.L.U., 96-5611 (1997).

39 U.S. v. Virginia, 116 S.Ct. 2264 (1996); Romer v. Evans, 116 S.Ct. 1620 (1996).

40 Peter Baker and Susan Schmidt, "Starr Searches for Sources of Staff Criticism: Private Investigator Says Clinton Team Hired Him," *Washington Post,* February 24, 1998, p. 1.

41 Howard Kurtz, "Starr Defends Background Talk," *Washington Post,* June 14, 1998, p. A10.

42 David Tell, "Washington Leak in Review," *Weekly Standard,* March 2, 1998, p. 17. See also Howard Kurtz, *Spin Cycle: Inside the Clinton Propaganda Machine* (New York: Free Press, 1998).

43 John F. Harris, "Office of Damage Control," *Washington Post,* January 31, 1998, p. 1.

44 Mark Cunningham, "Media Complex," *National Review* (February 23, 1998), p. 43.

45 Owen Ullman, "What Clinton Has to Fear from a Landslide," *Business Week* (November 11, 1996), p. 51.

46 John Yang, "Staff-Created Handout Prompts Ethics Charge," *Washington Post,* December 6, 1995, p. A8.

47 Jeffrey Katz, "Welfare: After 60 Years, Most Control Is Passing to States," *Congressional Quarterly Weekly Report,* vol. 54, no. 31 (August 3, 1996), pp. 2190–96.

48 Robert Pear, "Resignations Won't Disrupt Welfare Plans, Officials Say," *New York Times,* September 13, 1996, p. A26.

49 "Welfare Take-Back," *Wall Street Journal,* October 2, 1996, p. A18.

50 Judith Havemann and Barbara Vobejda, "Advocacy Groups across U.S. Preparing to Challenge Welfare Law," *Washington Post,* September 30, 1996, p. A8.

51 Alison Mitchell, "Stung by Defeats in '94, Clinton Regrouped and Co-opted G.O.P. Strategies," *New York Times,* November 7, 1996, p. B1.

52 Jeremy Rabkin, "The Reagan Revolution Meets the Regulatory Labyrinth," in *Do Elections Matter?,* ed. Benjamin Ginsberg and Alan Stone (Armonk, N.Y.: M. E. Sharpe, 1986), pp. 221–39.

53 See Terry M. Moe, "The Politics of Bureaucratic Structure," in *Can the Government Govern?*, ed. John Chubb and Paul Peterson (Washington, D.C.: Brookings Institution, 1989), pp. 267–331.

54 Reed Irvine, Letter to the Editor, *New York Times,* December 30, 1984, p. D12.

CHAPTER 6

1 D. W. Miller, "Election Results Leave Political Scientists Defensive over Forecasting Methods," *Chronicle of Higher Education,* November 17, 2000, p. A24.

2 Steven Schier, *By Inivtation Only: Contemporary Party, Interest Group and Campaign Strategies* (Pittsburgh: University of Pittsburgh Press, 2000).

3 John F. Harris, "Clinton and Gore Clashed Over Blame for Election," *Washington Post,* February 7, 2001, p. 1.

4 Ronald Dworkin, "The Phantom Poll Booth," *New York Review,* December 21, 2000, p. 96.

5 Chad Terhune and Joni James, "Presidential Race Brings Attention to Business of Voting Machines," *Wall Street Journal,* November 16, 2000, p. A16.

6 James B. Grimaldi and Roberto Suro, "Risky Bush Legal Strategy Paid Off: Equal Protection Argument, Initially Dismissed as Weak, Proved Pivotal," *Washington Post,* December 17, 2000, p. A32.

7 Adam Nagourney and David Barstow, "G.O.P.'s Depth Outdid Gore Team in Florida," *New York Times,* December 22, 2000, p. A1.

8 Dana Canedy, "How the Troops Were Mobilized for the Recount," *New York Times,* November 28, 2000, p. A23.

9 Susan Schmidt and John Mintz, "Florida's Instant Invasion: How Gore and Bush Rushed in Legal and Political Armies," *Washington Post,* November 26, 2000, p. A1.

10 Nagourney and Barstow, "G.O.P.'s Depth," p. A1.

11 Ibid.

12 Martin Peretz, "All Too Human," *New Republic,* January 1, 2001.

13 John D. McKinnon, "Florida's High Court Isn't Immune to Local Politics," *Wall Street Journal,* November 20, 2000, p. A12.

14 Peter Slevin, "Gore Lawyers Push Court to Include Recount Tally," *Washington Post,* November 19, 2000, p. A21.

15 Phil Kuntz, "What Happens If Florida Can't Declare a Winner?

Experts Debate Constitution," *Wall Street Journal,* November 13, 2000, p. A18.

16 William Glaberson, "Divergent Views Are Argued on the Functions of the Court," *New York Times,* November 21, 2000, p. A15.

17 Jess Bravin and Robert Greenberger, "Bush Warns Top Court of Electoral Catastrophe," *Wall Street Journal,* November 24, 2000, p. A7.

18 Ibid.

19 Lynette Holloway, "Most Populous Area Won't Seek Recount," *New York Times,* November 15, 2000, p. A19.

20 Don Van Natta, "Bush's Slim Lead Holds As Rules Change and Challenges Pile Up," *New York Times,* November 20, 2000, p. A1.

21 Lynette Holloway, "In Stress of Recount, Complaints Get Bizarre," *New York Times,* November 20, 2000, p. A15.

22 Schmidt and Mintz, "Florida's Instant Invasion," p. A1.

23 Susan Schmidt, "Republican Officials Complain About Military Vote Challenges," *Washington Post,* November 19, 2000, p. A23.

24 Richard Perez-Pena, "Military Ballots Merit a Review, Lieberman Says," *New York Times,* November 20, 2000, p. A1.

25 John Mintz, "Court Asked to Speed Action," *Washington Post,* November 28, 2000 p. A9.

26 Don Van Natta and Michael Moss, "New Dispute Over Florida Applications for Ballots," *New York Times,* November 13, 2000, p. A17.

27 Ibid.

28 Mary Leonard, "Justices' Ruling Unanimous, But Not Decisive: Case Sent Back to Florida's High Tribunal," *Boston Globe,* December 5, 2000, p. A39.

29 "Litigation May Prolong Process into 2001," *Washington Post,* November 19, 2000, p. A22.

30 David Barstow and Somini Sengupta, "Florida Governor Backs Lawmakers' Efforts to Bypass Courts and Select Electors," *New York Times,* November 30, 2000, p. A21.

31 David Rosenbaum, "What the House or Senate Could Do, or Not Do, in Picking the President," *New York Times,* November 30, 2000, p. A21.

32 Charles Holmes, "GOP Weighing the Right Time to Play Its Hand," *Atlanta Constitution,* December 11, 2000, p. 10A.

33 Roberto Suro, "Nation Awaits Court's Decision: Both Bush and Gore Camps Warn of Taint on Presidency, but Foresee Reconciliation," *Washington Post,* December 11, 2000, p. A1.

34 Ibid.

35 Linda Greenhouse, "U.S. Supreme Court Justices Grill Bush, Gore Lawyer in Effort to Close the Book on Presidential Race," *New Orleans Times-Picayune,* December 12, 2000, p. 1.

36 Ibid.

37 Charles Lane, "Divided High Court Grills Attorneys for Bush, Gore on Recount Options," *Washington Post,* December 12, 2000, p. A1.

38 All the litigation in the Florida election is discussed in E. J. Dionne and William Kristol, *Bush v. Gore: The Court Cases and the Commentary* (Washington, DC: Brookings, 2001).

39 "In the Courts," *San Diego Union-Tribune,* December 7, 2000, p. A14.

40 Quoted in "Today's News: Gore Pushes On," *Washington Post,* November 29, 2000, p. C15.

CHAPTER 7

1 James Bennet, "In Eerily Calm White House, Remaining in the Dark Helps," *New York Times,* February 12, 1998, p. 1.

2 Margaret Levi, *Of Rule and Revenue* (Berkeley and Los Angeles: University of California Press, 1988), chap. 5.

3 Robert Gilpin, *The Political Economy of International Relations* (Princeton: Princeton University Press, 1987), pp. 328–36.

4 William McNeill, *The Pursuit of Power* (Chicago: University of Chicago Press, 1982), chap. 3.

5 Barry Boyer and Errol Meidinger, "Privatizing Regulatory Enforcement," *Buffalo Law Review,* vol. 34 (1985), pp. 833–956.

6 John Brewer, *The Sinews of Power: War, Money, and the English State, 1688–1783* (New York: Knopf, 1989), p. 93.

7 See, for example, Bruce Ackerman and William Hassler, *Clean Coal/Dirty Air* (New Haven: Yale University Press, 1981); R. Shep Melnick, "Pollution Deadlines and the Coalition for Failure," *Public Interest,* vol. 75 (Spring 1984), pp. 123–34.

8 See, for instance, John Ferejohn and Charles Shipan, "Congressional Influence on Administrative Agencies: A Case Study of Telecommunications Policy," in *Congress Reconsidered,* 4th ed. (Washington, D.C.: Congressional Quarterly Press, 1989), pp. 393–410; Barry Weingast and Mark Moran, "Bureaucratic Discretion or Congressional Control? Regulatory Policy-

making by the Federal Trade Commission," *Journal of Political Economy,* vol. 91 (1983), pp. 765–800.

9 Michael Wallace, "Out of Control: Congress and the Legal Services Corporation," in *The Fettered Presidency,* ed. L. Gordon Crovitz and Jeremy Rabkin (Washington, D.C.: American Enterprise Institute, 1989), pp. 169–84.

10 Terry Moe, "The Politics of Bureaucratic Structure," in *Can the Government Govern?,* ed. John Chubb and Paul Peterson (Washington, D.C.: Brookings Institution, 1989), pp. 289–97.

11 Gary Bryner, *Bureaucratic Discretion* (New York: Pergamon Press, 1987).

12 Louis Fisher, "Micromanagement by Congress: Reality and Mythology," in *The Fettered Presidency,* loc. cit. 151.

13 Donald Lambro, "Sex Scandal Spooks Democratic Recruits: Would-Be Candidates Balk at Scrutiny," *Washington Times,* February 17, 1998, p. 1.

14 Adam Nagourney, "Working for the Clintons Can Mean Big Legal Bills," *New York Times,* February 20, 1998, p. 1.

15 Stephen Skowronek, *Building a New American State* (New York: Cambridge University Press, 1982), chaps. 6–8.

16 Richard L. McCormick, "The Discovery That Business Corrupts Politics: A Reappraisal of the Origins of Progressivism," *American Historical Review,* vol. 86 (April 1981), pp. 247–74.

17 Frances Fox Piven and Richard A. Cloward, *Why Americans Don't Vote* (New York: Pantheon, 1988), chap 3; cf. Philip Converse, "Change in the American Electorate," in *The Human Meaning of Social Change,* ed. Angus Campbell and Philip Converse (New York: Russell Sage Foundation, 1972), pp. 263–301.

18 Walter Dean Burnham, *The Current Crisis in American Politics* (New York: Oxford University Press, 1982), chaps. 1, 2, 4; Paul R. Abramson and John H. Aldrich, "The Decline of Electoral Participation in America," *American Political Science Review,* vol. 76 (September 1982), pp. 502–21; Raymond Wolfinger and Steven Rosenstone, *Who Votes?* (New Haven: Yale University Press, 1980).

19 Eric McKitrick, "Party Politics and the Union and Confederate War Efforts," in *The American Party Systems,* ed. William Nisbet Chambers and Walter Dean Burnham (New York: Oxford University Press, 1967), pp. 117–51.

20 See the essays in Margaret Weir, Ann Orloff, and Theda Skocpol,

eds., *The Politics of Social Policy in the United States* (Princeton: Princeton University Press, 1988).

21 Kristi Anderson, *The Creation of a Democratic Majority, 1928–1936* (Chicago: University of Chicago Press, 1979).

22 David Plotke, "The Wagner Act, Again: Politics and Labor, 1935–37," *Studies in American Political Development,* vol. 3 (1988), pp. 105–56.

23 Max Farrand, ed., *The Records of the Federal Convention of 1787,* vol. 1 (New Haven: Yale University Press, 1966), p. 49.

24 James DeNardo, "Turnout and the Vote: The Joke's on the Democrats," *American Political Science Review,* vol. 70 (June 1980), pp. 406–20.

25 John P. Diggins, *The Proud Decades: America in War and Peace, 1941–1960* (New York: W. W. Norton, 1988), p. 21.

Index

abortion, 19, 27, 54, 67, 148, 160, 164
    opposition to, 51, 64, 65, 68, 69, 114–17
    Supreme Court and, 116, 152, 153, 154,
        159
Abrams, Elliot, 24, 25
Abrams v. Johnson, 156
abstention doctrine, 147
Accuracy in Media, Inc., 169
Adarand Constructors v. Pena, 155
administrative capacity, destruction of,
        219–23
adversarial journalism, growth of, 31, 33
advertising:
    newspaper, 31, 183
    television, 19, 115, 122, 151, 167
affirmative action, 51, 78, 94, 110, 115,
        116, 154, 174
    Supreme Court and, 155, 158, 159
Afghanistan, 138
    Soviet invasion of, 92
African Americans, *see* blacks

Agent Orange, 141
Agostini v. Felton, 156
AIDS, 104
Aid to Families with Dependent Children
        (AFDC), 127, 130–31, 166
Alabama state prison system, 148
Aleutian Islands, 230
Alexander, Lamar, 77
Alliance for Justice, 166
Allison, Graham, 119–20
American Association of Retired Persons
        (AARP), 129
American Labor party, 87
American Legal Foundation, 169
American Legion, 141
American Spectator, 35
Americans with Disabilities Act (ADA), 72,
        136–37
Amish, 157
Angola, 138
antinuclear activists, 20, 231

antitrust laws, 105, 106
antiwar movement, 23, 33, 47, 138
Appleton, Ray, 68
Arizona, 76
  National Federation of Independent
    Business in, 71
Arizona v. Fulminante, 152–53
Arkansas:
  Clinton as governor of, 29, 39, 40, 162
  Clinton business dealings in, 39–40
Armey, Dick, 70
arms control, 140, 146
Arms Export Control Act, 22, 53
arms race, 47, 140
Aron, Nan, 166
Ash Council, 94
Aspin, Les, 120
assassinations, 142, 233*n*
autodollars, 122

Babbitt, Bruce, 25
Baker, James, 136
  election of 2000 and, 170, 181–82, 183,
    203–4
Bane, Mary Jo, 18
banks and banking, 105, 109, 121–22
  interstate, 60
  Japanese, 121–22, 139
Bauer, Gary, 78
Beck, Philip, 183
Berry, Mary Francis, 101
Bismarck, Otto von, 229
Blackmun, Justice Harry A., 150, 154
blacks, 155–56, 164, 238*n*
  conservatives' fear of, 231
  in Democratic party, 48, 50–51, 51, 56,
    58, 88–90, 93, 94, 95–96, 174
  in election of 2000, 175–76, 177
  as voters, 48, 50–51, 56, 68, 233*n*
  see also affirmative action; civil rights
Blackwill, Robert, 119–20
Bliley, Thomas, 124
block grants, 127–28, 166
blue-collar voters, *see* labor and labor unions;
    working class
Board of Education of Oklahoma City v. Dowell,
    152
Boies, David M., 182, 196–97, 202, 205,
    206
Boland amendments, 39, 142
bombing:
  of Cambodia, 37

  of Libya, 53, 115, 138
  of Oklahoma City Federal Building, 68
bonds and bond market, 114, 136
Bork, Robert, 150–51
Bosnia, U.S. troops in, 139
Boston school system, 148
bounty hunting, 218
bracket creep, 105
Brady Bill, 156
Brewer, John, 218–19
Breyer, Justice Stephen, 154, 198, 207, 208
Brooks, Jack, 59
Broward County, Florida, election of 2000
    and, 177, 180, 189, 190–91, 196,
    200
Brown, Floyd, 35
Brown, Ron, 25
B-2 stealth bomber, 141
Buchanan, Patrick, 77
Buchanan administration, 225
budget, New York State, 71
budget, U.S., 18, 68, 96
  balanced, 123, 126
  deficit, *see* budget deficit, U.S.
  1990 crisis, 73–74, 122
  1995-1996 battle over the, 74–75, 76,
    78, 167
  surplus, 174
Budget and Impoundment Act (1974), 22,
    53
budgetary incrementalism, 104–5
budget deficit, U.S., 60
  autodollars and, 122
  in Bush administration, 21, 97, 104, 105,
    122, 136, 139, 217
  Clinton administration and, 60, 137
  defense spending and, 104, 109, 121, 134
  in election of 1992, 122
  foreign financing of, 121–22, 139, 217
  Gramm-Rudman-Hollings and, 134
  institutional combat and, 132–37
  1990 budget crisis and, 122
  in Reagan administration, 72, 97, 105,
    108–9, 121, 132–34, 139, 141, 217
  social spending and, 122
  traditionalist vs. supply-sider view of,
    108–9
budget surplus, 174
Burford, Anne Gorsuch, 84, 120
Burger, Justice Warren, 150
Burnham, Walter D., 234*n*
Burton, Charles, 191

Bush, George H. W. (Bush administration), 33, 38, 66, 95, 105
 budget deficit and, 21, 97, 104, 105, 122, 136, 139
 court appointments of, 151, 153, 166
 defense policy of, 138, 139, 141
 dual sovereignty and, 216–19
 in election of 1988, 109, 111, 115, 146
 in election of 1992, 57, 58, 74, 122
 executive power measured by, 21–22
 Motor Voter vetoed by, 20
 1990 budget crisis and, 73–74, 122
 pardons granted by, 25
 political forces reorganized in, 109, 111, 113–15
Bush, George W. (Bush administration):
 appointments of, battle with Democrats over, 101, 159, 169
 in election of 2000, *see* election of 2000
 executive power exerted by, 22
 homeland security and war on terrorism, 120–21
Bush, Jeb, 181, 183, 185–89, 186, 196–99, 200–1
Bush v. Vera, 155
business, 107–9
 Democratic party and, 57, 94, 106, 107–8
 erosion of labor's accommodation with, 106–7
 Republican party and, 66, 69–71, 92, 107–9, 114, 130
 reunification of, 107–9
 state competition for, 129
 tort reform and, 130
busing, 51, 115, 116, 152
butterfly ballot, 177, 178–79

Cambodia, "secret bombing" of, 37
Campbell, Ben Nighthorse, 58
Campbell, Carlos, 168
capital punishment, 152
Capitol Legal Foundation, 169
Carswell, Judge G. Harrold, 150
Carter, Jimmy (Carter administration), 33, 55, 104
 defense spending in, 117
Casey, William, 142, 144
Catholics:
 in Democratic party, 47
 evangelical Protestants aligned with, 117
 in Republican party, 64, 114
CBS, 169

Central America, 138, 144, 215, 217
 see also individual countries
Central Intelligence Agency (CIA), 91, 138, 142
Chamber of Commerce, U.S., 66
Cheney, Dick, 79, 118–19, 171, 172
Chicago, Illinois, 87
Chief of Naval Operations (CNO), 118
child care, 100–1, 123, 128, 164
Children's Defense Fund, 130
Chiles, Lawton, 187
China, 23
Christian Broadcasting Network, 67
Christian Coalition, 35, 62, 63, 65, 67
Christopher, Warren, 170, 181, 182
CIA (Central Intelligence Agency), 91, 138, 142
Cisneros, Henry, 25, 31, 223
"citizens' militia," 66
"citizen suit" provisions, 148
Citizens United, 35
City of Boerne v. Flores, 156–58
civil rights, 27, 47, 48, 50–51, 88–90, 95, 173
 courts' defense of, 146, 148
 Supreme Court and, 152
Civil Rights Act of 1991, 152
Civil Rights Commission, 101, 223
civil service system, 85, 89, 94, 225
Civil War, 15, 226
class action suits, 146
class structure:
 Gingrich Republicanism and, 69–71
 middle class, *see* middle class
 poor people, *see* poverty and poor people
 upper class, 44, 45, 51, 69
 voter turnout and, 45
Clift, Eleanor, 164
Clinton, Bill (Clinton administration), 13–14, 26–31, 56–61, 72–79, 158–67
 budget deficit and, 60, 137
 compromises of, 18, 137
 congressional investigation of, 13, 22–23, 39, 40, 41, 160–61, 163
 court appointments of, 153–54
 crime bill of, 60–61, 66
 defense spending of, 99, 118
 in election of 1992, 13, 55, 56–58, 76, 103, 122, 154, 173
 in election of 1996, 13, 23, 28, 34, 78–79, 154, 166, 173, 214

Clinton, Bill (*continued*)
    ethics and morality of, 13, 18, 34, 78,
        173
    FBI files used by, 22–23, 40, 161
    financial dealings of, 13, 23, 28, 29,
        39–40
    foreign policy of, 139
    Gore's 2000 presidential campaign and,
        173, 176
    as governor, 29, 39, 40, 160–61
    health care and, 61, 66, 73, 98–100, 137,
        160
    impeachment and, 23, 41, 42
    innovative defenses against investigations
        of, 13, 161–65
    Jones suit and, 27, 35–36, 40, 158, 161
    Lewinsky affair and, 30, 36, 40–41, 162,
        164, 173, 176, 213
    liberal shift of, 59–61
    line-item veto and, 22, 158
    military relations in, 60, 118–20, 160
    Motor Voter Act and, 20
    murder allegations against, 35
    news media and, 13, 162, 164, 213–14
    1993 budget of, 122–23
    in 1995-1996 budget battle, 74–75, 77,
        167
    political reform and, 98–99
    probusiness policies of, 108
    RIP process in, 39–42, 160–63, 165,
        213–14
    social spending of, 123
    Starr investigation of, 13, 29, 30, 31,
        40–41, 161–64
    tobacco industry financing and, 100–1,
        217
    tort reform and, 130
    triangulation strategy of, 75, 173, 174
    welfare reform and, 18, 56, 75, 128,
        130–31, 165, 166, 167
    White House staffers in, fate of, 223–24
    Whitewater investigation of, 25, 29,
        35–36, 39–40, 161, 213
Clinton, Hillary Rodham, 35, 39, 40, 61,
        98, 160, 165, 223
    election to the Senate, 172
    welfare reform and, 167
    Whitewater investigation of, 29, 35, 39
Clinton v. Jones, 158
Clinton v. New York, 158
Coelho, Tony, 61
Cohen, William, 120

Cold War, 57, 91
Cole, James M., 25
Commerce Department, U.S., 127
commodities trading, 39
Common Cause, 92–93, 93
Communication Decency Act, 158
competition, 60, 106, 109
    foreign, 121, 122
    state, 129
Comprehensive Employment and Training
        Act (CETA), 113
compromise, political:
    in antebellum era, 15
    of Clinton, 18, 137
    in 1950s and 1960s, 18
Compromise of 1850, 15
Compromise of 1876, 15
Congress, U.S., 21–24, 28–33, 47–51,
        91–92
    attacks on leaders of, 14
    conflict measurement in, 18, 19
    courts and, 147–49, 156–58
    Democratic control of, *see* Democrats and
        Democratic party, Congress
        controlled by
    Democratic entrenchment and, 81–84
    destruction of administrative capacity
        and, 219–23
    dual sovereignty and, 214–16, 218
    elections, *see* congressional elections
    executive power vs., *see* executive branch,
        legislative power vs.
    independent counsel and, 27–31, 38
    leaks to, 37, 84
    104th, 71, 79, 123–30, 240*n*
    Rayburn-Johnson, Eisenhower White
        House and, 23
    Republican control of, *see* Republicans
        and Republican party, Congress
        controlled by
    spending of, 21, 37
    TV used by, 32, 39, 41, 144–45, 151
    see also House of Representatives, U.S.;
        Senate, U.S.
Congressional Budget Office (CBO), 125,
        215
congressional elections:
    Democratic success in, 41–42, 48–49
    midterm, 18, 40, 41–42, 58–59, 79, 123
    Republican failure in, 41–42, 52, 54
    role of volunteers and activists in, 62–63,
        80

voter turnout in, 16, 18, 79, 80
  see also specific elections
congressional investigations, 14, 124–26
  of Clinton, 13, 22–23, 39, 40, 41,
    160–61, 163
  of Gingrich, 25–26
  of Iran-contra scandal, 14, 22, 24–25, 53,
    142–46
  of Nixon, 38, 144–45
  in Watergate scandal, 22, 144–45
conservatives:
  court-stripping legislation and, 149
  Democratic, 53, 55, 56, 58, 61, 87, 96,
    119, 122–23
  judiciary used by, 27, 150, 151–52
  libel suits of, 168–69
  Lieberman's link to, 173
  news media of, 32, 35–36, 63, 67–68, 71
  Reaganism and, 64–66, 69–72
  religion and, 35, 54, 60, 62, 65, 67
  in Republican party, 18, 23, 54, 64–75,
    78, 92, 160, 173
  talk radio of, 35, 63, 67–68, 71
  voter mobilization feared by, 20, 231
Constitution, U.S.:
  First Amendment, 34, 147, 156, 157
  Article II, electoral college and, 171,
    187–88, 189, 197, 199–201, 204,
    206
  Fifth Amendment, 153
  Fourteenth Amendment, 181, 189, 208
  separation of powers in, 214
Constitutional Convention of 1787, 228
consumer movement, 33, 47, 92–93, 95, 97
  deregulation and, 105, 106, 108
Consumer Product Safety Commission
    (CPSC), 93, 222
Contract with America, 73, 123–24
contras, Nicaraguan, 39, 215
  Iran-contra scandal, *see* Iran-contra scandal
Converse, Philip, 234*n*
Corporation for Public Broadcasting, 127
corporations, 69, 70, 130
  profits of, 122
corruption charges against government
    officials, 25, 26, 114
cost-benefit analyses, 127
courts, *see* judiciary
Cox, Archibald, 27, 145
crime and criminals, 38, 75, 137, 152, 173
  rights of, 56, 115, 148
Cullum, Blanquita, 68

Cuomo, Mario, 59
Currie, Betty, 162

Daley, Richard J., 213
Daley, William, 182
Dalton, John, 118
Davis, Tom, 124
Deaver, Michael, 24
debt, national, 122
  see also budget deficit, U.S.
Defenders of Wildlife, 73
Defense Department, U.S., 91, 118,
    119–20, 144
defense spending, 54, 82, 91, 96
  budget deficits and, 104, 109, 121, 134
  cuts in, 99, 134, 136
  foreign policy and, 108, 117
  homeland security and, 120–21
  increase in, 52, 64, 69, 72, 121, 126, 169
  as industrial policy, 138, 140
  waste and fraud in, 140–41
DeLay, Tom, 183
demobilization, political, 225, 227–31
Democratic entrenchment, 81–101, 167
  bureaucratic, vs. mobilization, 95–101
  forms of, 81–84
  in 1960s and 1970s, 88–95
  origins of, 84–88
  party decline and, 86–88, 95
Democratic Leadership Council (DLC), 53,
    56
Democratic National Committee (DNC):
  break-in at, 37
  damage control of, 13, 163
Democratic National Convention (1968),
    49, 93
Democratic National Convention (1992), 57
Democratic Study Group, 125
Democrats and Democratic party, 21–45,
    81–120, 122–26, 128–34, 136–43,
    228–31
  antiwar, 23, 47
  arms control and, 140
  blacks in, *see* blacks, in Democratic party
  class structure of, 44; *see also* labor and
      labor unions, in Democratic party;
      middle class, Democratic party and
  Clinton bolstered by, 163
  Clinton compromises denounced by, 18
  Congress controlled by, 21, 22, 48–49,
    52–53, 62, 73, 79, 81, 82, 95, 96
  Congress strengthened by, 22, 53

Democrats and Democratic party (*continued*)
  conservatives in, 53, 55, 56, 58, 61, 87,
      96, 119, 122–23
  conservative talk radio criticized by, 68
  defection of, 53, 58, 59, 163
  defections from, 50
  domestic state and, 81–101
  election of 2000 and, *see* election of 2000
  electoral deadlock and, 47–67, 72–74,
      75–79
  incumbency effects and, 48, 143
  liberals in, *see* liberals, in Democratic party
  mobilization strategy and, 228, 231
  moderates in, 53–58, 75
  Motor Voter Act and, 20
  national security apparatus and, 138–42
  new rights created by, 136–37
  politics of, from 1968–1992, 47–55
  pork barrel politics of, 48, 52, 63
  reform of, 93–95
  Republican disruption of institutions of,
      103–7
  RIP process used against, 39–42, 160–63,
      165
  RIP process used by, 37–39, 161–62
  Southern, 15, 47, 50, 53–58, 84, 88, 96,
      115–16
  voter mobilization feared by, 20
  see also individual elections and people
Depression, Great, 224
deregulation, 64, 69, 102, 103, 105–8, 113,
      127
Dershowitz, Alan, 183
desegregation, school, 155
devolution, 127–29
Disability Rights Litigation and Defense
      Fund, 73
  disabled people, rights of, 47, 97, 136–37
discrimination:
  labor, 148, 152
  religious, 157
Disraeli, Benjamin, 229
Dobson, James, 67
Dole, Bob, 109, 184
  in election of 1996, 34, 76–79
dollar, value of U.S., 121, 135
Douglass, Dexter, 187
drug companies, 174
drugs, 151, 157
dual sovereignty, 214–19
  early modern monarchy compared with,
      216–19

Dukakis, Michael, 51, 83, 111, 115
Duke, David, 43

Easterbrook, Frank, 150
Eastland, Terry, 31
Economic Development Administration,
      223
economy and economic policy, 27, 82
  budget deficit and, 122
  Clinton programs for, 60, 98, 99–100
  in election of 1992, 56, 57, 58, 173
  in election of 2000, 172
  erosion of U.S. position and, 108
  health care and, 99–100, 160
  traditionalist vs. supply-sider view of,
      108–9
  see also individual economic issues
Edelman, Peter, 18, 167
education, 42, 110, 137
  desegregation of, 155
  in election of 2000, 174, 175
  home schooling, 65, 66–67, 70
  loans for, 60
  school choice and voucher programs, 169,
      174
  school prayer and, 51, 64, 67, 69, 75
Eighth Circuit Court of Appeals, 30
Eisenhower, Dwight D., 23
elderly, 174
  AARP and, 129
  balloting methods and, 179
  health insurance for, 105
  rights of, 97
  see also Medicaid; Medicare; Social Secu-
      rity
election of 1992, 13, 74, 76, 98, 103, 122,
      154, 159, 173
  electoral deadlock in, 55–58
  voter turnout, 43
election of 1994, 35, 40, 44, 73, 78, 79, 123
  electoral deadlock in, 58–61
election of 1996, 13, 23, 76–79, 131, 154,
      159, 161, 166–67, 173, 214
  campaign finances in, 19, 23, 25–26, 28
  media's role in, 34–35
  newly registered voters in, 21
  voter turnout, 18, 43
election of 2000, 46, 79, 170–211
  balloting methods, problems with, 177–
      79, 190, 191–92, 195–96, 207, 209
  the campaign, 172–76
  "contest" phase, 194–96

electoral votes, 170, 171, 176, 187–88,
199–201, 205, 206, 207, 208–9
Florida state legislature and, 170,
199–201
institutional combat in, 14, 209–11
legal battle, 27, 170, 181, 183, 185–89,
194–99, 202–9
mobilization of legal and political teams,
181–87
news media and, 170, 182–83, 184, 186,
194, 209
overseas ballots, 186, 193–94, 210
political conflict and institutional struggle, 209–11
popular vote, 14, 171, 176, 210
postelection struggle, 176–81
presidential debates, 174–75
recounts, 177–78, 180–81, 186, 188–89,
190–94, 203, 206, 207, 208
Supreme Court and, 170, 181, 183, 189,
197–99, 204–9
voter turnout in, 14, 175–76
elections, 13–21
of 1860, 226
of 1896, 17
of 1956, 32
of 1968, 49, 50, 94
of 1972, 37, 38, 49–50, 94
of 1976, 55
of 1980, 55, 102, 108, 110–11, 122, 143
of 1984, 50, 51, 111, 112–15, 122, 143,
239*n*
of 1986, 143
of 1988, 51, 109, 111, 115, 122, 146
of 1991, 43
of 1992, *see* election of 1992
of 1994, *see* election of 1994
of 1996, *see* election of 1996
of 1998, 41–43
of 2000, *see* election of 2000
advantages of incumbents in, 48, 143,
172
campaign spending and, 19, 23, 28, 30
congressional, *see* congressional elections
fraud, 18, 234*n*
gubernatorial, 43, 59
local, 49, 52, 54, 80
militarist campaigns and, 17, 19
presidential, *see* presidential elections
senatorial, 41–42, 52, 58
voter turnout in, *see* voter turnout
electoral college:

Article II of the Constitution, 171, 187–
88, 189, 197, 199–201, 204, 206
significance in election of 2000 of, 170,
171, 176, 187–88, 199–201, 205,
207, 208–9
electoral combat, 16–20
electoral deadlock, 46–80
in election of 1992, 55–58
in election of 1994, 58–61
in election of 2000, *see* election of 2000
Gingrich Republicanism and, 63–79
national party politics and, 1968-1992,
47–55
politics of stalemate and, 80
Republican strategy and, 61–63
electoral decay, 13–16, 19–21
election of 2000, *see* election of 2000
electoral mobilization, *see* voter mobilization
Eleventh Circuit U.S. Court of Appeals,
election of 2000 and, 170, 181
elites, political:
in electoral vs. institutional combat,
14–16
intensity of contemporary conflict of,
18–19
Employment Division v. Smith, 157
energy deregulation, 105
energy tax, 98, 100, 137
Engler, John, 184
entitlement programs, federal, 127–28
environmentalists and environmental issues,
20, 27, 33, 47, 70, 95, 112, 231
courts and, 148
deregulation and, 69, 105, 108, 127
regulatory policy and, 66, 92–93, 220
Environmental Protection Agency (EPA),
82, 84, 93, 119, 120, 130, 222, 223
equal protection under Fourteenth Amendment, 181, 189, 208
Ervin, Sam, 38
Espy, Mike, 25, 31, 223
Ethics in Government Act of 1978, 27, 28,
29–30, 38, 53, 149
evangelical Protestants, Republican appeal
to, 116–17
executive agencies, 16, 37, 86
congressional monitoring of, 22
presidential authority over, 21–22
executive branch:
increase in power of, 21–22, 53, 85–86
independent counsel vs., 13, 27–31, 38,
40, 161–64

executive branch (*continued*)
  legislative power vs., 21–24, 37, 52–53,
      94–95, 103–5, 133–34, 138,
      140–46, 168
Executive Order 12291, 215
executive privilege, 22, 120
exports, 121, 135

Fahrenkopf, Frank, 74
Falwell, Jerry, 35
family leave, 71, 72, 98, 136–37
Family Medical Leave Act, 66
Family Research Council, 67
family values, 57, 75, 76
Faris, Jack, 70
FBI (Federal Bureau of Investigation), 23,
      40, 161
Federal Election Commission, 210
Federal Register, 168
Federal Reserve, 121, 134, 215
Federal Rules of Civil Procedure, 147
Feeney, Thomas, 200
feminists, 27, 164–65
Fifth Amendment, 153
Filegate, 23, 40, 161
filibusters, 18, 166
First Amendment, 34, 147, 156, 157
fiscal policy, 22, 72, 102–5, 121–23,
      132–34, 167, 173
  see also monetary policy; taxes
Fiske, Robert, 29, 30
501(c)4 organizations, *see* not-for-profit groups
flag, American, 115
Florida and election of 2000, 46, 170–211
  balloting methods, problems with,
      177–80, 190, 191–92, 195–96, 207,
      209
  black voters in, 175–76, 177
  certification of the vote, 177, 185–86,
      187, 192–93, 194, 195, 196, 197,
      198, 200
  "contest" phase, 194–96
  electoral votes, 170, 176, 187–88,
      199–201, 205, 207, 208–9
  legal battle, 27, 181, 183, 185–89,
      194–99, 202–9
  mobilization of legal and political teams,
      181–87
  popular vote, 171, 177, 205
  postelection struggle, 176–81
  recounts, 177–78, 180–81, 186, 188–89,
      190–94, 203, 206, 207, 208

  state legislature and, 170, 188, 189,
      199–201, 203, 206, 207, 209
  Supreme Court and, 170, 181, 183, 189,
      197–99, 204–9
  see also individual Florida counties
Florida Supreme Court, 186–87, 188, 189,
      192, 197, 198, 200, 201, 202–3,
      205, 206, 208, 209
Flynt, Larry, 42–43
Focus on the Family, 67
Foley, Thomas, 59
Forbes, Malcolm (Steve), 77
Ford, Gerald, 55
Foreign Commitments Resolution, 22
foreign policy, U.S., 57, 91, 115
  bipartisan consensus on, 137–38
  congressional role in, 22, 37, 215–16
  defense spending and, 108, 117
  dual sovereignty and, 215–16
  institutional combat and, 137–42,
      215–16
  presidential role in, 53, 215
Foster, Vincent, 223
Fourteenth Amendment, 181, 189, 208
France, 135
fraud, 25
  in business dealings, 40
  electoral, 18, 234*n*
  in military procurement, 140–41
  welfare, 141
free speech, 34, 156, 158
free trade, 108, 113
Fulbright, J. William, 23, 33
fundamentalism, Protestant, 116–17
fund-raising, campaign, 23, 28, 30, 77, 80
  of Clinton, 79
  Clinton's reform of, 98
  direct-mail, 54, 62
  of Gingrich, 25–26
  Republican reforms in, 54

Garfield, James, 233*n*
Garin, Geoff, 75
gays, *see* homosexuals
General Accounting Office (GAO), 125, 215
Georgia, election districts in, 155, 156
Germany, 121, 134–35, 136
Gingrich, Newt, 59, 61, 74, 123–26, 213
  investigation of, 14, 25, 214
  resignation from House seat after 1998
      elections, 42
  weakening of, 75

Gingrich Republicanism, 63–79, 124–26
 aftermath of defeat of, 75–79
 class composition of, 69–71
 goals and methods of, 72–75
 GOP organization and mobilization and,
  64–69
 Reaganism compared with, 64–65, 69–72
Ginsberg, Benjamin L., 183
Ginsburg, Douglas, 150, 151
Ginsburg, Justice Ruth Bader, 154, 158,
  198, 206, 207, 208
GOPAC, 25–26
Gore, Al, 23, 28, 161
 in election of 1992, 56, 57
 in election of 2000, *see* election of 2000
government, U.S.:
 downsizing of, 60
 fragmentation of, 16, 19, 219
 local, *see* local government
 shutdowns of, 42, 74–75, 167
 Supreme Court decisions on power of,
  155, 156–57
 see also specific topics
governmental power, 212–31
 destruction of administrative capacity
  and, 219–23
 dual sovereignty and, 214–19
 electoral failure and, 212–14
 electoral mobilization and, 224–31
Gramm, Phil, 77, 134
Gramm-Rudman-Hollings deficit reduction
  act, 134
Grant, Bob, 68
grants, block, 127–28, 166
grants-in-aid, federal, 90
Gray, C. Boyden, 165
Great Britain, 134–35
Great Society, 89–90
Grenada, U.S. invasion of, 53, 115, 138
gross national product (GNP), 92
Group of Five, 134–35
gubernatorial elections, 43, 59
gun control, 47, 60, 66
gun owners, rights of, 69
gun sales, 156

Haiti, U.S. troops in, 139
Hakim, Albert, 218
Harris, Katherine, 177, 185–86, 187, 188,
  192, 195, 196, 197, 200, 203,
  205–6, 223
Harvard University, 119–20

Hastert, Dennis, 43
Hatch Act, 98–99
Haynsworth, Judge Clement, 150
Health and Human Services (HHS), U.S.
  Department of, 82, 130
health care, 61, 66, 73, 82, 98–100, 123,
  133, 137
 deregulation of, 105
 Medicaid, 127, 128, 129
 Medicare, 100, 126–27, 133, 167
 regulation of, 127
health insurance, 71, 98, 105
Helms, Jesse, 149
Hill, Anita, 151
Hispanics, 155
Holder v. Hall, 155
homeland security, 120–21
homelessness, 104
Home School Legal Defense Association
  (HSLDA), 65, 66–67, 70
homosexuals, 57, 66
 in the military, 60, 118, 160
 Supreme Court and, 158
Horton, Willie, 115
hostages in Iran, U.S., 143
House of Representatives, U.S., 18, 21, 26,
  52, 96
 Appropriations Committee, 124
 Banking Committee, 40
 Black Caucus, 125
 Commerce Committee, 124
 Democratic control of, 52, 59, 143
 District of Columbia Committee, 124–25
 Economic and Education Opportunities
  Committee, 125
 Ethics Committee, 25–26
 executive agencies monitored by, 22
 Gingrich's attacks on Democrats in, 61
 Gingrich's reorganization of, 124–26
 Government Reform and Oversight
  Committee, 40, 125
 growth of, 215, 220
 Hispanic Caucus, 125
 impeachment and, 41, 233*n*
 Judiciary Committee, 41, 124
  124–25
 Post Office Committee, 124–25
 presidential elections, role in deciding,
  188, 201–2
 Republican Conference, 68
 Republican control of, 42, 46, 58–59, 79,
  172, 188

House of Representatives, U.S., *(continued)*
  Subcommittee on Asian Affairs, 216
  Ways and Means Committee, 25
  Women's Caucus, 125
Housing and Urban Development (HUD),
  U.S. Department of, 130, 168
Hubbell, Webster, 40, 223
Hughes, Jerry, 68
Hyde, Henry, 124

Ickes, Harold, 76, 223
Immigration and Naturalization Service
  (INS), 147
impeachment, 233*n*
  Clinton and, 23, 41, 42
  Nixon and, 38, 145
imports, 109, 121, 122, 134, 139
income taxes, *see* taxes
incumbency, advantages of, 48, 143, 172
independent counsel, 26–31, 38, 161–63
Indian gambling casino license, 25
indictments, increase in federal, 24, 25,
  26–27
industrial policy, military procurement as,
  138, 140
inflation, 110, 117, 121, 134, 135, 141
  taxes and, 105, 110–11
influence peddling, 38
Inman, Bobby, 120
institutional combat, 13–16, 21–43,
  132–69, 212–31
  deficits and, 132–37
  destruction of administrative capacity
    and, 219–23
  dual sovereignty and, 214–19
  election of 2000 and, 14, 209–11
  electoral failure and, 212–14
  historical perspective of, 14–16
  judiciary in, 14, 16, 24–31, 146–59, 167,
    222
  national security apparatus and, 137–46,
    167
  news media in, 14, 16, 24, 31–36,
    144–45, 167
  as norm, 16
  political conflict and, 167–69
  president vs. Congress in, 21–24
  RIP process and, *see* RIP (revelation, in-
    vestigation, and prosecution) process
  social policy and, 159–67
  unified partisan control and, 23
  see also congressional investigations

insurance and insurance companies, 69, 71,
  98, 105
interest groups, 62, 69–70, 92–93, 99, 129,
  168, 174
  destruction of administrative capacity
    and, 219, 222
  liberals and, 110, 111, 129, 148
interest rates, 109, 110, 121, 122, 134, 135,
  136
Internet, 158
Iran, 217
Iran-contra scandal, 139, 142–46, 219
  investigation of, 14, 22, 24–25, 53,
    142–46
  RIP process in, 38–39
Iraq, U.S. relations with, 139
Irvine, Reed, 169
Israel, 224
  in Iran-contra affair, 139, 143

Jackson, Jesse, 58, 182
Jackson, Michael, 154
Japan, 134–35, 142, 217, 219, 224
  banks of, 121–22, 139
Japan-United States Yen-Dollar Committee,
  217
Jeffords, James, 46, 79
Jews in the Democratic party, 47
jobs:
  creation of, 71
  protection of, 134
Johnson, Andrew, 233*n*
Johnson, Lyndon B. (Johnson administration), 23, 89–90, 94
Johnson v. DeGrandy, 155
Joint Chiefs of Staff (JCS), 118–19
Jones, Paula, 27, 35–36, 40, 158, 161
Jordan, Vernon, 41
judiciary, 30
  in destruction of administrative capacity,
    222
  in election of 2000, 14, 27, 170, 181,
    183, 185–89, 196–99, 202–9
  in institutional combat, 14, 16, 24–31,
    146–59, 167, 222
  Iran-contra affair and, 144
  liberals' alliance with, 26–27, 146–50
  policy role of, 26–27
  see also Office of the Independent Counsel;
    Supreme Court, U.S.
Justice Department, U.S., 29, 114, 223
justiciability, rules of, 147

Kansas-Nebraska Act, 15
Kefauver, Estes, 32
Kemp, Jack, 78
Kennedy, Justice Anthony, 151, 152, 153, 154, 157, 198, 206
Kennedy, Edward (Ted), 164
Kennedy, John F., 32, 33, 89
Key, V. O., 17
Kirsanow, Peter, 101
Klain, Ron, 178, 182
Koppel, Ted, 34
Kristol, William, 160
Ku Klux Klan, 234*n*

labor and labor unions, 64, 85, 87, 227, 238*n*
    in Democratic party, 47, 49, 50, 56, 57, 83, 88, 94, 96, 113, 114, 174
    in election of 2000, 174, 175
    erosion of business's accommodation with, 106–7, 108
    liberal causes supported by, 106–7
    Republican attack on, 113, 114, 133
    in Republican party, 51, 69, 114
    see also working class
Labor Department, U.S. (DOL), 82
Labor party, Israeli, 224
LaHood, Ray, 75
lawyers, public interest, 20, 231
Lebanon, U.S. troops in, 138, 141
legal expenses:
    of Clinton staffers, 223–24
    in contesting election of 2000, 209
    of Katherine Harris, 223
Legal Services Corporation, 127, 147, 220–21
Legislative Service Organizations (LSOs), 125
Lehane, Chris, 186
Leon County Circuit Court, 196–97, 202, 203
lesbians, *see* homosexuals
Lewinsky, Monica, 30, 36, 40–41, 162, 164, 173, 176, 213
Lewis, Judge Terry P., 186, 187
libel suits, 168–69
liberals and liberalism:
    anger at Clinton's positions, 174
    in antiwar movement, 33, 47
    in Democratic party, 47–50, 52, 53, 55, 59–61, 64, 73, 75, 84, 86–95, 99, 110, 111, 140, 141, 150, 167, 173, 174

interest groups, 110, 111, 129, 148, 174
    judiciary's alliance with, 146–50
    labor's coalition with, 106–7
    news media and, 33–36, 164, 168
    in veteran's groups, 141
    voter mobilization feared by, 20, 231
Library of Congress, 125, 152
Libya, U.S. bombing of, 53, 115, 138
Liddy, G. Gordon, 67
Lieberman, Joseph, 171, 172, 173, 194
Likud party, Israeli, 224
Limbaugh, Rush, 35, 67
limitation amendments, 126
Lincoln, Abraham, 15, 226, 229, 233*n*
line-item veto, 22, 158, 227
Livingston, Bob, 42–43, 124
loans, education, 60
lobbyists, 70, 99, 105, 129–30, 165, 166
local elections, 80
    Democratic success in, 49
    Republican failure in, 52, 54
local government, 65, 68–69, 85, 87, 113–14, 148, 225
    grants-in-aid to, 90
Louisiana election of 1991, 43
Louvre Accords of 1987, 135–36
Lucas v. South Carolina Coastal Council, 153

McCarthy, Joseph, 23, 32
McClure, Kirby, 68
McDougal, James, 40
McDougal, Susan, 40
McGovern, George, 50, 173
McIntosh, David, 124, 166
Mack, Connie, 179–80
McKay, John, 201, 203
McKinley, William, 17, 233*n*
Mack v. United States, 156
McLaughlin Group, The, 164
magazines, 32
manufacturing, 134, 218, 219
Marcos, Ferdinand, 142, 216
mark, German, 135
Marshall, Justice Thurgood, 151, 152
Martin County, Florida, 195, 196, 202, 209, 210
Maryland, balloting methods in, 179
Massachusetts, 115, 148
media, *see* news media
Medicaid, 127, 128, 129
Medicare, 100, 126–27, 133, 167, 174
Meese, Edwin, 24

mercenaries, 217–18, 219
Miami-Dade County, Florida, election of
    2000 and, 177, 180, 189, 190, 196,
    203
Michigan:
    Democrats in, 87
    voter registration in, 175
middle class, 173
    Democratic party and, 20, 44, 57, 60, 83,
        88, 89, 94, 110, 228, 231
    lower, 20, 70, 89, 228, 231
    Republican party and, 44, 47, 64, 69,
        110–15
    as target of political advertising, 19
    upper, 20, 44, 45, 47, 51, 61, 89, 91, 94,
        114, 231
    as voters, 19, 20, 44, 51
middle-income suburbanites, Republican
    appeal to, 110
Midwest, 47, 65, 68, 88
militarist campaigns, 17, 19
military:
    defense spending, *see* defense spending
    homosexuals in, 60, 118, 160
Miller v. Johnson, 155
minimum wage, 174
Minnesota, Democrats in, 87
minorities, 45, 98
    as court appointments, 154
    in Democratic party, 47, 56, 84, 89, 231;
        see also blacks, in Democratic party
Missouri Compromise (1820), 15
Missouri v. Jenkins, 155
mobilization, political, 225, 226–27
    see also voter mobilization
monarchs, dual sovereignty compared with
    early modern, 216–19
Mondale, Walter F., 50, 111, 173
monetary policy, 102, 121, 134
    see also fiscal policy; interest rates
Moorhead, Carlos, 124
moral issues in election of 1984,
    114
Moral Majority, 64, 65
Morris, Richard (Dick), 75, 76, 173
mortgages, 110
Motor Voter Act of 1993, 20–21, 230

Nader, Ralph, 73, 92, 166
    in election of 2000, 174
Nassau County, Florida, election of 2000
    and, 196–97

National Association for the Advancement
    of Colored People (NAACP),
    175–76
National Federation of Independent Busi-
    ness (NFIB), 62–63, 65, 66, 70–71
National Labor Relations Act, 85
National Labor Relations Board, 113
National Rifle Association (NRA), 62–63,
    66
national security, 82, 91–92, 102, 123, 167
    institutional combat and, 137–46, 167
    Republican offensive and, 117–21
    see also defense spending
National Security Council, 142, 146, 215
National Taxpayers Union, 65
Native Americans, 157
Natural Resources Defense Council, 93
Navy, U.S., 138, 230
neo-Nazism, 43
New Deal, 47, 83–87, 93, 104, 105, 106,
    112–13, 160
New Frontier, 89–90
New Hampshire, National Federal of Inde-
    pendent Business in, 70–71
news media:
    ancillary institutions and, 36
    budget crisis and, 75
    Clinton and, 13, 162, 164, 213–14
    conservative, 32, 35–36, 63, 67–68, 71
    in institutional combat, 14, 16, 24,
        31–36, 144–45, 167
    leaks to, 32, 37, 84, 162, 168
    liberal, 33–36, 164, 168
    in nineteenth-century politics, 17
    in presidential elections, 19, 49, 52, 62,
        115, 170, 176, 182–83, 184, 186,
        194
    presidential power supported by, 32
    Reaganism and, 64, 144
    rise in power of, 24, 31–36
    senatorial elections and, 52
    Vietnam War's effects on, 32–33
    see also specific publications
newspapers, 31, 183
    see also individual newspapers
Newsweek, 37
New York State:
    National Federation of Independent Busi-
        ness in, 71
New York Times, 33, 36, 37, 183
Nicaraguan contras, 39, 215
    see also Iran-contra scandal

Nightline, 34
nineteenth century:
  news media in, 31
  voter mobilization and turnout in, 15,
    16–17, 20, 229, 233*n*
Nixon, Richard M. (Nixon administration),
  33, 95
  court appointments of, 37, 150
  Cox dismissed by, 27
  destruction of administrative capacity
    and, 222
  in election of 1968, 50
  in election of 1972, 37, 38
  executive power increased by, 21, 37, 94
  impeachment and, 38, 145
  news media's influence threatened by, 37
  resignation of, 14, 38
  RIP process vs., 37
  Watergate and, 14, 27, 37–38, 145, 149,
    163, 164, 213
Nofziger, Lyn, 24
Noonan, John, 150
Noriega, Manuel, 139
North, Oliver, 24, 67, 142–45
North American Free Trade Agreement
  (NAFTA), 60
North Carolina, voting districts in, 155–56
Northeast, 47, 88
not-for-profit groups, 130, 168, 236*n*–37*n*
  Democratic entrenchment in, 81, 82, 83
nuclear freeze, 106, 140
nuclear weapons, 140

occupational safety, 70, 71, 93
Occupational Safety and Health Administra-
  tion (OSHA), 71, 93
Occupational Safety and Health Administra-
  tion Reform Act, 71
O'Connor, Justice Sandra Day, 150, 152,
  153, 154, 198, 206
Office of Management and Budget (OMB),
  22, 168, 215
Office of Technology Assessment, 125
Office of the Independent Counsel, 26–31,
  38, 161–63
Ohio, McKinley's "front porch" campaign
  in, 17
Oklahoma City Federal Building, bombing
  of, 68
Olson, Ted, 183, 197, 198, 205, 206–7
opposition research, 36
Oregon, narcotics laws of, 157

Packwood, Bob, 165
Palestine Liberation Organization (PLO),
  224
Palm Beach County, Florida, election of
  2000 and, 177, 178–79, 180–81,
  189, 191–92, 196, 197, 200, 203
Panama, U.S. invasion of, 139
pardons, 25
Pataki, George, 71, 184
patriotism, 115, 117
Pennsylvania, voter registration in, 175
Pentagon Papers, 37, 149
People's Radio Network, 68
Perington, Philip, 223
Perot, Ross, 122
Perry, William, 120
Persian Gulf, 138, 218
petrochemical companies, lobbyists for, 70
Philippines, 142, 216
Phillips, Howard, 116
physically disabled, rights of, 47, 97,
  136–37
Pickering, Judge Thomas, 159
Pierce, Samuel, 168
Pittsburgh, Pennsylvania, 87
Planned Parenthood, 129
*Planned Parenthood of Southeastern Pennsylva-
  nia v. Casey,* 153
Plaza agreement, 135
plumbers squad, 37
Poindexter, John, 145
political compromise:
  in antebellum era, 15
  of Clinton, 18, 137
  in 1950s and 1960s, 18
political conflict, institutional combat and,
  167–69
political machines, 81, 85, 86–88, 87, 113,
  213
political parties and political party
  organizations:
  decline of, 32, 44, 86–88, 95
  Democrats, *see* Democrats and Democratic
    Party
  nineteenth-century press subordination
    to, 31
  Republicans, *see* Republicans and
    Republican party
political questions doctrine, 147
"politics by other means," growing importance of, 14
pork barrel politics, 48, 52, 63, 91

Posner, Richard, 150
postelectoral era, 14
posttraumatic stress syndrome, 141
poverty and poor people:
    as voters, 19, 20, 83, 228, 231
    welfare reform and, 18, 56, 68, 75,
        127–29, 130–31, 165, 166–67
Powell, Colin, 78, 118–19
Powell, Lewis F., 150
president, U.S.:
    Congress vs., *see* executive branch, legisla-
        tive power vs.
    destruction of, administrative capacity
        and, 219–23
    dual sovereignty and, 214–19
    press support of, 32–33
    see also individual presidents
presidential elections, 23
    Democratic problems in, 49–51, 64, 94
    Democratic success in, 54–57, 78–79
    news media in, 19, 49, 52, 62, 115
    Republican failure in, 64
    Republican success in, 51–52, 54, 57, 102
    voter turnout in, 16, 18
    see also elections; *specific elections*
presidential privilege, claims of, 162–63
price competition, 106
Printz v. United States, 156
privateering, 217–18, 219
Professional Air Traffic Controllers Organi-
    zation, 113
Progress and Freedom Foundation, 26
Progressives, 15, 225–26, 227
property rights, 65, 66, 68–69, 70
    Supreme Court and, 152, 153
property taxes, 71, 89
protectionism, 107, 134, 139, 142
Protestants:
    fundamentalist, 116–17
    in Republican party, 47, 64
Public Citizen, 92–93
public interest groups, *see* interest groups
public interest law centers, conservative, 66
Public Interest Research Group, 73
public relations firms, 36
punch card ballots, 177

Quayle, Dan, 57, 160

Racicot, Marc, 184, 191, 193–94
radio programs, 32, 184
    conservative, 35, 63, 67–68

Raines v. Byrd, 158
Rayburn, Sam, 23
Reagan, Michael, 68
Reagan, Ronald (Reagan administration;
        Reaganism), 33, 37, 64–66, 95
    antiunion practices in, 113
    budget deficit and, 72, 97, 105, 108–9,
        121, 132–34, 139, 141, 217
    class composition of, 69–71
    defense in, 117–18, 134, 138–42
    Democratic accommodation with, 72
    Democratic institutions disrupted in,
        103–7
    dual sovereignty and, 214–17, 219
    in election of 1980, 55, 108, 110–11
    in election of 1984, 50, 111, 114
    EPA and, 84, 120
    executive power increased by, 21–22
    goals and methods of, 72
    GOP organization and mobilization and,
        64–66
    as Great Communicator, 64
    Iran-contra scandal and, 14, 139, 142–46,
        163–64, 213
    new media and, 64, 65, 144
    OMB in, 168
    political forces reorganized in, 108, 111,
        113–15
    RIP process vs., 38–39, 213
    Supreme Court and, 149–53, 166
    tax reform and, 112, 132–33, 134
Reagan Diaspora, 65–66
Reconstruction, 15
redistricting plans, election, 155–56
regulatory policy and regulatory agencies,
        33, 51, 166
    cost-benefit analysis and, 127
    Democratic entrenchment and, 81–84,
        92–93, 96, 97
    Reaganism and, 64, 68–69
    Republican offensive against, 105–8, 127
Rehnquist, Justice William, 150, 152, 154,
        158, 159, 198, 206, 207, 208
religious conservatives, 35, 54, 60, 62, 65,
        67
    Lieberman's link with, 173
Religious Freedom Restoration Act of 1993,
        157
Reno, Janet, 25, 28, 29, 30
Reno v. American Civil Liberties Union, 158
Reorganization Act of 1937, 84
Republican National Committee (RNC), 54

Republican National Convention of 1996, 34

Republican offensive, 102–31
 Democratic institutions disrupted in, 103–7
 mechanisms of government constructed in, 117–23
 Phase 2 of, 103, 123–31
 political forces reorganized in, 107–17

Republicans and Republican party, 15, 21–25, 37–40, 92, 96–134, 136–46, 149–53, 165–68, 229–31
 class structure of, 44; *see also* middle class, Republican party and
 Clinton's compromises with, 18, 60
 Congress controlled by, 22–23, 31, 40, 44, 58–59, 61–63, 79, 100, 103, 123–31, 160–61, 165; *see also* Gingrich Republicanism
 conservatives in, *see* conservatives, in Republican party
 defection of, 163–64
 Democrats' shift to, 58, 59
 election of 2000 and, *see* election of 2000
 electoral deadlock and, 49–80
 entrenchment of, forms of, 82
 executive power increased by, 21–22
 filibusters of, 18
 Gingrich, *see* Gingrich Republicanism
 mobilization strategy and, 229, 231
 moderates in, 23, 78
 Motor Voter Act opposed by, 20
 national security apparatus and, 117–21, 137–42
 in 1995-1996 budget battle, 74–75, 76, 78
 organization and mobilization of, 64–69
 politics of, from 1968-1992, 47, 50–55
 RIP process used against, 37–39, 161–62
 RIP process used by, 37, 39–42, 161–63
 southern strategy of, 51
 southern whites and, 116–17
 traditionalists vs. supply-siders in, 108–9
 voter mobilization as threat to, 20
 welfare reform and, 18
 see also individual elections and people

Reykjavik summit of 1986, 144
Richard, Barry, 183
Ridge, Tom, 120
rights expansion, 136–37
right-to-life issue, *see* abortion, opposition to

RIP (revelation, investigation, and prosecution) process, 36–45, 213–14
 in Clinton administration, 39–42, 160–63, 165, 213–14
 for democratic politics, 43–45
 institutionalization of, 39
 in Iran-contra scandal, 38–39
 legal expenses and, 223–24
 in Watergate, 37–38

Robertson, Pat, 35, 67
Roe v. Wade, 116, 152, 153
Romer v. Evans, 158
Roosevelt, Franklin D., 32, 47, 84–88, 91, 226–27, 230
Roosevelt, Theodore, 32
Rose law firm, 40
Rosenberger v. University of Virginia, 156
Rostenkowski, Dan, 25, 59, 61
Ruckelshaus, William, 84
Russia, 119
Rust v. Sullivan, 152
Rutherford Institute, 27

safety, 105, 127
 consumer, 93, 222
 occupational, 70, 71, 93
St. Louis Globe-Democrat, 31
sales tax, 113–14
Salisbury, Robert, 89
Sandanistas, 148, 153
Sasser, Jim, 59
Saturday Night Massacre, 27
Saudi Arabia, U.S. relations with, 139
Sauls, Judge L. Sanders, 196–97, 202–3
Scalia, Justice Antonin, 150, 152, 154, 158, 159, 198, 205, 206–7
Scalia, Eugene, 101, 159
Schattschneider, E. E., 17
Schier, Steven, 175
school busing, 51, 115, 116, 152
school desegregation, 155
school prayer, 51, 64, 67, 69, 75
school vouchers, 169, 174
Schwartzkopf, Norman, 194
secession, 15
Secord, Richard, 142, 144, 218
Secret Service, 162–63
Seminole County, Florida, 195, 196, 202, 209, 210
Senate, U.S., 18, 21, 52, 96, 215
 appointments confirmed by, 119, 120
 Armed Services Committee of, 120

Senate, U.S., (*continued*)
  Banking Committee, 40
  Democratic control of, 133, 143
  Dole's resignation from, 77
  Ervin committee, 38
  executive agencies monitored by, 22
  filibusters in, 18, 166
  Foreign Relations Committee, 33
  impeachment and, 233*n*
  Judiciary Committee, 150–51, 154
  news media used by, 32
  presidential elections, role in deciding,
      201–2
  Republican control of, 42, 46, 58, 59, 79,
      149, 172
senatorial elections, 41–42, 52, 58
separation of church and state, 155, 156,
    159
separation of powers, 188, 189, 214
sexual abuse, 118
sexual harassment, 118, 151, 165
  in Jones suit, 35, 40, 158, 161
Shaw v. Hunt, 155–56
Shaw v. Reno, 153
Shelby, Richard, 58
Slaughter, Louise, 166
slavery, 15, 229
Smith, Linda, 124
Smith, Ron, 68
Smoot-Hawley Tariff, 224
social class, *see* class structure
social programs (social welfare), 27, 50, 60,
    69
  Democratic entrenchment and, 81–84,
      96, 97
  devolution and, 127–29
  institutional combat and, 159–67
  as "investment," 60, 137
  new rights and, 136–37
  spending cuts from, 53, 73, 102–5, 113,
      121, 123, 130, 133, 134, 136, 138
  spending increases for, 48, 49, 60, 72–73,
      97, 110, 123
Social Security, 42, 99, 104, 149, 160, 174
Social Security Act and amendments, 84
Social Security Administration, 149
Social Security Board, 85
Social Security Disability Reform Act of
    1984, 149
Solarz, Stephen, 216
Somalia, U.S. forces in, 139
Sony, 217

Sosnick, Douglas, 151, 153, 154
Souter, Justice David, 151, 153, 154, 198,
    206, 207, 208
South Africa, 216
South and Southerners, 92
  defense industry in, 117
  as Democrats, 15, 47, 50, 51, 53–58, 84,
      88, 96, 115–16
  extralegal violence in, 234*n*
  Republican appeal to, 116–17
  in Republican party, 52, 59, 116–17
  secession of, 15
  voter turnout in, 16, 233*n*
South Carolina, in election of 1996, 77
Soviet Union, 92, 138
  U.S relations with, 140, 146
Springfield Republican, 31
standing, doctrine of, 147
Starr, Kenneth:
  Clinton investigated by, 13, 29, 30, 31,
      40–41, 161–64
  Clinton's investigation of staff of, 13,
      161–62
State Department, U.S., 144
state government, 65, 68, 85, 87, 148, 225
  block grants to, 127–28, 166
  social programs controlled by, 128
  states' rights, 198
  Supreme Court decisions on relationship
      of federal and, 156–58
state prisons, 148
Stephanopoulos, George, 76
Stevens, Justice John P., 158, 198, 207, 208
stock and stock market, 135, 136
Stockman, David, 72
stonewalling, 161
Strategic Defense Initiative ("Star Wars"),
    140
strikes, 113, 227
supply-side economics, budget deficit and,
    108–9
Supreme Court, U.S., 30, 147, 149–59
  abortion and, 116, 152, 153, 154, 159
  affirmative action and, 155, 158, 159
  appointments to, 37, 150–54
  conservative members of, 27, 151,
      155–56
  election of 2000 and, 170, 181, 183, 189,
      197–99, 204–9
  line-item veto and, 22
  on power of federal government versus
      state goverment, 155, 156–57

property rights and, 152, 163
voting rights and, 155–56
Warren court, 115

Tailhook affair, 118
Tailhook Association, 118
"takings impact analysis," 68
Tammany Hall, 87
tariffs, 224–25
tax-deductible contributions, 26
taxes, 54, 216–17
  bracket creep, 105
  Civil War and, 226
  cuts in, 51, 64, 69, 71, 72, 75, 78, 98,
    102, 103–4, 109, 110, 111, 112,
    121, 122, 123, 126, 132–33, 169,
    174, 175
  deductions from, 99, 104, 133
  energy, 98, 100, 137
  increase in, 50, 57–58, 60, 71, 98, 109,
    110, 122, 126, 134, 136
  inflation and, 105, 110–11
  National Federation of Independent Busi-
    ness's agenda on, 71
  property, 71, 89
  Republican emphasis on, 111–12
  sales, 113–14
tax farming, 216–19
Tax Reform Act of 1981, 72, 216
Tax Reform Act of 1986, 104, 133
teachers' unions, 174
teenage mothers, unwed, 128
television, 37, 140, 164
  congressional use of, 32, 39, 41, 144–45,
    151
  conservative use of, 35, 67
  convention coverage, 174
  local stations, 37
  political advertising on, 19, 115, 122,
    151, 167
  presidential elections influenced by, 19,
    49, 52, 62, 115, 122, 182–83, 184,
    194
  presidents' use of, 32
  sex and violence on, 75
Texas, congressional districts in, 155
"think tanks," 36
third-party movements, 87, 122
Thomas, Justice Clarence, 151, 154, 158,
    159, 165, 198
Time, 37
tobacco industry, 100–1, 217

tort law, reform of, 69, 129, 130, 166
Tower Commission, 146
Toyota, 217
trade:
  deficits, 108, 109, 121, 122, 132–37
  free, 108, 113
  sanctions and, 216
  tariffs and, 224–25
traditionalism, 134
transportation, 110
  deregulation of, 105, 107
Travelgate affair, 40, 161
Treasury Department, U.S., 29, 73, 133,
    134, 215, 218, 234n
  securities of, 121–22, 134, 135, 139, 217
triangulation strategy, 75, 173, 174
Tribe, Lawrence, 182, 197, 198
Tripp, Linda, 40
Truman, Harry, 91
Tucker, Jim Guy, 40
Tyson Foods, Inc., 39

unemployment, 92, 111, 113, 122
unemployment insurance, 71
unions, *see* labor and labor unions
United Parcel Service, 70
U.S. Congress, *see* Congress, U.S.; House
    of Representatives, U.S.; Senate,
    U.S.
United States v. Lopez, 156
United States v. Tucker, 30
United States v. Virginia, 158
upper class, 44, 45, 51, 69

veterans, Vietnam, 141
Veterans Administration, 138
Veterans Affairs Department, U.S., 141
Veterans of Foreign Wars, 141
veto power, line-item, 22, 158, 227
Vietnam War, 32–33, 91, 112, 138, 139,
    217
  veterans of, 141
Viguerie, Richard, 116
Virginia Military Institute, 158
Volcker, Paul, 111
volunteers and activists, 80
  Democratic, 47–48, 49, 54, 62, 92–93,
    94, 97, 183
  Republican, 54, 62–63, 64–65, 65–66,
    68, 79, 183–84, 210
Volusia County, Florida, election of 2000
    and, 177, 180, 186

voter mobilization, 15–21, 43–44, 82, 225
    election of 2000, 171, 175
    fears about, 20, 231
    governmental power and, 224–31
    Motor Voter Act and, 20–21, 230
    in nineteenth century, 15, 16–17, 20, 229
    twentieth-century failure of, 19–21, 44,
        95, 97, 212–14, 229–30
voter registration, 20–21, 43, 116
    in election of 2000, 175
voter turnout, 43, 59, 79
    class bias in, 45
    in election of 1994, 63, 79
    in election of 2000, 14, 175–76
    electoral fraud and, 234n
    high levels of, 16–17
    low levels of, 18, 19–21, 80, 95, 225–26
    in the South, 16, 233n
Voting Rights Act of 1965, 50, 116, 155,
    159
"Votomatic" punch card machines, 179–80

Wagner Act of 1935, 84
Wallace, George, 50
Wall Street Journal, 35
Walsh, Lawrence, 145
Wards Cove v. Atonio, 151–52
war on terrorism, 120–21
War Powers Act, 22, 64, 141
Washington on Trial, 68
Washington Post, 33, 36, 37, 57, 183
Washington Times, 35
Watergate:
    break-in at Watergate Hotel, 37
investigations of, 14, 22, 27, 37–38, 163,
        164, 213
    Iran-contra affair compared with, 144,
        145, 146
    political effects of, 26
    tapes, 145, 149
Webster v. Reproductive Health Services, 152
Weinberger, Caspar, 24, 25, 119
Weir, Margaret, 129
welfare, 82
    fraud, 141

reform of, 18, 56, 68, 75, 127–29,
        130–31, 165, 166–67, 173
welfare offices, voter registration in, 20
Wells, Judge Charles T., 203
West, 92
    property rights in, 65, 66, 70
    as Republican stronghold, 52
Westmoreland, William, 168–69
Weyrich, Paul, 116
Whiskey Ring scandals, 234n
White, Justice Byron, 152, 154
whites, 20
    Clinton's appeal to, 56, 58
    defection from Democrats of, 50, 53–54
white southerners:
    as Democrats, 15, 50, 53–58, 84, 88, 96,
        115–16
    Republican appeal to, 116–17
Whitewater Development Corporation, 29,
        35
Whitewater investigation, 25, 29, 35–36,
        39–40, 161, 213
Whitman, Christine, 184
Wildavsky, Aaron, 104–5
Wilkinson, J. Harvie, 150
Williams, Margaret, 223
Wilson, James, 228
Wilson, Woodrow, 32
Winter, Ralph K., 150
women, 56
    court appointments, 154
    courts and, 148, 154, 158
    in Democratic party, 93, 164–65
    in the military, 118
    pregnant, 128
    rights of, 47
worker compensation, 71
working class, 88, 94, 228
    in election of 1984, 114
    liberal fears of, 20, 231
    see also labor and labor unions
World War II, 91
Wright, Jim, 24, 61, 215

yen, Japanese, 135